THE ABLE GARDENER

Overcoming Barriers of Age & Physical Limitations

by

Kathleen Yeomans, R.N.

A Garden Way Publishing Book

Storey Communications, Inc.
Schoolhouse Road
Pownal, Vermont 05261

Copyright © 1992 by Kathleen Yeomans

Published by Storey Communications, Inc., Schoolhouse Rd., Pownal, Vermont 05261.

Edited by Gwen W. Steege
Cover design, text design, and production by Cindy McFarland
Cover photographs by Charles Mann, Photo/Nats, Gardener's Supply Co., and Walter Chandoha
Line drawings by Alison Kolesar, except on the following pages: 98, 100, 102, 104, 118, 149 (bottom), 150, 158–61, 169–71, 199 by Judy Eliason; 49, 103, 149 (top), 165, 237, 241, 245, 250 by Brigita Fuhrmann; 154, 199 by Elayne Sears; 117, 176 by David Sylvester
Indexed by Little Chicago Editorial Services

Printed in the United States by The Book Press
First Printing, November 1992

The information in this book is true and complete to the best of our knowledge. All recommendations are made without guarantee on the part of the author or Storey Communications, Inc. The author and publisher disclaim any liability in connection with the use of this information. For additional information please contact Storey Communications, Inc., Schoolhouse Road, Pownal, Vermont 05261.

Garden Way Publishing was founded in 1973 as part of the Garden Way Incorporated Group of Companies, dedicated to bringing gardening information and equipment to as many people as possible. Today the name "Garden Way Publishing" is licensed to Storey Communications, Inc., in Pownal, Vermont. For a complete list of Garden Way Publishing titles call 1-800-827-8673. Garden Way Incorporated manufactures products in Troy, New York, under the Troy-Bilt® brand including garden tillers, chipper/shredders, mulching mowers, sicklebar mowers, and tractors. For information on any Garden Way Incorporated product, please call 1-800-345-4454.

Library of Congress Cataloging-in-Publication Data

Yeomans, Kathleen, 1947–
    The able gardener : overcoming barriers of age & physical limitations / by Kathleen Yeomans.
        p.   cm.
    Includes bibliographical references and index.
    ISBN 0-88266-790-4 — ISBN 0-88266-789-0 (lie-flat)
    1. Gardening for the aged.   2. Gardening for the physically handicapped.   I. Title.
    SB457.4.A34Y46   1992
    635'.087—dc20   91-58925
                                                                   CIP

CONTENTS

To my mother, Alyce Steiskal,
who waited so long for her garden;
and to my gardening friends, young, old, or in-between —
Able Gardeners, one and all.

ACKNOWLEDGMENTS

Thanks to my clients, patients, and friends, who shared their gardening experiences with me, and to the many Physical and Occupational Therapists who offered helpful recommendations for easier gardening. In addition, I would like to thank Suzanne Michaud, M.P.H., former Community Service Coordinator, Santa Barbara Branch of the Arthritis Foundation, for her enthusiastic interest in this project.

I would like to express sincere thanks to my editor, Gwen Steege, for her professional guidance, unerring suggestions, and long-distance friendship.

I am indebted to those who kindly loaned photographs and sent good wishes: Paul Conrad of Gardener's Supply; Pat Lawless and Melinda Lawson of Smith & Hawken; Michelle Addy of W. Atlee Burpee and Co.; Melissa Deason and Michelle Kidd of Breaking New Ground, Purdue University; Katrina Nicke, Walt Nicke Company; and Nancy Andrews, No Bend Garden.

I am most grateful to Curtiss Madison for his endless patience, loyal support, and continuing encouragement.

Finally, I extend very special thanks to Librarian Rebecca J. Eldridge of the Santa Barbara Botanic Garden for her research assistance and courtesy.

INTRODUCTION

Food, recreation, exercise, and peace of mind — gardening offers all these and more to many dedicated gardeners. But what if your energy isn't what it used to be? Perhaps your back isn't as strong or arthritis, a heart condition, or some other disability interferes with this integral part of your life? You can overcome barriers of age or physical limitation: Just use your head, not your back! If you're not gardening because you think it's too hard, grab your hoe and let's go — this book will show you an easier way to make gardening fun again.

> *"But though I am an old man, I am but a young gardener."*
>
> — Thomas Jefferson
> Letter to Charles Wilson
> Peale, August 20, 1811

There are as many kinds of gardeners as there are gardens. You may be the kind of gardener who likes to sit back, sip a lemonade, and contemplate a peaceful landscape. Or maybe you're one of those diehards, rubber-booted to the knee, who slogs around in the muck, so anxious to get digging that you can't wait for the weather to improve. Some folks like to design their gardens, but rely on assistants to do the actual digging and hoeing. Others don't feel right unless they have green-stained hands and dirt under their nails. This garden book is for every kind of gardener. It's a book to make gardening easier and more fun for everyone.

I've been gardening for over twenty years. I started young, and my first awkward gardens soon became elaborate showpieces. Wheelbarrows full of soil were moved from one end of the yard to the other. Rocks were piled, moved, and moved again. Lawns disappeared, and then reappeared elsewhere. Haphazard gardens became formal, color-coordinated works of art. In all my gardening days, I must have shifted tons and tons of soil. And, I'm not tired of gardening yet. The process of planning, planting, waiting, and growing has gotten under my skin, and I would now no more give up gardening than I would forgo eating.

> Special tips for the physically limited gardener are included in every chapter; some of these hints can be helpful for any gardener who wants to save time and energy. You can find them quickly by looking for this "Special Help" symbol:

As the years have gone by, however, the *way* I garden has changed. My body is getting a little tired. Those wheelbarrows get heavier and the yard seems to get bigger. Dragging hoses and dirt around isn't as much fun anymore. My gardening friends and I are "getting on in years"; some of us have physical conditions that limit our work capabilities. But that doesn't stop us.

Lately, I think often of my grandmother, who was one of the most determined gardeners I've known. I spent some of my happiest gardening hours with her. As she grew older and her arthritis worsened, she modified her gardening techniques. Her gardens became smaller and closer to the house. She used a cart to pull her tools along and brought a stool to sit on. Instead of dragging hoses around, she kept one within easy reach of every garden area. As time passed, she spent fewer hours in the garden, yet her gardens flourished. We always had an abundance of sweet, crunchy carrots and sun-warmed tomatoes. My grandmother's motto was, "If you can't do it one way, learn to do it another!

Research has shown that if we maintain good health

habits and exercise regularly, we can remain strong and vital throughout our lives. Proper nutrition and frequent exercise are as important to the health of a seventy year old as they are to the health of a thirty year old. It's essential, therefore, that we enjoy active pastimes and challenge our physical abilities throughout our lives. Gardening is one of the most healthful activities. It gives us the exercise and fresh air that "stir the bones" and "fire the pumps."

In this book, I'd like to share the tips and tools I've discovered that make gardening easier. Whether you need to conserve time and energy, or you have developed arthritis or a heart condition, or you require a wheelchair, you can still grow flowers and vegetables in your own garden. "Gardening easy" is often simply "gardening smart." I hope the suggestions that follow will make your garden a source of pleasure rather than a lot of work. So, don't let anything stop you — get out there and keep on growing!

CHAPTER 1

CUSTOM DESIGNING YOUR GARDEN AND YARD

A STORY ABOUT GARDEN PLANNING

I remember my first garden. After living in apartments for many years, I finally had a house, and I was excited to have some earth of my own to dig up. I couldn't wait to get the garden in.

As soon as the boxes were unpacked, I started planting. I wanted a privacy hedge, so I planted a line of mixed trees. A few friends brought their "living Christmas trees" and we set out those as well. Voilà — instant hedge! I delighted in flowers — the more exotic the better — and added them to my steadily growing garden. I also wanted one of those lush, vibrant, romantic, English-looking perennial borders — a *real* garden. Out came the nursery catalogs and in went bulbs, roots, corms, and seedlings. Next, I decided I needed vegetables. I planted squash and twenty-four tomato plants, which didn't seem like too many at the time. There was all that wonderful space! I never drew any plans for that garden, or even stopped to think about it. I "designed" the garden as I went along, perfectly happy to be digging the soil and popping in another plant or two every day. I didn't think of the "big picture"; I just wanted to be surrounded by beautiful plants. Well, I was surrounded all right.

By midsummer I started to see some real growth in the garden. Flowers were blooming, tomatoes were ripening, the grass was growing, and the trees were taller. I found myself out in the yard, weeding, hoeing, snipping, and staking almost every day. The trees began to shade the perennial border, and the sun-loving flowers started to droop. The privacy hedge blocked the driveway, so I had to park on the street. The tomatoes all ripened at the same time, and because I couldn't harvest them fast enough, they began to rot. When I returned from a two-week vacation, I could hardly believe my eyes! Those neatly trimmed plants and well-weeded beds looked as though they'd been fed a growth hormone.

Things didn't improve over the next few years, either. Some exotics became invasive pests; others just disappeared. Tree crowns touched, cutting out most of the light. In that dim suburban forest, the flowers quietly strangled each other. The pruning shears wouldn't do — a machete would have been more appropriate. Even now, after years of thinning, pruning, and weeding, some awful plants still left over from that first naive and energetic garden rear their pesky leaves now and then to remind me of past mistakes and poor judgment.

PLANNING AN EASY-CARE GARDEN

A carefully researched garden plan would have avoided some of my problems. I've learned my lesson, and now I offer this advice: Think twice, maybe three times, before setting out a plant. What will it look like in ten years? How much care does it take? Will it drop fruit or blossoms on a patio or deck? Is it a water guzzler or a potential weed? Never underestimate the vigor of a plant. Some of the lowliest, most innocent-looking seedlings can become space-greedy monsters.

Whether you have an acre of land or ten square feet, if you take time to plan your garden, you can create one that is convenient, functional, efficient, and, most important, suited to your own taste, needs, and capabilities. Those time-consuming and back-breaking chores that always seem to go along with the pleasures of gardening can be eliminated. If there's something about gardening you don't like or can't do, plan it right out of your garden! You can have a garden that's made just for you.

Thinking about Your Needs

The first step in designing your easy-care garden is to determine what special obstacles you may face and then to eliminate them. We will discuss all of these in detail in the chapters that follow, but here are some examples:

★ If bending over is hard for you, design a garden with raised beds, built waist-high if you wish, so you can sit while you work.
★ If you use a cane, a walker, or a wheelchair, plan a garden with wide, level paths and convenient turnaround areas.
★ If you get short of breath when you exercise, locate the garden close to the house and have all your tools and supplies within easy reach.

The next step in custom designing your garden is to decide how you want to use your outdoor space. Do you want a special place for entertaining, sitting and relaxing, eating outdoors, hanging laundry to dry, or exercising the dog? Tailor your design to the land's use. For instance, the outer limits of your yard are less likely to be used for lounging or socializing; plant these areas with low-maintenance trees and shrubs that offer privacy and shade, and ground covers that visually tie the larger plantings together. Plantings can also enhance the view from a window. Outdoor areas near the kitchen, porch, or dining room are probably most convenient for entertaining and relaxing, and this is where you may want to concentrate your gardening efforts.

Evaluating Your Site

Once you know your needs, evaluate your property and

decide where to put your plantings. This part of the process should be done on paper. You can use graph paper to make a scale drawing that shows all the permanent features you will be working around. Deed maps, architect's plans, or contour maps of your site will save you a lot of time and measuring. Here's what to include:

★ Your lot's boundaries, dimensions, and orientation to the compass
★ Spots of sun and shade during the summer months
★ The direction of winds, in both winter and summer
★ The location of such elements as underground utilities, septic tanks, and water faucets
★ The house, including windows, doors, walls, and walkways
★ Notes on soil conditions (for instance, an area where the soil is particularly sandy or one with poor drainage)
★ Existing plants, and especially large trees

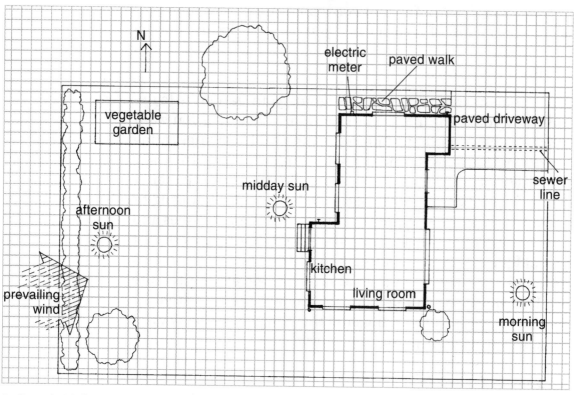

▲ *Step 1: Make a scale drawing of your property*

Trace or photocopy your map, so that you can design your garden as many times as you wish without redrawing the map each time.

Before you site any plantings, consider the following characteristics of your property: weather conditions, the availability of water, convenience, and the quality of the soil. Here's what to look for:

Weather conditions. In addition to the general climatic conditions of the region where you live, even a small lot has *microclimates* — areas that are warmer, colder, windier, or drier than other parts of the yard. The conditions in the particular area where you locate your garden will determine the kinds of plants you can grow. For instance, hillsides are usually less windy than hilltops; they are also warmer than the bottom of a hill. A south-facing plot gets more sun, while east-facing plots shelter heat-sensitive plants during the summer. The south side of a house protects plants against cold north winds. In addition, a south wall retains heat during the day, which it releases at night.

Many flowers and most crops need about six to eight hours of full sun daily, so watch the sun patterns in your yard. The sunniest areas should be reserved for fruits, vegetables, and cutting flowers. Note where the rain drains and puddles and where frost appears first and remains longest. These clues will help you identify the microclimates in your yard.

Availability of water. Where are your water sources? Are there enough of them, or will you be dragging hoses to the far corners of your yard? It's important to provide for the watering needs of your plants without great effort. (See pages 51-53, 62-63, 124-131 for more on watering techniques.)

Convenience. Locating a garden near the house will make your work easier. Long trips "out to the garden" discourage regular maintenance. A vegetable or herb garden near the kitchen is convenient and practical. A small flower garden right outside the dining room can be easily reached and offers a lovely view at mealtime.

Soil. Look at the soil in the site or sites you've chosen. Good soil reduces garden work, because healthy plants are less susceptible to disease and pest attack. Soil can be improved (see chapter 4, but it saves time and energy if you can garden in areas that already have good soil — these are the spots on which to focus your first efforts.

Creating Your Plan

Now, take a copy of your property plan and draw in plantings where you think you'd like them. Let your imagination run free, and experiment with many possibilities. Don't think this is a waste of time. Planning on paper, a

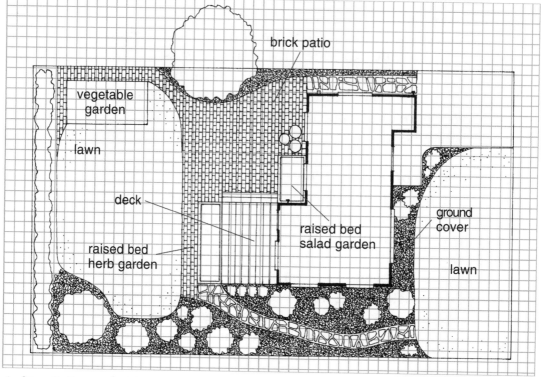

▲ *Step 2: Draw plantings on your scale drawing.*

step many eager gardeners omit, is vital to easy gardening. It's a lot less expensive and less time-consuming to experiment on paper than in the ground.

Develop one small section at a time. The most effective and efficient gardens are designed as small, manageable units. Even in a large yard, several small gardens with definite boundaries are more easily maintained than a big, unbordered garden. Square or round shapes, too, are easier to manage than free-form beds. (Round the corners of square or rectangular beds, however, to make mowing easier.) Although exotic and complicated garden designs are fun and a challenge to the accomplished gardener with unlimited time and energy, if you are a new gardener, it's particularly important to start small. A compact garden will give you important experience and with less to care for, you'll have more time to do things right.

Plan your garden in rectangles, each no wider than 4 feet and no longer than 10 feet. Walking back and forth to care for a garden over 10 feet long can be exhausting. You should also be able to reach the middle of the garden from either side. A 2-foot reach is comfortable for most people, but if you are unable to reach that far, make the bed as wide as suits your physical abilities. ☛ **Don't lay out a garden based on your maximum reach; the strain can be quite tiring when you are working for any length of time. Don't stretch it!**

Working with Nature

With your site or sites chosen, consider what to grow. One of the first rules of easy gardening is to work *with* nature rather than against it. Use plants that thrive in the conditions your site offers. Plants that need shade, acid soil, and/or lots of moisture are best planted in a garden that already provides these necessities. If you put shade-loving plants in the sun, you'll have to water them frequently, just to keep them alive. Other plants prefer hot, sunny areas. If you plant sun-loving plants in the shade, they will languish and die. Select hardy plants that are suitable for your region and climate. Plants native to your area are often the best and most logical choices. A bed of self-sowing wildflowers or a hedge of native plants needs little upkeep. Plant tropicals and exotics only if you live in a warm climate or plan to devote a lot of time to "babying" your garden. A local nursery will know the plants that grow well in your area. Also, ask your neighbors which plants grow well for them. Most gardeners love sharing, and when you ask for information you may come away with a handful of cuttings and some heirloom seeds, as well.

It is equally important to choose plants that are easy to grow and that can survive occasional neglect or abuse. For general landscaping, use plants that require little upkeep and grow at a moderate rate (see page 261 for suggestions). You don't want to be cutting and trimming rampant growth every time you go out to the garden. Instead of grass that needs constant mowing, use ground covers, bark chips, gravel, or even concrete, asphalt, or pre-cast pavers. If you combine these with shrubs, rocks, and trees, you can achieve a natural look.

Plant at the time of year when that particular plant is likely to get off to the best start. Bulbs, for instance, generally like to be planted in the fall, so their roots can become established before bloom time. Many perennials and shrubs do better if planted in the spring, when the weather is mild and light rainfall is frequent.

If you use plants to screen windows and provide privacy, remember that shrubs and trees grow, and if planted too close to the house may need to be pruned frequently to keep them in bounds. Tree roots can disrupt plumbing or even cause your foundation to crack. Shrubbery planted right next to a house or window can also make your garden look small and crowded. Obtain the privacy you want by planting along the perimeter of the yard, or use fences or trellises.

BEYOND THE GARDEN BEDS: LAWNS AND LANDSCAPES

Everyone loves a beautiful garden, and to many people that means a lush lawn and extravagant flower beds. Just as my first gardens quickly grew out of control, any landscape can become an energy-eating monster. A lot of time, effort, and muscle is needed to manage those lavish lawns and flower beds. You may need to renovate your landscape to suit your time and abilities. Here are some more ideas for designing easy-care landscapes.

EASY-PLANTING BASICS

★ *Put plants where they like to grow.* Put shade-loving plants in the shade and sun-loving plants in the sun.

★ *Plant at the right time.* Fall planting is usually best for bulbs, and spring planting, for perennials and shrubs.

★ *Plant sparingly.* Crowded plants and plants that require constant pruning are harder to take care of. Find out how big a plant will get before adding it to the garden.

★ *Plant in easy-to-reach areas.* If you have to climb between shrubs or squeeze into narrow pathways, your work will be harder.

★ *Avoid planting under eaves.* Plants will need frequent pruning and hand watering.

★ *Plant in healthy, weed-free soil.* Garden beds that have been infested with disease or weeds should be avoided, as these same problems are likely to plague your newly planted garden.

★ *Put plants with similar needs together.* Place all the drought-tolerant plants together, all the moisture lovers together, and all the heavy feeders in another spot. Organized gardening is easier gardening.

★ *Use mulches and ground covers.* They reduce watering and weeding chores.

▲ *A nearly rectangular garden with rounded corners is one of the easiest to mow.*

LAWN SHAPES TO AVOID

★ *Hourglass shapes or double triangles.* These require you to keep going over the same ground in the middle to reach the outer ends.

★ *Dead-end areas.* If you must stop and move the mower to a separate, enclosed area of the lawn, you're wasting time and energy.

★ *Sharp curves and scallops.* These require unnatural movements and repeated mowing to get a good cut. You almost always end up hand-trimming these places.

★ *Sharp angles.* These are the most common cause of stop-and-turn mowing movements. Save your back by rounding out the sharp angles.

A Few Words about Lawns

Lawns should be easy to mow. A hilly lawn can be tiresome and dangerous to mow. If you have a slope that rises more than 1 foot in every 3 horizontal feet, it is too steep for a lawn and is best planted in ground covers. Even if your yard is fairly flat, you don't have to cover the entire area with grass. If you are the lawn mower in the family, limit the size of your lawn to suit your physical capabilities. You can modify the shape of your lawn, too, to make mowing easier.

☛ **If you have to stop and turn, or stop and angle the mower, you're asking for a back injury.** Mowing that puts more strain on one side of the body than the other — mowing in a tight circle for instance — is tiring. If you have a circular lawn, do not mow around and around the circle. A rectangular or square lawn with rounded corners is one of the most efficient shapes for mowing. Another good shape is a lozenge shape, consisting of two parallel sides with semicircular ends.

Keep obstacles out of the lawn. Trees, small flower beds, rocks, birdbaths, and garden ornaments can make mowing exhausting. If such obstacles cannot be moved, create a mowing strip around them by installing strips of gravel, bricks, concrete, paving stones, or railroad ties flush with the lawn around them. The strips should be wide enough to support one wheel of the lawn mower — about 4 to 6 inches wide. Similar mowing strips make mowing easier wherever the lawn does not adjoin a paved area.

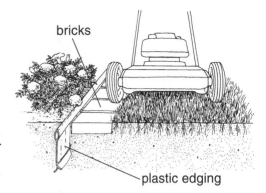

bricks

plastic edging

▲ *Create a mowing strip to carry the mower wheel — you won't have to trim edges.*

How to Limit Lawn Maintenance

★ Avoid work-intensive lawn care by using paving and low-maintenance ground covers where possible.

★ Use rocks and stepping stones in your garden if you wish, but don't place them in the lawn where they can be a problem to mow around.

★ Avoid planting trees and shrubs in the middle of a lawn, where they obstruct mowing.

★ Keep your lawn small; avoid irregular shapes.

★ Add mowing strips to lawn areas to limit trimming and edging tasks.

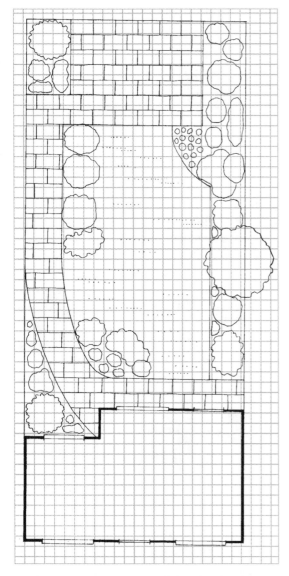

▲ *Create an attractive, low-maintenance garden on a small narrow lot by using paving materials, small shrubs, and ground covers.*

Working with Your Unique Yard

The size and shape, as well as the topography of your yard, form the "canvas" on which your landscape "painting" will appear. Here are some suggestions for making the idiosyncracies of your property work for you.

A *flat, rectangular lot.* Flat land is easily planted, but may have drainage problems. To make flat yards more interesting, owners often overplant, which makes the yard seem walled in. Avoid this by planting only a few background plants of varying heights along the perimeter of the yard. If you use evergreen trees and shrubs, you'll have less maintenance. Be sure to choose a combination of leaf sizes and colors, or the effect can be boring. Avoid planting deciduous trees and shrubs near patios or pools, where leaf and blossom clean-up can be a never-ending task. Located in shrub beds, on the other hand, deciduous plants shed their leaves inconspicuously under the shrubs, where they eventually degrade. Railroad ties, fences, ground covers, and paving break a rectangular yard into attractive garden areas.

Small, narrow yards. Although small yards are sometimes considered problematic — not even worth gardening in — these can be some of the easiest and most delightful gardens, so low-maintenance that you'll have more time to relax and enjoy your garden. Cover part of the area with stones, brick, or paving to make a sitting area and choose plants that are of moderate size when mature. Leave a few spots among the trees and shrubs for colorful annuals or bulbs for seasonal interest. Oriental-type gardens work especially well in small yards.

Pie-shaped lots. Oddly shaped areas confound some folks, especially when the arrangement is a very small front yard with a large, triangular-shaped backyard. I have a pie-shaped lot, and I consider my minimal front yard a real advantage; it means even less to diligently maintain for the sake of neighborhood neatness. By using concrete, asphalt, or pre-cast pavers, ground covers, and evergreen shrubs in the narrow front of such a wedge, you can provide an attractive, low-maintenance entry. Your "room in the back" can then be developed to suit your personal needs without concern about rigorous neatness. Wooden decks, patios, and wide paths can make this part of your yard easy to access, as well as easy to maintain. If you have a large garden area, include rest stops and contemplation seats.

The hillside lot. Sloped yards can be a challenge, especially if you have difficulty getting around. ☞ **One hillside gardener's advice is to "take it slow and easy" to prevent accidental slips, trips, and falls. Plant steep areas with native material and low-care ground covers.** Groups of blossoming trees and shrubs add color without requiring continual care. Restrict areas that need your attention to the flat, easily reached parts of your yard. Container gardening on the deck or patio may be your best choice. A veteran hillside gardener recently told me that the drought in California turned out to be the best thing that's happened to her garden in years! All her high-maintenance plants died, so she replaced them with native or drought-tolerant plants that require minimal care, and therefore, less climbing up and down the slopes.

Condominiums and mobile home parks. The more restricted your space, the more important it is to develop a design that maximizes your garden area. Don't overplant a small area, or you will be thrashing about in a jungle to find the garden bench. Besides, too many plants make a small garden look even smaller. Warm-colored paving or paving stones,

★ Avoid such shrubs as hydrangea, eugenia, privet, and many deciduous flowering shrubs that need regular pruning.

★ For color and visual interest, plant flowering shrubs like azalea, lavender, rosemary, and gardenia. Less trouble than annuals, these may be good choices for an easy garden, depending on where you live. Consult a garden reference for hardiness requirements.

★ Avoid trees and shrubs that create litter. All deciduous trees drop leaves, and flowering trees like acacia, olive, and jacaranda (all warm-climate plants) also drop blossoms and seedpods. I still bear a grudge against an acacia tree planted near a patio that required daily clean-up almost seven months of the year.

★ Don't plant trees and shrubs too close together; you won't be able to get in to do whatever pruning is needed.

---

with one or two medium-sized plants as focal points, surrounded by low-growing shrubbery, gives a small garden a feeling of spaciousness. Arrange container plants in groups for colorful interest. Hanging plants are a good solution to lack of space. (For more on container gardening, see pages 48-71 and 215-222.) The very small garden is an ideal spot for a hummingbird feeder. These little visitors add color and activity to even the tiniest garden. And don't forget your recliner! For a sample mobile home garden, see pages 252-258.

DESIGNING A BARRIER-FREE GARDEN

You can't garden if you can't get there! Providing safe, convenient access to the gardening area is an important part of garden design. Steep stairs, uneven risers, and awkward entryways are real problems for gardeners whose mobility is limited. The height of planting boxes, hanging plants, work tables, and tool-storage areas should be determined by the height and reach of the gardener. Measurements that may be helpful in designing your garden are listed in appendix 2.

With a few minor adjustments, any garden can be wheel-chair-friendly. As a matter of fact, the tips and tricks that make gardening easier for people who use wheelchairs can be used by anyone who wants to give his or her back a rest.

If need be, you can design a garden so you never have to leave your seat. Keep your garden beds and containers within reach. The most convenient garden beds should be no wider than 4 feet; 3 feet may be even more comfortable for you. Keep in mind that if you can't reach it, you can't weed it. If raised beds don't fit into your garden plan, garden in containers on a table top. Card tables will support a number of small pots, and old picnic tables are sturdy enough to handle larger containers. Garden benches, or even just a strong board set on top of two concrete blocks, make a useful staging area for sit-down gardening. The distance from the floor to your lap, plus 4 inches, is a good height for both raised beds and benches or tables for containers. The most comfortable garden "tables" allow for knee room, so you don't have to lean over to work. (For more on container gardening, see pages 48-71 and 215-222.)

If possible, keep your tools and supplies in the garden area. A roofed tool shed should be at least 48 inches wide, if you need to allow for wheelchair access. It should contain a pegboard wall for hanging large tools and a few storage shelves. Measure the distance from the floor to the top of your head for the maximum height of shelves. Keep potting soil and soil amendments in wheeled plastic trash containers, so they may be easily moved to your work area when necessary. For convenience, carry your tools in a bag on the back

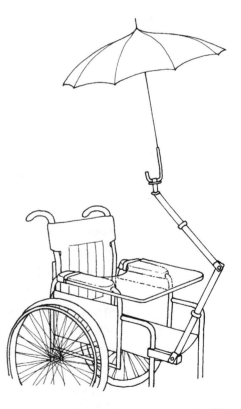

▲ *A wheelchair support arm can hold an umbrella to protect you from strong sun.*

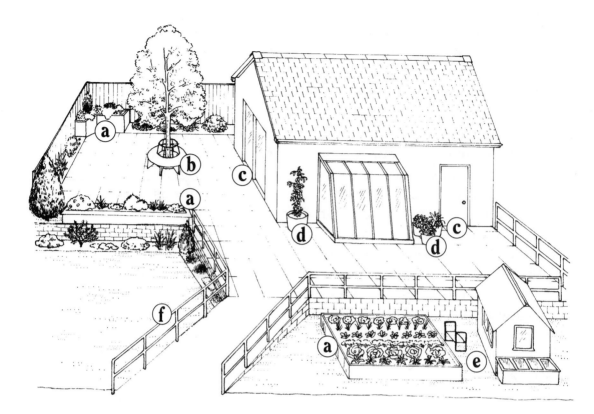

▲ *Paved areas and a wide ramp (slope ratio 1:12) make it easy to get around if you use a walker or wheelchair. Other features:* ⓐ *raised beds,* ⓑ *sitting area,* ⓒ *doors at ground level,* ⓓ *container plants,* ⓔ *kneeling bench, and* ⓕ *sturdy rounded handrails.*

or arm of your wheelchair. Those who do not use a wheelchair but like to sit to garden can carry their tools in a pocketed apron or in a backpack. For more information about tools and tool storage, see chapter 2.

Water should be readily available. If you have no faucets in the immediate garden area, run a hose out and leave it there, or leave a plastic trash container full of water near your work site and fill watering cans as needed — you'll save going back and forth to the main faucet for frequent refills. For more about watering techniques, see pages 124-131.

If you're going to be sitting in the garden for an extended period of time, bring a pillow to cushion your bottom or to support your back. Clamp-on umbrellas, which fit most wheelchairs, will protect you from the hot sun. Attachable trays and lapboards make convenient work surfaces for small garden tasks like repotting and sowing seeds in containers. Stop and stretch, or change position, once in awhile so you don't get stiff or overwork certain joints.

Steps

Treads. If treads are too narrow (federal accessibility standards require stair treads to be at least 11 inches wide), widen them, if possible.

Nosings. Protruding nosings (the overhang on stair treads) can cause you to trip if you catch your toe on them.

Risers. Open risers are also dangerous; your foot can slip through the hole, or you can trip in the openings if you don't step just right on them.

Surfaces. Nonskid surfaces on stair treads are good insurance against slipping. Securely attach indoor-outdoor carpeting or textured rubber mats to treads for traction and a firm footing, especially in wet weather.

Railings. Add a railing both for safety and to make getting up and down the stairs easier. The most useful handrails run along both sides of a stairway. They should be rounded to make them easy to grip, and they shouldn't rotate or wiggle within their fittings. A rail that runs 30 to 34 inches above stair nosings is right for most people.

Ramps

Ideally, gardens for people with physical limitations should be on smooth, level surfaces. When that is not possible, or when it's necessary to provide transitions from one area to another, well-designed and -built ramps are a good solution.

Ramp slope. Ramps should not be too steep. A slope ratio of no more than 1 inch of rise in 12 inches is best.

Ramp width. Make the ramp at least 36 inches wide, so that there is enough room to maneuver a wheelchair or walker, as well as to carry an armload of gardening supplies or move wheelbarrows and other gardening equipment.

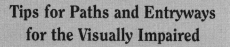

Ramp surface. The ramp surface should be of nonskid material. This is especially important in wet weather. Textured concrete, brickwork, roughened wood, or crushed gravel are good surfaces for ramps.

Doors

Door width. Doorways out to the garden can be widened, if necessary. Most wheelchairs fit through a 36-inch doorway.

Thresholds. Door sills can be removed to reduce the chance of tripping, as well as to allow wheelchairs to roll through the opening more easily, or you can get special door sills that depress under the weight of a wheelchair. If you don't want to be "climbing" in and out of the doorway, lower the threshold to ¾ inch or less.

Ease of opening. It shouldn't take too much force to open and close your doors. If doors stick, oil the hinges and other hardware or plane the door edge, as needed. Reduce the tension on spring-loaded hardware, if necessary. Replace doors that are too heavy.

If you have a weak grip, replace round door knobs with lever handles, U-shaped handles, or push-type mechanisms. Hardware stores and mail-order houses that specialize in assistive devices offer a good selection of handles (see appendix 5).

Door hardware should be mounted no higher than 48 inches above the floor. If you need to push the door open with your knees, feet, or wheelchair, have a kickplate installed to save wear and tear on the door.

Paths and Passageways

When you're traveling on wheels, consider what is underneath you before you proceed.

Path width. Most garden paths are about 2½ feet wide. If you use a walker or wheelchair, you will need pathways about 4 feet wide. This allows enough room for an ambulatory person and a wheelchair to pass and for a wheelchair to make a 90-degree turn without backing up. A 5-foot path will let a wheelchair make a complete 180-degree turn without reversing. If you don't have room for a 5-foot turnaround, make two 3-foot pathways that meet in a T (see page 271).

Wide paths also make it easier to move wheelbarrows and other large equipment around in the garden area. All gates, passageways, and other openings should be at least 42 inches wide — the width of a wheelbarrow measured from knuckle to knuckle.

Path surface. All pathway materials should be firm and even. Good materials include textured concrete, brick paving, interlocking concrete blocks, asphalt, wood decking, and epoxy-bonded resin aggregate. You may need to hire someone to install these, and they can be expensive. The upkeep is minimal, however, and they offer tough, nonskid surfaces for easy walking and wheeling.

Gravel is readily obtained and inexpensive, but wheels sink into it, making travel by wheelchair exhausting, and pushing a heavy wheelbarrow full of garden materials nearly impossible. Crushed gravel set into a clay binder is better, but it needs some upkeep and can get muddy in wet areas. Anything larger than "pea" gravel is slippery and hard to walk on. You can modify a gravel path by covering it with indoor-outdoor carpeting or artificial grass.

Hard-packed soil is cheap, but although it is fine in dry weather, pathway use will be limited in rainy weather. Wood,

The Barrier-Free Garden

★ Provide wide doorways. Doors to the garden area should allow easy entry and exit for a wheelchair or a person with assistive devices.

★ Consider safety of stairs and steps. Avoid narrow treads, open risers, and protruding nosings, and provide railings and nonskid surfaces.

★ Provide minimally sloped ramps. Hard, level, nonskid surfaces with a slope gradient of no more than 1:12 are the most functional.

★ Maintain wide, firm paths and walkways of nonskid material; turn-around room for a wheelchair may be required.

★ Keep it small. Design gardens that you can easily reach without tiring. Use raised beds and container plants to keep work areas manageable.

★ Keep tools and water in easy-to-access places.

especially long-lasting railroad ties, makes a good pathway surface. Shredded bark, if laid on a firm, well-drained surface, is a suitable and attractive material for most paths.

Garden Beds

Raised beds are a great help to the gardener who cannot stoop, bend, or kneel. A raised bed no wider than a comfortable reach is the easiest garden bed to weed or work in. (For more on raised-bed gardening, see pages 43-47).

PURCHASING SEEDS AND PLANTS

To further streamline the gardening process, obtain seeds and plants by mail order. Garden catalogs are full of information and planting ideas. Unusual and special-use plants that can be found nowhere else are available by mail. Gardening by mail helps you to keep up with the latest advances in specialty tools and new plant offerings, and part of the fun of gardening is to try new things. You can't beat doorstep delivery for convenience!

Some catalogs offer more information than many garden encyclopedias. Browsing through the catalogs between planting seasons can be an entertaining and educational pastime for the "armchair" gardener. You may even find yourself ordering more plants or seeds than you can possibly use, if you aren't careful. Remember that the longevity of some seeds is limited to a very short period of time, so don't order more seeds than you can plant in one year. See appendix 5 for a list of mail-order suppliers.

Local nurseries are also good sources for seeds. There you will find informed salespeople who can help you choose plants that

The Most Important Rules to Easier Gardening

★ Know your soil.

★ Know your climate.

★ Limit lawn areas.

★ Use disease- and insect-resistant plants.

★ Keep garden beds, tools, and supplies within reach.

★ Locate your garden near a water source.

★ Mulch to control weeds.

★ Start small — don't try for the perfect garden.

★ Stop to sit and enjoy!

are easily grown and do well in your area. In addition, these folks are usually trained to recognize common plant diseases; bring your problem plants to them for diagnosis and advice.

I often receive many seed packets at one time, and I find it helpful to organize them by planting date. The ones I intend to start early are stored together, as are those for midseason and later, so that I can find them easily. I also separate these holdings into further groups divided by care requirements: those requiring cool starts and those requiring warm starts; those that need long germination times and those that need shorter times. Anything that helps garden organization cuts down on your workload.

If you mail order herb and perennial plant material or shrubs and trees, be prepared to plant them immediately. Reputable mail-order nurseries send plants only during their proper planting times in your area, unless you request otherwise. Because of this shipping policy, you may wait some time for your order. Don't be overly anxious, your plants will survive and grow better if shipped and planted at the optimal time.

Plants usually suffer in transport and should not be left out of the ground for too long. If you must store them, a cool, shady place is best, but beware of dampness that can cause rot or disease. Keep them in their original packages if they are delivered wrapped in sphagnum moss or some other root-protecting material. Check them frequently and don't allow the roots to dry out. Trees and shrubs that are sent when dormant can be *heeled in* until planting time (see illustration at right). Unpack your new arrivals in a cool, shady place and examine them for injuries. Cut off broken or ragged roots and heel in. Plant them in their perma-

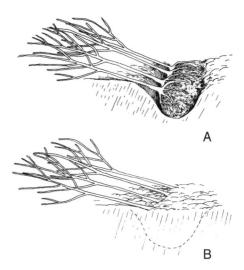

▲ *To heel in, choose a spot in a bright, well-drained area. (A) Dig a trench that is vertical on one side and sloped on the other. Lay the bare-root plants close together, with the stems or trunks resting on the sloped side of the trench. (B) Cover the roots completely with soil, and water them thoroughly. Firm the soil around the roots. Cover the stems and trunks with protective earth if the plants are to be heeled in through the winter.*

nent positions as soon as possible. Bulbs, of course, are dormant when shipped and are more tolerant of delay, but they, too, should be planted as soon as possible.

Don't be disappointed by the appearance of your mail-order plants. They often look pretty homely. Some may be nothing but shriveled-up roots in plastic bags, but they will grow quite nicely if planted correctly.

Leave the plant labels attached, if possible. One naked stick looks like another until it starts to grow and bloom. It's too easy to tromp over newly planted roots, or even to yank them out if they are not marked in some way.

CHAPTER 2

TOOLS FOR ABLE GARDENERS

The well-planned, well-equipped garden saves time and energy. Think about what you need to accomplish, and then get the right tools for the job. At the very least, you need a digging tool, a clipping tool, and a cultivating tool. For raised beds and containers, hand tools are sufficient. For a larger garden, you'll need a spade, a turning fork, and a hoe. The gardener who faces lots of pruning and shaping should think about buying some power tools to make the work go faster.

"Test drive" tools before you buy them. Lift and manipulate the tool from the position in which you'll be using it. Whether you stand, stoop, or sit to garden will determine the handle length you require. For example, if you expect to be sitting while you garden, sit down and go through the motions of using the tool. You'll be surprised at how different a tool can feel when you're sitting, standing, or stooping. Make sure the handle is the right length and the grip is the right size. A tool that's too big for your hand can't be fixed, but if it's too small, wrap the handle to make it bigger. Hold the tool at arm's length. Is it awkward or weighty? A tool that feels heavy in the store will feel twice as heavy out in the garden. Look for good workmanship — a tool that's solid and safe.

Spades and rakes that break when you lean on them are especially dangerous. Look for bright-colored handles that make tools easy to find.

Gardeners come in all sizes and strengths. Mobility restrictions and physical limitations don't have to keep you out of the garden. With a little planning and the right tools anyone can continue to garden independently. You can buy special "enabling" tools, or you can adapt tools you already own to suit your particular needs. These tools not only save time and energy but also help you avoid unnecessary stress or pain.

> **Tool Tip:**
> Use the right tool for each job. Hacking at a large branch with a pair of hand clippers, for example, is a waste of energy.

MARTHA STOREY

▲ *Clean and oil garden tools by plunging them up and down in a bucket of sand combined with used motor oil.*

CARING FOR TOOLS

Good garden tools should last a long time. Don't leave them out to weather and rust. Clean mud and dirt off tools before putting them away. A piece of wood makes a good scraper. Plunging tools up and down in a bucket of sand combined with used motor oil is an easy way to clean and oil them at the same time. Keep hoe and shovel edges sharp by filing them occasionally; the sharper the tool, the easier it is to dig with. Check wooden handles for slivers, and sand them to keep them smooth. Replace broken handles, and make sure the connections are tight.

Locate your tools in an accessible and convenient place. If you have room for a tool shed near the garden, you're in luck. Make sure doorways are wide enough to let you and your tools out at the same time. This is especially important if you use a wheelchair

Possibilities for good tool holders and carriers are all around you, if you use your imagination. No matter what you carry your tools in, keep the load reasonable — don't strain your back just to save a trip! Try these:

★ An old golf-bag and cart — you can wheel your tools right out to the garden

★ Wall-mounted storage bins

★ A mobile mechanic's toolbox with drawers

★ Two pegboards fastened together A-frame fashion

★ Aprons with large pockets

★ Wicker or plastic baskets

★ A backpack

★ A child's wagon

GARDENER'S SUPPLY

★ A plastic bucket

★ A collapsible shopping cart

or some other assistive device. Pegboard or other types of hangers will help you organize your tool storage area.

HOMEMADE TOOLS

It's not hard to make your own special tools. The following ideas solve some common problems many gardeners face. You may think of other ways to accommodate your own needs.

Trouble "making a fist." Wrap the handles of hand tools, shovels, and garden forks with soft fabric to enlarge them. The rubber hand grips made for crutches are great for wrapping around tool handles; they are available at pharmacies or from medical suppliers. Self-adhesive foam, found in the foot-care section of your drugstore, can also be used to pad tool handles. Bicycle handle grips, foam pipe insulation,

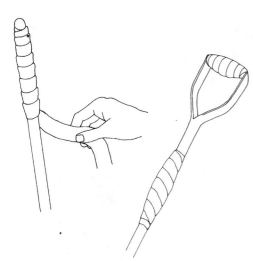

▲ *Wrap tool handles with tape.*

▲ *If your grip is weak, use a cup as a digging tool.*

tennis racket grip tape, and elastic bandages are other good handle-pads.

Weak fingers. Try using a cup with a large handle as a digging tool. Put your hand through the handle, and even if you can't grip, the handle will hold the cup on your hand. Use the cup to dip water from a bucket or to move dirt. People who cannot lift even the smallest watering utensil are able to use a sponge dipped in water and dribble it over the plant.

Trouble reaching or bending. Long handles, such as those on barbecue tools, are a great help when you must pull weeds, transplant, or remove dead leaves from hard-to-reach areas. Slip a tube-shaped elastic arm bandage over your arm and the long handle of a tool. This allows you to use your forearm for leverage, and takes the stress off your hand and wrist.

Fatigue. Bring a stool out to the garden to sit on while you work. A stool with a carrying handle is easy to move. Make a padded board to place between two raised beds for easy "sit-down" gardening. Cut a board long enough to reach between two raised beds, and staple some cotton or polyester batting

HOUSEHOLD TRANSPLANTING AIDS

★ Scissors to thin seedlings

★ A teaspoon or fork to cultivate in containers

★ The handle-end of a wooden spoon for a dibble to make planting holes for small transplants

★ Tweezers to pick up tiny seeds

★ Salt shakers filled with a mixture of sand and seed for sowing the tiniest seeds

and oilcloth over the top of a board.

If you know a child who has abandoned his or her skate-board, see if you can "borrow" it. A skateboard can be pretty handy for scooting around the garden. One with fat tires will be more stable and easier to move over dirt than one with narrow wheels.

 TOOLS YOU CAN BUY

Sources of enabling tools include mail-order houses, local nurseries, and home-improvement suppliers, as well as your own kitchen. Shop for quality; nothing is more frustrating than a cheap, ill-designed tool.

There are as many different ways of doing things in the garden as there are gardeners. Use the tool and technique that work best for you. Some mail-order suppliers that can be depended on for quality goods are listed in appendix 5.

Back savers. Use long-handled tools to avoid bending over in the garden. Some tools come with interchangeable handles, a longer one to extend your reach and a shorter one for closer work. Well-made children's tools are an excellent choice for no-bend gardening. Buy quality products, not toys, that will serve you long and well. Specialty tools, such as long-handled bulb planters, weed pullers, and grass shears are available from many garden supply catalogs, if you can't find them at your local nursery.

▲ *Long-handled grass shears take the back strain out of edging tasks.*

Wrist savers. If your wrists tire or your grip is weak, trigger-grip tools made of cast aluminum are designed so that your index and middle finger have a resting place under the handle that makes them easier to hold securely. You can find

▲ *One-handed lopper*

▲ *Ratchet-action pruners*

▲ *Kneeling bench*

▲ *Knee pads*

trowels that are designed to rest against the palm of your hand, so that a tight grip isn't necessary to push the trowel into the soil. Ratchet-action pruners and lopping shears make branch-cutting easier. Florist's pruners are lightweight, have blunt ends, and sharp blades for smooth cutting. The handle springs open, so those who have limited hand strength can use them easily. They come with different sized handles; even people who can't bend their fingers can slip their hand through the large openings. Flower cutters that hold the stem of a flower after it's cut make one-handed flower harvesting possible.

Knee savers. Kneeling or squatting in garden beds strains your joints, and some folks have trouble rising from that position. Look for assistive devices that make kneeling easier or that allow you to scoot about the garden while sitting. A kneeler with handles that provide support for getting up and down is especially helpful. This same kind of kneeler, when turned over, becomes a handy seat! You can make your own kneeling stool; be sure to give yourself plenty of padding. Attach a tool carrier to your stool for additional efficiency. Kneeling pads that attach directly to your knees and pants with built-in knee pads protect your joints while you are working on the ground.

A comfortable alternative to all that squatting and kneeling is a seat with wheels. These "garden scoots" have wide rubber tires that move through the garden easily.

Muscle savers. Move your tools and equipment around the garden the easy way — on wheels! Lightweight carts come in many sizes. Plastic carts are the easiest to move; large carts with detachable sides are the easiest to unload. And telescoping handles that adjust to your height are a real advantage. Balance is important, so test them out before you buy. A cart with four wheels is more stable than the traditional three-wheeled barrow, and it puts less strain on the arms and back.

Finger savers. Seed-sowing helpers are available through most mail-order houses. They are a boon to those who have lost finger flexibility. Some seed-sowers are adjustable to accommodate small and large seeds. Row seeders that drop one seed at a time as you walk through the garden eliminate bending.

Watering aids. Keeping a garden well-watered can be a burden, but there are tools to make the job easier. Water nozzles with trigger grips or that shut off when dropped are easy on the weak wrist or poor grip. Long-handled nozzles extend your reach and allow access to overhead plants. Lightweight hoses and hose carriers with wheels lessen hose-dragging chores. Hose nozzles with snap-on fixtures are easier to use than the screw-on types. Some holders grip the hose for you; all you have to do is direct the spray.

Plastic watering cans with long spouts and well-balanced handles are easy for anyone to use. Water is heavy, so choose cans that hold no more than 1 gallon.

Drip irrigation is the most convenient way to water, and installing a drip system is worth the initial effort and investment. Kits

▲ *This lightweight plastic cart is more stable than a wheelbarrow.*

▲ *A long-handled seed sower*

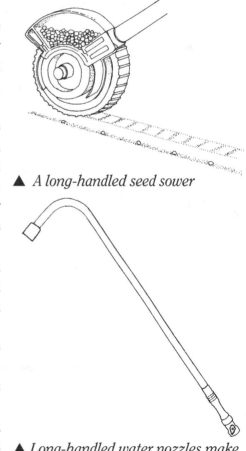

▲ *Long-handled water nozzles make it easy to reach overhead plants.*

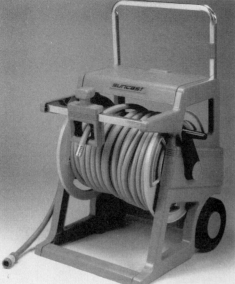

▲ *A wheeled hose carrier*

▲ *A lightweight watering can with a well-balanced handle*

are available that make start-up pretty simple. If you can't have a drip system, a water timer is the next best choice. Automating your sprinklers and soakers cuts down on watering chores. (For more on watering, see pages 124-131.)

Digging aids. A well-balanced, sharp spade or shovel makes digging go more smoothly. Spades with D–grips are easier to grasp than straight-shafted tools. For heavy digging, a long-handled shovel gives you good leverage and is therefore easier on the back. Remember your individual needs when selecting equipment. A spade should be easy to lift and feel comfortable. Choose tools that suit your height, weight, and strength. And, be sure to heft it before you buy it! A too-heavy or clumsy tool can cause accidents.

Garden forks are easier on your back than shovels, since you have only to turn the soil, not lift it. The gardener with a weak back will want to use a small-headed fork, which is lighter because its soil-moving capacity is smaller.

Power tillers weighing as little as 17 pounds come with various attachments to make many jobs easier. They are either gasoline- or electric-powered. The electric-powered tools are lighter in weight. A rear-end tiller is the safest and easiest kind of tiller to use. Remember to wear safety goggles when using power equipment.

Weeding aids. I have a gardening friend who beats weeds

▲ *Spades with D-grips are easier to grasp than straight handles.*

to death with his cane — he says it works better than pulling them up, and it gives him great satisfaction!  **Another friend, whose hands are affected by arthritis, uses a Bowie knife for many garden jobs, including weeding.** You can adapt many everyday objects to make weeding easier. In addition, many special tools have been developed to make this least-favorite chore as painless as possible. You'll find lightweight hoes in various shapes and sizes. For weeding, the sharper, the better. My favorite tool is a Cape Cod weeder. This L-shaped tool allows you to work closely around the stem of a plant with less risk of damage than some of the other weeding tools. The "elbow" part of the blade pulls up weed roots with little effort.

A tool called the Queensland backsaving weeder is said to have been invented in Australia. This 34½-inch-long device lets you reach weeds without bending or straining your back. To use it, position the pronged weeding claw over the weed's center. As you step down on the foot plate, the claws close tightly around the weed so that you can pull it up.

Weed whackers and other power weeding tools give the home gardener all the advantages of the landscape professional. Many string trimmers are so light and well-balanced that anyone can quickly and easily clean up the shaggy edges of the garden.

Eye savers. Perfect eyesight isn't necessary for good gardening. Vision-enhancing tools are easily found. A magnifying glass can be used for seed-sowing or insect inspection. Magnifiers that hang from the neck and leave one's hands free are especially helpful. Tools with bright-colored handles are easier to see and less likely to get lost out in the yard. Seed tape and pre-planted seed trays are a big help to the gardener with limited sight.

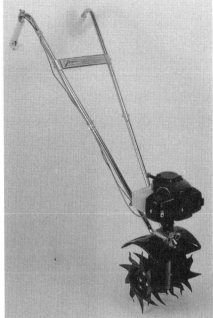

GARDENER'S SUPPLY

▲ *Portable tiller*

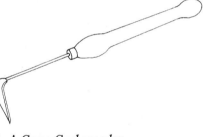

▲ *A Cape Cod weeder*

Some Tool Safety Rules

★ Use long-handled tools; avoid bending and save your back!

★ Use tools with trigger grips or wrapped handles — they are easier to use and cause less stress to small hand joints.

★ Use lightweight tools (including lightweight power tools) to avoid the fatigue caused by working with heavy tools.

★ Use kneelers or padded pants to protect your knees.

★ Use a cart with wheels to move your tools and garden waste.

★ Keep garden paths clear. Always move garden carts, hoses, and tools out of the paths.

★ Don't leave tools lying around. It hurts when you step on hand tools or trip over long-handled tools (remember the old "rake-in-the-face" trick?). Put them away when you've finished, it's easy to forget where you left them.

★ Store and use pesticides safely. Maintain a special area, away from foodstuffs, for toxic chemicals. This should be a locked cupboard if there are small children in your home. Be aware that pets may try to get into pesticides. Mix these chemicals in a safe place and wear protective clothing. Do not carry breakable containers around the garden.

★ Organize your tools. Keep frequently used items near at hand in an easily accessible location. If possible, keep duplicates of harder-to-transport tools at various working locations.

★ Wear safety gear. Use eye protection goggles when spraying, pruning, or using power tools. Stout gloves will protect your hands from cuts and thorns. Wear closed-toe shoes with nonslip soles.

★ Keep your tools sharp. Dull, rusty tools cause accidents.

★ Install a drip system or place hoses at convenient spots to decrease watering chores.

★ Lightweight power tools can save work.

★ Adapt your own tools and assistive devices for safer and easier work in the garden.

Less is more. Gardening can be heavy work. If you are gardening in containers, plastic pots and gardening implements make heavy tools a thing of the past. Use heavy-duty plastic spoons for moving dirt and heavy-duty plastic knives for transplanting.

Safety first! Wear protective gloves when working with thorns, branches, or power equipment. Gloves help you maintain your grip as well as protect your hands from cuts and scratches. Don't forget to put them on at the start of your gardening day, *before* you get blisters!

Protect your feet. Wear supportive shoes with nonslip soles. If you are doing any heavy work, wear heavy-duty protective boots or hard-toed shoes. Wear a hat and/or sunscreen to protect yourself from the sun's rays. Remember to apply sunscreen or cover your arms as well as your face. Sturdy, comfortable clothing is advisable; don't wear anything that might trip you or get caught in equipment. As mentioned earlier, wear safety goggles to protect your eyes when using power equipment or when working in brush. Make sure they don't fog up and restrict your vision.

Tips for Assistive Devices

If you use assistive devices to get around, adapt them to make your gardening tasks easier. Almost any plastic or metal basket can be attached to a walker to get your tools to the work area. Use your imagination! Some gardeners use bicycle baskets and backpacks to increase their tool-carrying capacity.

Replace walker wheels with fat tires to move through the garden more easily, or put runners on the back legs so they

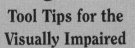

Tool Tips for the Visually Impaired

★ Keep tools hanging on a pegboard with outlines that show where each tool belongs. You'll spend much less time searching for what you need.

★ Use tools with bright-colored handles.

▲ *Use a magnifying glass when working with small seeds.*

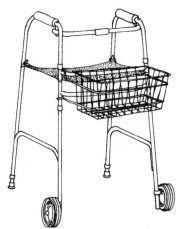

▲ *A basket and fat tires make this walker garden ready.*

won't get stuck in the dirt. Add a seat for resting, and you've got the perfect garden walker! Custom-fit wheelchairs with trays or lapboards for convenient tool-carriers or work stations. Pockets that attach to the arms or the back of the wheelchair are also handy.

A NEW GARDENING TOOL: YOUR COMPUTER

Imagine a cold and dreary day — you're sitting comfortably in your cozy house with a fire crackling and your favorite music playing in the background, and you're gardening. You don't believe it? With a home computer and some gardening software you can do almost everything but poke the seeds in the ground.

The newest and most fascinating garden tool is the home computer. Now that many households have computers for home accounting, record keeping, writing, and amusement, people who can't get out easily are finding that computers are great for keeping up. Special Interest Groups (SIG's) and forums that run on computer bulletin boards communicate via computer modem (a device that allows computer-generated messages to be sent and received over telephone lines) at any time of the day or night. These bulletin boards are accessed by members from all over the world. Think about how much fun it would be to talk with gardeners from other countries and other walks of life. In researching this book, for instance, I accessed information by asking gardeners all over the United States to send me their ideas about barrier-free gardening.

Fortunately, modern advances have made computers simple to master. For people with limited manual dexterity, computer keyboards are easier to use than standard typewriters. Computer-assisted drawing makes creative artwork and graphics, such as garden designs, possible for those who are unable to hold conventional artist's tools.

With a computer as a gardening tool, you can work in the

garden regardless of what the weather is like. When rain keeps you indoors, you can plan and rearrange your garden design, organize your seed inventory, update your gardening notes, and make planting lists, so you'll be ready to go when the sun comes out. You can even buy plant-information programs that help you choose the right plants for your garden. You input your particular soil, moisture, site, and plant zone, and the software creates a plant list suited to your particular garden. Some programs even "age" your garden graphically, so that you can see what it will look like when mature. This is especially valuable if you have limited space.

Garden Recordkeeping

Garden recordkeeping is a much-touted, and often ignored, garden practice. Not only do you have to develop some system that makes sense to you, but you have to keep your records in an accessible place. No one wants to go sifting through five years of scattered notes just to find one little bit of information. Here's where a computer has the advantage.

GARDEN TABLE

Seed	planted	germinated	harvested	source
Kandy Korn	May 15, 91	May 24, 91	Aug 30, 91	Shepherd's
carrot, Rondino	Feb 14, 91	Mar 3, 91	Apr 30, 91	Johnny's
carrot, Rumba	Feb 14, 91	Mar 1, 91	Apr 15, 91	Johnny's
carrot, Mokum	Feb 14, 91	Feb 28, 91	Apr 15, 91	Thompson & Morgan
peas, Sugar Daddy	Mar 15, 91	Mar 22, 91	Apr 30, 91	Burpee
peas, Snappy	Mar 15, 91	Mar 30, 91	May 14, 91	Burpee

▲ *Garden records created in a computer database are easy to access.*

Most computers have search-and-find programs that can locate a specific piece of information once you type one or two commands.

To keep your records straight, create your own gardening database. The term *database* may seem sophisticated and high tech, but you probably use one every day. A phone book is a type of database, as is an index-card file. A computer database is simply an electronic list for saving information; you can use your computer to organize, re-organize, and retrieve your data at will. For example, enter certain categories of information about all of your plants — type (flower, vegetable, annual, perennial), season of bloom, color, where you obtained the plant, and so on. Then, sort your data by any of these criteria to retrieve lists of all the plants that will bloom in the spring, for instance, or all those with a red flower. Some other things you might want to sort for include:

★ Planting date
★ Water needs (dry, moist)
★ Soil preference (acid, alkaline)
★ Light requirements
★ Bloom color
★ Harvest time

Can't remember when you last fertilized the roses? Need to be reminded to plant the tulips? In addition to your garden records, keep your personal garden calendar on your computer. Record yearly temperatures, first and last frost dates, rainfall, and so on. These will be easy to access in an electronic file. Some software programs print calendars by the week, month, or year, with space for you to add your own to-do notes.

Design a Garden

Most gardening books (this one included!) advise planning your garden on paper, but they don't always recognize what a problem that can be. Garden plans are difficult to draw, aggravating to change, and get lost just about the time you need to refer to them. With a computer, however, you can produce scale drawings faster than you can with paper and pencil. The plans can be quickly changed and modified, and you can keep multiple versions on hand for comparison. With the aid of a computer, you can even plot the sun's movement across your yard.

So-called *draw programs* are particularly useful for generating garden plans to scale, and for giving you a bird's-eye view of the whole yard or a specific garden area. *Paint programs* help you visualize how groups of plants will look. You can fill various geometric and free-form shapes with distinct shades and patterns to represent different plant beds. These beds can be rearranged and resized at will until you find a grouping that suits you. Landscape design programs combine the advantages of draw and paint programs — they are set up to make garden planning as automatic and painless as

MARCH

Sunday	Monday	Tuesday	Wednesday	Thursday	Friday	Saturday
30 *order vegetable seeds*	31	1	2 *plant tomato seeds*	3	4	5 *prune roses*
6	7	8	9	10	11 *tomatoes germinated*	12 *32 degrees last night*
13	14 *receive seeds from Parks*	15	16	17	18	19
20	21	22	23 *garden plan*	24	25	26
27	28	29	30	31	1	2

▲ *Keep your garden calendar on your computer.*

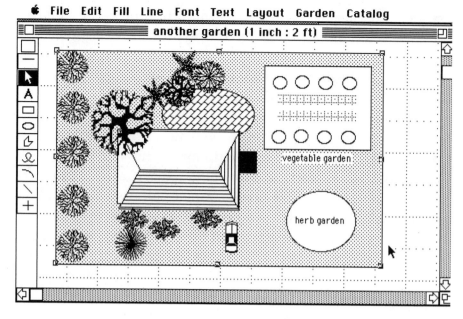

another garden (1 inch : 2 ft)

vegetable garden

herb garden

▶ *Some landscape design programs allow you to make graphic plans that you can change at will. This design was created using the garden software "Mum's the Word" from Terrace Software.*

possible. (See appendix 5 for sources of garden software.)

I've changed my garden the "old-fashioned way" — toting plants and hauling soil from one end of the garden to the other — so many times that my back aches just thinking about it. From now on, I'll let my computer do some of that work for me. The next time I need to find the source for my favorite tomato seeds, I won't be down on my knees hunting through old notebooks — I'll just ask my friendly computer to retrieve that information for me. Try some armchair gardening with these modern tools that can help make you a gardening wizard! Don't pass up the opportunity to use your computer in the garden.

CHAPTER 3

THE EASIEST-CARE GARDENS:
RAISED BEDS, CONTAINER GARDENS, INDOOR PLANTS, AND WINDOW GARDENS

Gardens come in as many shapes and styles as gardeners do. Some gardens are easier to work than others. Raised-bed gardens and container gardens, for instance, are real time and energy savers. One or both of these may be the perfect answer for you if you don't want to deal with the demands of in-ground gardening. Indoor gardens can fulfill the desire to keep on gardening, even when the weather outside prohibits it. They are also good alternatives for those with little garden space or for those who can't get outdoors very often.

RAISED-BED GARDENING

The term *raised bed* refers to any technique that raises the growing bed above the garden level. It may be as simple as mounding the soil in your garden or as complicated as constructing special growing boxes. Even if your raised bed is only a few inches high, it will be neater and last longer if it is framed with wood, stone, or other suitable material. If you raise the bed enough to eliminate the need to bend over, you'll have created a real back saver. Sitting edges around the bed provide a convenient and safe working position. Waist-high

▲ *Waist-high raised beds allow you to garden sitting down.*

beds are ideal for a wheelchair gardener or anyone else who wants to sit while working. Raised beds can be placed anywhere, even over an existing lawn or patio, if you provide good drainage.

In the confined area of a raised bed, it's easy and economical to mix soil to suit each plant's specific needs. You can have separate beds of acidic, sandy, and loamy soils. Because you never walk in these beds, the dirt doesn't get compacted and is therefore easier to dig.

Constructing Your Raised Bed

If possible, lay out your beds in a north/south orientation. Because the sun will pass over your plants from east to west, keep tall plants on the north side of the garden, where they are less likely to shade the shorter ones.

▶ *All plants in a garden with a north-south orientation receive equal sunlight throughout the day.*

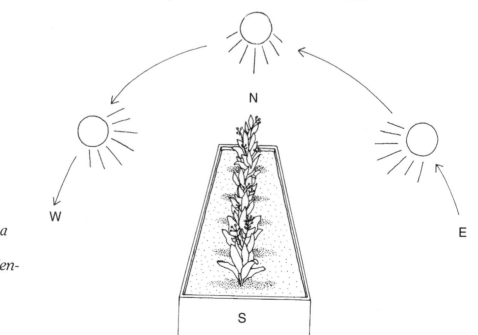

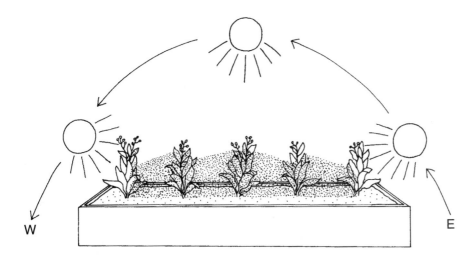

◄ Plants in a garden with an east-west orientation shade one another as the sun moves across them.

A raised bed can be any length, but no more than 10 feet is optimal. If you make it 25 feet from one end to the other, you'll be doing more walking than gardening. Make the bed width no more than twice the distance you can comfortably reach without straining. A bed 4 feet wide requires a 2-foot reach to get to the middle of the bed. You don't need very large beds. I've grown even that old space-hog corn in 4-foot square boxes.

Dig the bed and prepare the soil (see chapter 4). Use a lightweight power tiller to make this job easier. Frame your raised bed with anything that is strong and resists weather. Railroad ties or concrete blocks make sturdy raised beds. Boards (2"x8" preferably) are equally appropriate. Redwood and cedar, although somewhat costly, are long lasting and attractive. You can also use pressure-treated wood or treat your lumber with a water-repellant preservative. Be certain, however, to choose a product that can be safely used around plants, particularly food plants. Lumber treated with copper chromate arsenicals, for example, is considered safe. Many preservatives are highly toxic or possibly carcinogenic. Current research promises to develop safer alternatives.

When choosing wood for your raised bed, use the straightest pieces. Buy wood that is at least 1½ inches thick; boards thinner than that don't hold up well. Used bricks, paving blocks, or leftover stones from a rock garden are other possibilities. Look around — you may already have your building material stashed in the yard somewhere.

If you are building a wooden frame, nail together the measured and cut boards. If you wish, reinforce the corners with metal angle braces. These are not absolutely necessary, but they do give the box extra strength.

Place the box around the soil in the prepared bed. Use a level to make sure the box is plumb and level. To give the box more stability, on the inside of the cold frame at each corner insert one large screw eye at the top and one at the bottom of the side boards. Line these screw eyes up so that you can drive 18-inch metal stakes through them, as shown. It's easier to pound the stakes into damp ground than into dry, so soak the earth before you start your work.

▶ *A 4'x5' raised bed makes a compact growing area. Note the extra stability provided at the corners by the metal stakes.*

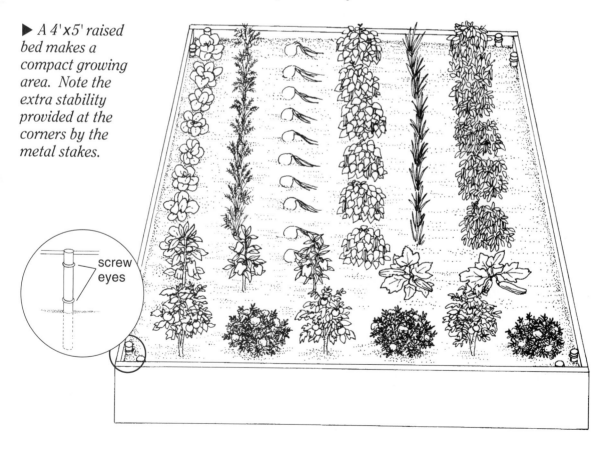

screw eyes

After the box is in place and staked, fill it with additional soil or soil substitute (peat moss or soil mix, for instance; see pages 53-54 for soil mix formulas). Level the surface with a rake or a board, and water well to help the soil settle. Wait about a week for the soil to settle completely, and your raised bed is ready to plant! This model can be adjusted for height, width, length, and materials: Choose the one that suits your gardening needs.

For a strong garden bed, convenient for use when seated, pile concrete blocks, three or four blocks high. Most elevated garden beds do not need to be any higher than 3 feet. For safety's sake, get an experienced person to build concrete-block garden beds. It is necessary to prepare a firm, flat foundation for a concrete-block structure so that it doesn't crack or wobble. Any concrete-block structure that is over 3 feet high requires both vertical and horizontal reinforcement. To reinforce horizontally, mortar galvanized mesh across the joints between the blocks. For vertical stability, run steel reinforcing rods through the blocks and into the soil.

Successful Raised Beds

★ Design small beds — they are easier to use. Beds should be no wider than twice a comfortable reach (4 feet or less).

★ Waist-high beds eliminate the need to bend over while working.

★ Fill the beds with a light soil mix, which drains well and is easy to dig.

★ Give your raised beds sitting edges — these make built-in rest areas.

OTHER ELEVATED GARDENING TECHNIQUES

If raised beds aren't possible, miniature garden beds can be created on a sturdy old table, a strong bench, stair steps, sawhorses, or other support that gets them up to waist level. Fill a few small boxes with lightweight soil mix and place them on the base. Soil is heavy, so be sure your elevated garden bed is on a strong base. So-called pyramid gardens, available at many garden supply centers, are also good for waist-high gardening. Old tires, stacked three high, make an easy, inexpensive garden.

If you garden on a patio, rooftop, or balcony, where deep

beds are not feasible, you can get good yields of strawberries, onions, radishes, lettuce, spinach, and bush beans in beds only 3 inches deep. A shallow-bed device used frequently in Europe is the *pillow-pack,* a large plastic bag filled with a light soil mix and laid on its side. Plants are inserted into the bag through holes cut in the top. Drainage holes should be provided in the bottom or sides of this type of container. (See appendix 5 for source of supply.) Taking this idea to its simplest form, you could even plant right in purchased soil mix bags.

OUTDOOR CONTAINER GARDENING

Outdoor container gardening is ideal for the "sit-down gardener," someone who doesn't get around easily, or someone who can't invest a lot of time and energy in garden chores. You don't even need a yard to enjoy gardening. Any patio, balcony, deck, or even doorstep can be your growing area for bright flowers and delicious vegetables. You can grow a whole garden in pots, cans, or window boxes — in fact, in any container with holes for drainage. And, you can have an instant garden anywhere simply by moving the containers. In fact,

▲ *Create a versatile, movable garden by placing plants in a child's wagon.*

create a truly movable garden by filling a child's wagon with potted plants. Very little weeding is necessary and plants can be kept attractive with a few pinches or snips. What could be easier?

Filled containers are heavy, so put them where you want them *before* you add the soil, or put them on a wheeled platform for easy mobility.

Choosing the Container

Containers come in a variety of styles, sizes, and materials. In addition to those available commercially, you may find other suitable containers. Each type of plant container has both advantages and disadvantages.

Unglazed clay pots. Although easy to find and inexpensive, clay pots can be heavy, and if you are physically limited, this must be a consideration. Clay pots are porous and allow air to circulate to plant roots, but the roots also dry out quickly and need extra watering. If you set the pot on a tray of moistened pebbles, you can increase the surrounding humidity and reduce water requirements. Mulch also helps.

Clay pots can be re-used only if you're willing to spend some of your garden time to clean them thoroughly. Salts and other minerals build up on the outside of clay pots. This build-up is not only unattractive but can cause burns of sensitive plant roots. The mineral accumulation can be scrubbed off easily if tackled right away, but turns into a major job if left too long. After scrubbing, dip the pots in a chlorine bleach bath (1 cup bleach to 1 gallon water), rinse

▲ *Heavy containers are easier to manage if placed on a wheeled platform.*

CINDY MCFARLAND

▲ *The salts and other minerals that build up on clay pots should be scrubbed off before re-use.*

thoroughly, and allow the pots to stand for three days to break down the chlorine. Chlorine kills viruses and other plant diseases that may be left over from previous plantings.

Plastic pots. Available in assorted styles, colors, and sizes, plastic pots are light, reusable, and inexpensive. Unlike clay pots, plastic ones are easy to clean; you can even run them through the dishwasher (on the upper rack, where it is usually a little cooler than the bottom, to avoid melting the plastic). One problem with plastic pots is that water cannot evaporate through the sides. This means that although you have to water your plants less frequently, it's easy to overwater and drown plants. The light weight of plastic makes these containers a good choice for the physically limited gardener. On the other hand, plastic pots can be too light to support the weight of very tall plants. Add stones to the bottom before the plant is potted to solve the tip-over problem.

Wooden containers. Make your own wooden containers in any shape and size that suits your particular garden spot, or purchase ready-made containers of redwood and cedar, which resist decay and age beautifully. The soft gray color of an unpainted redwood or cedar box harmonizes nicely with green plant foliage and bright-colored blossoms. Fir is often used for large planters because it is stronger than redwood or cedar. In order for this wood to last a long time, it should be treated with a preservative (see page 45). Pine is soft and easy to work with, but it also needs preserving. Exterior plywood is lightweight and strong, but is unattractive unless painted. If you don't mind a rustic look, wooden planter boxes can be built of almost any leftover wood. I've had surprising success by just nailing together five pieces of scrap redwood, with the bottom piece drilled for drainage. These quick-and-easy plant containers lasted over 10 years before they started to fall apart.

Styrofoam containers. Although not as attractive as some materials, Styrofoam is lightweight, and also insulates the roots from temperature extremes. A good way to use a pretty pot with no drainage holes is to *double pot;* place the

Easy Container Gardening
for Physically Limited Gardeners

★ Garden on the doorstep. Keep plants within easy reach.

★ Garden on the table. Table-top lights offer indoor convenience and good growing conditions.

★ Garden in the window. Get outdoor conditions with indoor convenience.

★ Use lightweight containers that are portable and easy to handle.

★ Limit soil preparation chores: use commercial soil mixes.

★ Choose the right plants — those that can tolerate your particular conditions and some neglect.

★ Assemble your tools in a convenient area, or keep them in a wheeled cart.

★ Don't plant more than you can care for.

well-drained, but homely Styrofoam container inside the more appealing pot.

Metal, stoneware, glass, and porcelain containers. Old olive-oil and other bright-colored cans can be used for plants. Provide drainage by making holes in the bottoms with a bottle opener. Stoneware, glass, and porcelain are good-looking, but usually nonporous and lacking drainage holes. It is difficult to gauge how much water to give, even with the assistance of a water meter, and inevitably, if you plant directly in these pots, excess water builds up and the plant roots rot. For this reason, use them only as the outside pot in a double-pot arrangement.

Managing Your Container Gardens

Water. Container plants require more water than in-ground plants. Small pots, in particular, tend to overheat and dry out quickly, and during hot weather they require frequent watering — always once, and sometimes even twice, a day. Here are some things that will make watering less of a chore:

★ Install an automatic-drip watering system to cut down on

▲ An automatic-drip watering system is a real asset if you have many hanging plants.

watering chores. Many drip-irrigation supply companies offer kits that are especially made for container plants. They include all the materials needed for a basic drip system and are convenient and easy to set up. Small tubing connected to a larger feeder line delivers water to flowerpots, planter boxes, and hanging plants with mist, spray, or drip emitters placed in each container. The feeder lines to hanging plants can be hidden along the edge of a patio or along the roof line. It's a good idea to plan your drip system on paper first. You may want to rearrange some of your plants to make the watering system more efficient. (For more on drip watering, see pages 129-131).

★ Suspend over the tops of a row of plants a piece of gutter material, with the ends sealed and holes punched in the bottom. Fill the gutter, allowing water to drip through each hole into the pot below.

★ Use heavy cotton cord as watering wicks for container plants. Insert a piece of cord all the way to the bottom of a container plant. Put the other end of the cord into a dish or bucket of water. When the soil dries out in the pot, water will move by osmosis from the water bucket into the pot. This homemade self-watering device is handy if you are not going to be around to water your plants for a few days.

★ If you are unable to set up a drip watering system, keep hoses and lightweight watering cans at hand, so you don't have to pull heavy hoses around or carry water any great distance. You can even place a sprinkler among a group of containers to water many plants all at once.

★ Choose plants that can tolerate an occasional dry spell; there will be days when you can't keep up with the evaporation.

★ Mulch each container with stones or decorative bark chips.

★ Locate containers out of the wind.

★ Group containers so they shade one another. This helps to moderate temperatures around their roots and reduces evaporation.

▲ *Cluster small plants in a large container. Surround the pots with Styrofoam "peanuts," hidden by a top layer of peat moss.*

★ Place containers in the deepest shade they can tolerate.

★ Add water-holding soil polymers to the potting soil. These are available at most nurseries.

★ Use light-colored pots, which reflect the sun's heat and slow evaporation.

★ Cluster small plants in a larger container of a more moisture-retentive material, such as plastic, Styrofoam, sealed redwood, or glazed clay.

★ Double-pot by setting small pots inside larger ones, with a layer of sand, gravel, vermiculite, or damp peat moss in between. Styrofoam "peanut" packing material keeps a cool layer between pots.

★ Sink pots into the ground.

Soil. Good soil mixes for outdoor containers should be light, loose, and moisture retentive. Because container gardens require frequent watering, nutrients quickly wash out. Your soil must therefore contain plenty of organic matter, vermiculite, and/or peat moss. If you have only a few containers, buy premixed soil. If you need quite a lot of soil, you may wish to prepare your own container mix. Use one third each of peat moss, vermiculite, and perlite. This mix is light and moisture retentive, but offers few nutrients, so be sure to fertilize regularly. If compost is available, use it instead of peat moss for a richer mix. Avoid using regular garden soil, which may be too heavy or compact and drain poorly in a container.

Fertilizer. Fertilization is important to container plants because they are especially susceptible to malnutrition. The limited nutrients available in the container are soon exhausted and must be replaced, or the plant will eventually starve. An all-purpose, easily dissolved plant food works well for most container plants. Plants grown for their flowers, however, need a fertilizer with a high percentage of phosphorus (the "P" in the NPK formula on fertilizer labels; see page 76). Use fertilizer at half strength every two weeks to keep plants growing vigorously. Beware of mixing too strong a fertilizer solution. Because container plants are limited to the amount of soil in the pot, there is a greater risk of chemical burn and root damage from overfertilization. You can also use time-release fertilizer, which needs to be applied only a few times a year.

Repotting. If you notice your plants are drying out quickly and beginning to droop, they may have outgrown their containers. Move rootbound plants into containers that are 1 or 2 inches larger than their current pots. An alternative, if you don't want your plants to crowd you out of living space, is to prune their roots. Root-pruning is a technique used by bonsai gardeners to keep plants growing in very small containers. Remove the plant from the pot, prune the roots back by half, replace the plant in the same container, and add new soil mix. Most plants tolerate this quite nicely as long as the weather is mild and they are protected from direct sun for about two weeks while they recover.

Successful Container Gardens

★ Provide good drainage — you'll have fewer problems with root rot.

★ Use a light soil mix — containers will be easier to move and drainage will be improved.

★ Group plants — humidity will be improved, soil temperatures will be more stable, and watering needs will be decreased.

★ Automate your water system.

★ Fertilize regularly — frequent, light fertilizing keeps container plants growing well.

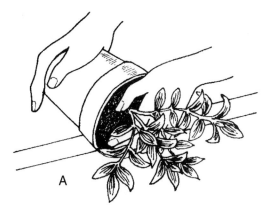
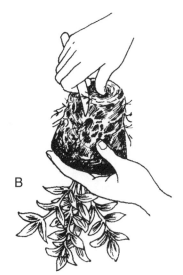

▲ *To root prune pot-bound plants, (A) gently remove plant from pot, and then (B) with a sharp knife, trim away about one-half of the roots. Replant.*

Selecting Plants for Container Gardening

Choose slow-growing plants that don't need frequent pruning or repotting, and those that don't mind having their roots confined.

Herbs and vegetables grow well in sunny locations. Eight 16-inch containers can supply fresh vegetables all season long for one or two people. Space-loving plants like tomatoes, peppers, and cucumbers should be grown one to a container. Lettuce, carrots, spinach, and beets can share a container; sow them thickly, and when you thin, use the shoots for salad. Attach trellises to containers full of beans and peas; they will happily grow upright, and yet remain within easy reach. Tuck herbs among the lettuce and spinach plants, or devote a container to them. Strawberry jars, which have pockets for individual plants, make attractive, easy-to-care-for herb gardens.

It's easy to grow flowers in containers, and you can move them around to give them

Container Gardening Tips for the Visually Impaired

★ Keep hanging plants clear of walkways and doorways; you don't want to bump your head on your garden!

★ Situate container plants around the edge of the gardening area to keep them out of walkways.

★ Bright-colored containers offer a contrast with the background and are easier to see.

▶ *You can grow an entire vegetable garden in containers: (right, clockwise from top) beans on a teepee; tomatoes; lettuce, carrots, and spinach; herbs (parsley and basil); peppers; cucumber; (below) tomatoes.*

the best light exposure or to enjoy seasonal blooms. Perennials need only basic care and will give you pleasure year after year. An added advantage of container-grown perennials is that you can grow perennials that are not winter hardy in your location, if you have a place to put them indoors when cold weather sets in. For bright color in your garden, it's fun to try annuals and bulbs in various combinations.

You can even have a "sit-down" orchard! Grow dwarf fruit trees in large pots and strawberries in jars. Fruits grown in containers are more sensitive to heat and cold, so if you grow a plant that is not hardy in your area, be sure to protect the roots during extreme weather conditions, or move it indoors for winter protection. If you plan to move plants, remember that containers filled with soil can be very heavy and hard to grip. Either keep your plants on permanent wheels, or use a hand truck, rollers, or a strong assistant to help you move them. In mild-winter areas, you can protect plants against cold by double-potting, arranging them in groups, and/or wrapping their containers.

Cacti and succulents are undemanding container plants. Their shallow root systems and modest water needs make them ideal for sit-down gardening. They are easy to plant, good-looking, and long-lived. Even in very

▲ *To grow daylilies in a container, choose one large enough to accommodate their roots and water frequently.*

hot weather, cacti and succulents may need only weekly watering. In cool weather, water only enough to keep them from shriveling. You don't need a sunny area to grow cacti and succulents; there are varieties that tolerate almost every garden situation, except winter freeze. In cold-winter areas, move them indoors for protection. Many have attractive blooms that rival even the showiest annuals.

INDOOR CONTAINER GARDENING

You don't have to go outdoors to enjoy growing plants. You can create a thriving indoor garden on a windowsill, in a well-lit room, or under special grow lights, which plants like almost as well as natural sunlight. Or, choose plants that don't need much light.

If you put your plants on or near a windowsill, give them a half turn every week so that all sides receive equal light; this will keep your plants "well-rounded." Although windowsills

GOOD CONTAINER PLANTS

COMMON NAME	BOTANIC NAME	HARDINESS ZONES*
Bulbs, Corms, and Tubers		
Amaryllis	*Amaryllis* spp.	9–10
Canna	*Canna* spp.	8
Crocus	*Crocus* spp.	4–8
Freesia	*Freesia* x *hybrida*	9
Hyacinth	*Hyacinthus* spp.	5
Iris	*Iris* spp.	5–9
Kaffir lily	*Clivia* x *cyrtanthiflora*	10
Lily	*Lilium* spp.	4–8
Lily-of-the-Nile	*Agapanthus orientalis*	8
Narcissus and daffodil	*Narcissus* spp.	4–7
Scilla	*Scilla* spp.	4–9
Tuberous begonia	*Begonia* x *tuberhybrida*	10
Tulip	*Tulipa* spp.	4–5
Annuals		
Basil	*Ocimum basilicum*	
Coleus	*Coleus* spp.	
Lobelia	*Lobelia* spp.	
Marigold	*Tagetes* spp.	
Nasturtium	*Tropaelom* spp.	
Parsley	*Petrocelinum crispum*	
Petunia	*Petunia* spp.	
Sweet pea	*Lathyrus odoratus*	
Perennials		
Alyssum	*Alyssum* spp.	3–6
Carnation	*Dianthus caryophyllus*	8
Chrysanthemum	*Chrysanthemum* spp.	3–6
Daylily	*Hemerocallis* spp.	3–9
Geranium, including scented geranium	*Pelargonium* spp.	9–10
Lavender	*Lavandula* spp.	5–8
Marguerite	*Chrysanthemum frutescens*	9
Ranunculus	*Ranunculus* spp.	4
Rosemary	*Rosmarinus officinalis*	8
Sage	*Salvia* spp.	3–8
Thyme	*Thymus* spp.	5–9
Viola	*Viola* spp.	5–8

GOOD CONTAINER PLANTS (CONT.)

COMMON NAME	BOTANIC NAME	HARDINESS ZONES*
Slow-Growing Trees and Shrubs		
Some bamboos	*Arundinaria disticha*	7
	A. variegata	7
	Bambusa glaucescens	9
Camellia	*Camellia* spp.	8–9
Fuchsia	*Fuchsia* x *hybrida*	9
Japanese maple	*Acer palmatum*	5
Palms for containers		
Mediterranean fan palm	*Chamaerops humulis*	9
Sentry palm	*Howea belmoreana*	
Parlor palm	*Chamaedorea elegans*	
	Chamaedorea seifrizii	
Evergreens for containers		
Mugho pine	*Pinus mugo mughus*	3
Japanese black pine	*Pinus thunbergiana*	5
Yew	*Podocarpus macrophyllus*	7
Fruits for Containers		
Dwarf apple	*Malus* spp.	4–8
Dwarf apricot	*Prunus armeniaca*	5
Dwarf citrus	*Citrus* spp.	10
Dwarf peach/nectarine	*Prunus persica*	5
Fig	*Ficus carica*	10
Strawberry	*Fragraria* spp.	4–8
Cacti and Succulents		
Aloe	*Aloe* spp.	9–10
Christmas cactus	*Schlumbergera* spp.	10
Crassula	*Crassula* spp.	9–10
Echeveria	*Echeveria* spp.	7–10
Haworthia	*Haworthia* spp.	9–10
Old-man cactus	*Cephalocereus senilis*	
Sedum	*Sedum* spp.	3–10

* Chart shows coldest hardiness zone tolerated by a species. Where a specific species is not named on the chart, look for a species appropriate to the hardiness range indicated.

▲ *Commercially made plant shelving with built-in lighting*

☞ If you use grow lights, make sure the wires are out of the way, so you don't trip over them.

work well for many plants, they may be too hot or too cold for some. The sun coming through an unshaded window can overheat and burn unprotected plants, while on cold nights, they can become chilled. The most sensitive plants are unable to tolerate these conditions. Provide shade during hot days, and move sensitive plants when the temperatures are extreme.

Put your indoor garden within easy reach; you don't want to climb to upper shelves every time you need to water or groom your plants. Set plants in a waterproof tray, near a source of water, if possible, for more convenient upkeep.

The most important tip for a successful indoor garden is to choose the right plant, one that will survive in your particular indoor "climate" conditions. Light and temperature are a plant's most critical needs. You may find that because of the light quality and room temperature you can provide, you will be limited to certain plants. Stick with these, for it's an uphill battle to change your whole house or apartment just for the sake of a few plants. If one of your favorite plants doesn't fall into the category of those that thrive in the conditions you offer, you may be able to grow them outdoors until they reach their most attractive stage, then bring them inside to enjoy.

Buy plants from a nursery or garden center that is likely to have taken good care of them. Nothing is more discouraging than to bring a plant home, only to have it succumb to some unknown disease within a week or two — or worse still, to infect plants you already own. Knowledgeable nursery personnel can help you choose the right plants for your gardening situation and can offer good advice about plant care.

Good Indoor Plants

Normal Indoor Temperature (nights 50°-65°F)

Sunlight

*Aloe   (Aloe spp.)
*Amaryllis   (Hippeastrum hortorum)
*Geranium   (Pelargonium spp.)
 Jade tree   (Crassula ovata)
*Kalanchoe   (Kalanchoe spp.)
*Miniature rose   (Rosa spp.)
*Orchid cactus   (Epiphyllum spp.)
*Passionflower   (Passiflora caerula)
*Rosemary   (Rosmarinus officinalis)
*Wax begonia   (Begonia x semperflorens
          cultorum)

Bright, Indirect Light

 Artillery plant   (Pilea microphylla)
 Boston fern   (Nephrolepsis exaltata cv.)
 Cast-iron plant   (Aspidistra elatior)
 English ivy   (Hedera helix)
*Impatiens   (Impatiens spp.)
*Jasmine   (Jasminum polyanthum)
 Maidenhair fern   (Adiantum capillus
          veneris)
 Spider plant   (Chlorophytum comosum)

Cool Indoor Temperature (nights below 50°F)

Sunlight

*Camellia   (Camellia japonica)
*Chrysanthemum   (Chrysanthemum spp.)
*Cineraria   (Senecio hybridus)
*Cyclamen   (Cyclamen persicum)
*Freesia   (Freesia refracta)
*Gardenia   (Gardenia jasminoides)

Bright ,Indirect Light

*Azalea   (Rhododenderon simsii)
*Fuchsia   (Fuchsia spp.)
 Piggy-back plant   (Tolmeia menziesii)
*Primrose   (Primula spp.)

Warm Indoor Temperature (nights above 65°F)

Sunlight

 Croton   (Codiaeum variegatum)
 Hawaiian ti plant   (Cordyline terminalis)
^Mother-in-law's tongue   (Sansevieria
          trifasciata)
 Umbrella tree   (Schefflera arboricola)

Bright, Indirect Light

*African violet   (Saintpaulia ionantha)
 Coffee plant   (Coffea arabica)
 Dumb cane   (Dieffenbachia maculata)
*Gloxinia   (Sinningia speciosa)
*Moth orchid   (Phalaenopsis spp.)
 Philodendron   (Philodendron spp.)
 Weeping fig   (Ficus benjamina)

Low-Light Plants

 Auricula   (Primula auricula)
 Bromeliads   (Bromelia spp.)
 Cast-iron plant   (Aspidistra elatior)
 Chinese evergreen   (Aglaonema spp.)
 Dragon tree   (Dracaena fragrans)
 Dumb cane   (Dieffenbachia maculata)
 Kentia palms   (Howea forsterana)
 Mother-in-law's tongue   (Sansevieria
          trifasciata)
 Philodendron   (Philodendron spp.)
 Podocarpus   (Podocarpus spp.)
 Rubber plant   (Ficus elastica)
*Wax plant   (Hoya carnosa)

*Blossoms on some species
^Will also survive in shade

★ Provide adequate light. Supplement natural light with artificial lights, if necessary.

★ Locate plants near a convenient water source, so you don't have to lug heavy watering containers.

★ Watch for pests and diseases, and treat them immediately.

★ Provide good air circulation, a natural preventative of disease.

★ Choose appropriate plants, those that will tolerate your indoor conditions.

★ Water and fertilize carefully. Indoor plants grow relatively slowly, so their water and fertilizer needs are minimal. Do not overwater; fertilize at half-strength weekly.

GROWING HEALTHY CONTAINER PLANTS: GIVE THEM A GOOD HOME!

Like plants grown outdoors, indoor plants need adequate water, air, light, and nutrients, as well as the right kind of soil.

Watering: Don't Kill Them with Kindness

More indoor plants are killed by overwatering than by any other cause. The plant's root system needs air to breathe, just as your lungs do. If soil is too wet, air is unavailable to the roots and the plant drowns.

Test the soil with your finger. If a few soil particles stick to your finger and the soil gives a little, the plant probably does not need watering. You can also poke a toothpick or stick into the pot, and if a few soil particles cling to it, the soil is still moist underneath. Lift the pot; if it feels very light (you'll soon learn to judge the proper weight), give it water. For indoor plants, underwatering is safer than overwatering, so if you're unsure, wait a day or two before you water. A water meter is a "high-tech" gardening tool that takes the guesswork out of watering. Stick the meter into the soil to measure the degree of wetness — very wet, moderate, moist, and dry.

When it's time to water, do so *thoroughly.* Soaking the soil washes out excess fertilizers and minerals, and therefore prevents root burn. Distilled water or, better yet, rainwater is excellent for watering indoor plants. Chemically softened water is never acceptable; the salts will kill your plants. Cold water can cause plant damage, and it, too, should never be used. Some gardeners find it convenient to keep containers filled with room-temperature water.

Be sure pots have good drainage and are not sitting in a puddle of water — most plants don't like wet feet.

Mist daily with a spray bottle, and increase surrounding humidity to reduce the amount of water a plant needs.

Some plants, especially the succulents, but also orchids, cacti, bulbs, some blooming shrubs, and many perennials, go dormant at certain times of the year. Dormancy is the period during which a plant makes no active growth. Think of it as a plant's "rest period." For plants native to the northern hemisphere, December and January and right after blooming are the most common dormant times, even for indoor plants (for plants native to southern hemisphere, dormancy may occur in June and July). It is easy to tell when deciduous plants are dormant, because they lose their leaves. Other plants seem to stop growing for awhile, even though they are receiving the proper amount of food, water, and light. Cut back on watering or stop altogether, and don't feed them at this time. A plant-care encyclopedia is an indispensable gardening tool for an indoor gardener. It can tell you about the life cycle needs of all your plants.

Feed Them When They're Hungry

Proper fertilizing is even more important for potted plants than it is for those grown in the ground, since container-grown plants are limited to the nutrients contained in the soil of the pot. Apply fertilizer weekly to moistened soil. Reduce fertilizer when a plant is dormant. Plants do most of their growing from March to September, and then take a rest. During the winter months (October through February) fertilize only once a month, since growth slows down and plant food is not needed as often. Do not fertilize when a plant has been stressed in any manner — for instance, when it has been allowed to dry out too much or has a disease. Fertilizer stimulates growth, which in turn can further stress an already weakened plant.

Use only water-soluble fertilizer mixed at half-strength. Once a month, wash out fertilizer build-up by watering heavily and letting the water flow through the pots freely, or by plunging them in a water-filled container.

Give 'Em Good Soil

Healthy plants can be grown in a number of different soil mixes. Commercially manufactured, lightweight, sterile mixes are the most convenient. If you use these mixes, you won't have to sterilize garden soil. Sterilized soil is recommended for indoor plants because they are often under more stress (such as low light, roots restricted in pots, low humidity, and high temperatures) than in-ground plants and so are more vulnerable to disease.

Mixes are formulated to meet the needs of many different plants. You can purchase special orchid mixes and cactus mixes, for example, as well as mixes for both acid- and lime-loving plants. If you want to prepare your own potting soil, use one of the recipes shown in box, above.

Pick a Pot, Any Pot!

Selecting a pot for your indoor container plant is easy, if you remember a few rules. It is essential to use clean pots, free of disease. You may want your indoor containers to be a bit more decorative than outdoor containers, but the criteria for choosing them are essentially the same as those discussed on pages 49-51.

Keep Them Healthy

Plants that are cared for properly are less likely to suffer insect or disease damage, but dry air and limited light often make indoor plants more susceptible to disease and pest attack. Watch your plants carefully and treat them as soon as you see any unhealthy signs, such as wilting, dwarfed growth, leaf burn, white or brown spots on leaves, graying, a "dusty" appearance of leaves, or leaf drop.

The most common indoor pests are aphids, mealybugs, spider mites, scale, and whiteflies. It is an unusual indoor garden that never suffers one of these problems. A magnifying glass can help you see these minute pests. Magnifiers that hang from your neck and leave your hands free are great for plant inspection. You can sometimes keep problems at bay by dunking your plants in a weak soap solution once every two weeks — be sure to rinse off soap solution.

If you notice that one of your plants looks unhealthy, either from disease or pest attack, remove it immediately from the vicinity of your other plants. It is far easier to prevent plant disorders than to cure them. The most common pests and diseases that attack indoor plants are listed on pages 66-67.

WINDOW GARDENING

Window gardens offer some of the advantages of outdoor growing along with the convenience of working indoors. With a window greenhouse, you can maintain excellent environmental conditions for your plants. Bright light, combined with the high humidity of grouped plants and the good air circulation provided by the window itself, promotes a successful garden. Although a window greenhouse costs money and effort to install, the advantages easily compensate the investment. In a window greenhouse you can grow almost any plant that appeals to you, and you are not usually restricted to those few plants that tolerate average indoor conditions. Many tropical plants will not tolerate temperatures below 55°F, so

PEST	SYMPTOM	CURE
Aphids or plant lice (3 mm): White, red, green, or black, these small, soft-bodied insects suck plant juices and carry fungus and disease.	Foliage deformation Sticky, curled, or yellowed leaves Sometimes a sooty mold	Remove aphids with an alcohol-dipped cotton swab. Rinse plant in a soapy solution and then in lukewarm water. Spray with pyrethrin, if necessary.
Mealybugs (6 mm): These white, oval, hairy-looking insects with a cottony appearance suck plant juices.	Pale foliage Leaf drop Stunted growth	Remove mealybugs with an alcohol-dipped cotton swab. Wash with soapy water. Spray only if necessary.
Mites (7 mm): Very hard to see without a magnifying glass, mites suck plant juices.	Leaf curl Leaf drop Stunted growth Blackened buds Grayish, dusty look to the plant Webs on the under-side of the plant	Very difficult to eradicate. Try soapy water. Remove from the rest of your plants. Spray with insecticide. Put plant outside. High humidity sometimes helps.
Scales (3 mm): Hard-shelled lumps on stems and leaves attach so tightly they sometimes look like part of the plant.	Yellowed foliage Dropping leaves	Scrub off with alcohol-soaked swab. Rinse in soapy water. Spray as necessary. Very difficult to eradicate if the infestation is heavy.
Whiteflies (1.60 mm): White, wedge-shaped winged insects that suck plant juices and spread diseases, especially viruses.	Yellowing leaves Dropping leaves Swarms when plant is disturbed	Wash with strong water spray. Difficult to eradicate. Sometimes a hot pepper spray solution helps. Quarantine the plant.

INDOOR DISEASES

DISEASE	SYMPTOM	CURE
Bacterial infection	Graying and yellow-ing leaves Crown rot	Use antifungal spray. Water from the bottom.
Botrytis blight	Gray mold on all parts of the plant	Avoid overcrowding, overfeeding, and overwatering. Provide good air circulation. Spray with antifungals. Dispose of infected plants.
Edema	Plants rapidly absorb water, but transpi-ration is slow and cells burst. Swelling on leaves and corky ridges	Increase temperature and lower humidity. Allow soil to dry out before watering.
Fungal diseases	Stem and root rot	Increase air circulation. Decrease humidity.
Powdery mildew	Leaves covered with white powder	Use antifungal spray. Let dry between waterings. Usually can't be saved.
Virus	Mottled, yellowing leaves Leaf curl Spotted flowers Stunted growth	Remove and destroy infected plant promptly. Watch out for the insects that spread these diseases! (See page 182)

if your windows are chilly, install weatherstripping and heat-ing cables (which can serve as "electric hot pads" for the plants). You can also use your window greenhouse as a place to start seeds. What you grow depends only on space.

Commercially made window greenhouses are available at many home-improvement centers and by mail order. Made of metal or wood, these prefabricated kits are relatively easy to insert in almost any window. Window greenhouses are usu-ally attached to the outside of a window, but if you live in an

▲ *A window greenhouse makes it possible to enjoy outdoor-style gardening year round.*

apartment, or there is no room outside to extend your window (because of a narrow walkway or very small patio against the house), some can be attached to the inside. If you are handy you can install a custom-made window greenhouse.

Where to Put a Window Greenhouse

Try to put your greenhouse in a room near water; you don't want to be lugging water containers up and down stairs, if you can avoid it. A convenient location for your window greenhouse is the kitchen, where water is readily available; you'll be able to enjoy your garden fully while you go about your daily activities. Another good place is the bathroom, which also provides extra humidity and easy access to water.

Generally, a south-, west-, or east-facing window works well for a greenhouse. Don't despair if the only window available to you is a north-facing one, however; many plants grow well in the shade. The south-facing window, although it gets wonderful light, may actually be too hot for some plants, and you may need to provide shade.

Construction

Whether you buy a prefabricated window greenhouse or build it yourself, it must be attached properly. The seal between the house and the window should be free of leaks or cracks. Apply caulking compound or strips of wood, metal flashing, or sealing tape to keep the window draft-free.

If you're building your own, use moisture-, decay-, and insect-resistant redwood or cedar heartwood for the frame. Build the frame first and then install the glass. Make a slanted top to allow for rain run-off and reduce snow build-up. If you make a greenhouse more than 30 inches wide, install supports at the midpoint for strength. Attach your greenhouse to 2"x6" boards that have been bolted to the house wall around the window opening.

The best window greenhouses have a provision for ventilation; both you and your plants will appreciate the good air circulation. A hinged top makes ventilation easy and helps moderate temperatures.

Plant shelves should be sturdy and easy to clean. Glass, acrylic, wood slats, and metal mesh have been used successfully. Glass and acrylic allow maximum light to reach all your plants; slats and mesh are attractive and easy to clean.

Plant Care in Window Greenhouses

Caring for the plants in your window greenhouse is a pleasure. Your greenhouse plants may need watering less frequently than other house plants because extra humidity is created by grouping them. If you are growing tropical plants, increase this humidity by setting your pots on a tray of moist gravel or perlite. On hot summer days, you may need to water more frequently.

Plants in window greenhouses are susceptible to the same pests and diseases as other indoor plants, but your problems may be fewer because the growing conditions are better and therefore the plants are healthier. Whiteflies, mealybugs, aphids, and red spider mites are typical pests. Watch for them and eliminate them immediately; don't let them get a grip on your garden! Since your window greenhouse is at eye-level, it is easy to spot these culprits when they arrive. I avoid the use of pesticides and fungicides in the house, especially in the kitchen. Soap-and-water solutions, alcohol-dipped cotton swabs, and red-pepper and herb sprays can help keep these pests under control without resorting to chemicals. Plants growing vigorously in a window greenhouse resist many plant diseases, but botrytis, fungi, and other "high-humidity" diseases can cause trouble. If you treat your plants with fungicides or other chemicals, remove them from

PLANTS FOR A SOUTH OR EAST WINDOW

Vegetables

Carrots

Cucumbers (midget)

Eggplant

Lettuce

Peppers

Radishes

Tomatoes

Herbs

Catnip

Marjoram

Parsley

Rosemary

Sage

Tarragon

Thyme

Flowering Plants

Cacti and succulents

Christmas cactus (*Schlumbergera* spp.)

Dipladenia (*Mandevilla x amabilis*)

Firecracker flower (*Crossandra* spp.)

Gardenia (*Gardenia* spp.)

Jade tree (*Crassula ovata*)

Thunbergia (*Thunbergia* spp.)

Foliage Plants

Any type

PLANTS FOR A WEST WINDOW

Vegetables and Herbs

Basil

Lettuce

Spinach

Foliage Plants

Any type

Flowering Plants

Begonia (*Begonia* spp.)

Bromeliads (*Bromelia* spp.)

Columnea (*Columnea* spp.)

Dendrobium (*Dendrobium* spp.)

Kohleria (*Kohleria* spp.)

Orchids (various spp.)

Wax plant (*Hoya* spp.)

PLANTS FOR A NORTH WINDOW

Flowering Plants

African violet (*Saintpaulia ionantha*)

Anthurium (*Anthurium* spp.)

Begonia (*Begonia* spp.)

Bellflower (*Campanula* spp.)

Bromeliads (*Bromelia* spp.)

Gloxinia (*Gloxinia* spp.)

Lantana (*Lantana* spp.)

Foliage Plants

Dragon tree (*Dracaena fragrans*)

Dumb cane (*Dieffenbachia maculata*)

Philodendron (*Philodendron* spp.)

the house for treatment. Sometimes simply providing more ventilation and removing infected plants will control the problem. (See chapters 7 and 8 for more on pest and disease control.)

What to Grow in Window Greenhouses

In addition to the usual house plants that do well on a windowsill, you can grow orchids, begonias, and other exotic plants that love the light and humidity of a greenhouse. Vegetables, including tomatoes, peppers, and eggplants, also do well in a window greenhouse. Give them plenty of room and grow them vertically on trellises for easy harvest. Miniature varieties of all these vegetables are available and will fit into this space. Herbs are good candidates, too; you will especially enjoy having them close at hand if your greenhouse is in the kitchen.

Nontoxic Disease and Pest Control

Researchers at Cornell University recently reported that a dilute solution of sodium bicarbonate (baking soda) is an effective treatment for powdery mildew and blackspot. Mix 5 level teaspoons of baking soda with 1 gallon of water. For best results, spray this solution on affected plants every other week from spring until fall.

To overcome spider mites, thrips, and aphid infestations mix 1 tablespoon of kelp powder with 1 gallon of water, and spray on plants three or four times a week during the growing season.

CHAPTER 4

EASY GARDENS START WITH GOOD SOIL

Soil is essential to successful gardening. Good soil makes gardening easier because it minimizes the need for fertilizer and water. Plants growing happily in nutrient-rich soil are more resistant to plant disease and insect pests. The ideal soil is medium grained, moisture retentive, and rich in essential ingredients.

Soil texture, structure, acidity, and fertility are some of the elements that combine to make different types of soil. Serious soil deficiencies can ruin all your gardening efforts, but most soils can be improved, once you understand what is lacking and what you can add — ingredients called *soil amendments* — to improve it. Here are some tips about garden soil and how to condition it.

SOIL STRUCTURE

Let's first consider the two basic types of soil: heavy clay and light sand.

Heavy soil, called clay or adobe, is easy to recognize and difficult to work. When you squeeze a handful of moist soil together and get a sticky, gummy mass that won't break apart, you know you have clay soil. Although often rich in nutrients, clay soil contains very little air space for roots, and plants growing in clay can easily die from lack of oxygen. Clay soil takes a long time to dry out, and when it does, it becomes cement-like. It's very difficult to re-wet because water just runs right off of it. Clay soil can be a real obstacle to easy gardening, because it's so heavy and difficult to dig.

Sandy soil creates problems of a different sort. Water drains through it so quickly that roots barely have time to take up the moisture. Any plant nutrients in the soil leach out with the water as it runs through, leaving the plants not only dry, but starving. If the sand particles are large, the spaces between them can be so great that some roots cannot establish good contact with the soil, and they, too, starve to death.

Poor drainage is also a consequence of thin topsoil or rock- and gravel-filled soil.

SOIL pH AND MINERAL CONTENT

Soil acidity or alkalinity is measured by the *pH scale*, which runs from 0 to 14. The 0 end of the scale is acid and the 14 end is alkaline. A soil test reading of 7.0 means the soil is neutral — neither acid nor alkaline.

Acid soils. Many vegetables, fruits, and flowers do well in soils that are neutral, or even a little on the acid side. Most

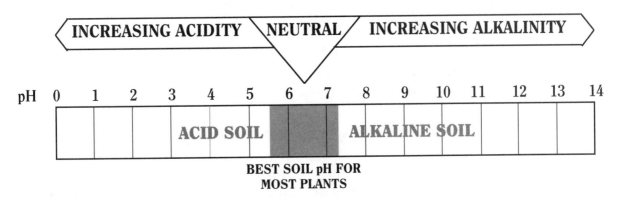

▲ *Soil acidity or alkalinity is measured on the pH scale.*

soils that contain large amounts of organic material have a pH of about 6.5. Overly acid soils, however, bind certain nutrients and make them unavailable to plants. In the United States, the high rainfall areas of the East Coast and the Pacific Northwest generally suffer from overly acid soils. The addition of calcium (lime) to these soils helps to neutralize and improve them for gardening.

Alkaline soils. A soil test reading above 7.0 means the soil is alkaline, which some plants do not tolerate. Alkaline soils may contain large amounts of sodium and other soluble salts that are toxic to plants or make the soil impermeable to water. Areas with light rainfall commonly have alkaline soils. Most plants will grow in slightly alkaline soil, but in order to grow such acid-loving plants as azaleas, rhododendrons, and gardenias, you'll need to adjust alkaline soil to suit their needs. The addition of sulfur or iron sulfate will acidify alkaline soils.

Mineral content. In addition to alkalinity, desert and semi-arid regions also have a high concentration of salts and minerals and low humus content. These soils can stunt plant growth, cause germination problems, and turn leaves yellow or brown. Occasional deep flooding, or *leaching,* sometimes washes the harsher salts out, but this is a rather extravagant use of water, especially in a desert region. It's more efficient and less wasteful to garden in raised beds, where you can provide the correct soil.

Lack of iron is another common deficiency associated with alkaline soil. If plant growth is stunted, leaves are yellow and the veins remain green, iron deficiency may be the culprit. Acid-loving plants are especially affected. Acidifying the soil as described above will often correct this problem.

ANALYZING YOUR SOIL

What kind of soil do you have? A little digging will give you the answer. Take a look at a spadeful of soil. Is it heavy or light? wet or dry? loose or tightly packed? If it's hard to dig,

it's probably going to be difficult for plants to grow in it —
think about the little root hairs that have to make their way
through it! If you see a lot of earthworms, you're in luck. They
are nature's soil builders and can make any soil better. (For
more about earthworms, see pages 89-92.) If you're not sure
about the acidity and fertility of your soil, have it chemically
analyzed. You can do this yourself with a soil-testing kit, or
ask your local Cooperative Extension Service if they will do
it for a fee. Ask other gardeners and local landscape nursery
personnel about their experience with soil in your area.

IMPROVING YOUR SOIL

After you analyze your soil, you can work on improving it. If
your soil is very poor, you may have to buy good topsoil, but
usually the addition of soil amendments will solve the problem. Topsoil can be obtained by the truckload for filling large
gardens, but it's easier and less expensive to improve the soil
you have than to import all new soil.
Remember the basic principles: sandy
soils need moisture-holding particles
and heavy soils need to be lightened.

Organic matter, such as peat moss,
ground bark, or leaf mold, are excellent
amendments for sandy soil. The spongy
particles fill empty spaces between the
grains of sand and help the soil retain
water and nutrients. On the other
hand, sand or other mineral amendments, such as vermiculite, perlite, or
gypsum, make heavy clay soil lighter
and allow water to drain faster. Compost is the best all-around amendment
for every kind of soil. It's cheap, easy to
use, and available to every gardener.
For information about composting see
pages 80-88.

Soil Basics

★ Plants in good soil will be
healthy and less prone to disease
and pest infestation.
★ The ideal soil is a combination of
sand, clay, and moisture-retentive organic material.
★ Improve soil quality by adding
amendments and/or using green
manures.
★ Soil types differ according to the
climate and geography of the
area in which you live.
★ Learn your soil type.

Fertilizing Your Soil

The major "food groups" necessary to healthy plant growth are nitrogen, phosphorus, and potassium. *Nitrogen* (N) promotes rapid growth of stems and leaves, and gives plants a deep green color; *phosphorus* (P) encourages root formation, flowers, and fruit; *potassium* (K) aids in root growth and seed production, and is necessary to all plant functions.

Organic or Synthetic?

You can feed or fertilize your plants with synthetic additives or with organic fertilizers, whichever is easier for you to obtain and use. Many people prefer organic fertilizers, which are based on plant material. They are as easily obtained as chemical additives, safer to use, and much healthier for our earth. They not only add nutrients, but at the same time, improve the texture of the soil.

Natural Sources of NPK

Nitrogen

Blood meal

Cottonseed meal

Fish scraps

Guano

Phosphorus

Bonemeal

Fish scraps, dried

Phosphate rock

Sugar wastes, raw

Potassium

Granite dust

Seaweed

Tobacco stems and powder

Wood ashes

Organic fertilizers. Organic fertilizers are derived from plant and animal residues. Examples of organic fertilizers include fish meal, bonemeal, cottonseed meal, blood meal, and seaweed extract. Organic fertilizers are not as concentrated as chemical fertilizers, and few, used alone, contain all the elements needed for healthy plant growth. A combination of additives, therefore, might be necessary. They also may need to be applied more frequently than time-release synthetic fertilizers.

Organic fertilizers are nontoxic and can safely be used in your food garden, around your home, and in a yard where pets and children play. I should warn you about bonemeal, though — dogs love it. I once left a 5-pound bag within my labrador's reach and

TABLE OF ORGANIC FERTILIZERS

FERTILIZER	NUTRIENTS	APPLICATION RATE	USES
Blood meal	N 15% P 1.3% K 7%	Up to 3 lbs. per 100 sq. ft. (more will burn plants)	Readily available nitrogen Speeds decomposition of compost
Bonemeal	N 3% P 20% K 0% Calcium 24–30%	Up to 5 lbs. per 100 sq. ft.	Raises pH Excellent source of potassium Good for fruit, bulbs, flowers
Cow manure	N 2% P 1% K 1%	40 lbs. per 50–100 sq. ft.	If fresh, will burn plants Because slow releasing, a valuable soil additive
Cottonseed meal	N 6% P 3% K 2%	2–5 lbs. per 100 sq. ft.	Acidifies soil Lasts 4–6 months
Fish emulsion, fish meal	N 5–8% P 4–6% K 0–1%	Meal: Up to 5 lbs. per 100 sq. ft. Emulsion: 20:1	In early spring, as a foliar spray Lasts 6–8 months
Gypsum	Calcium 23–57% Sulfur 17%	Up to 4 lbs. per 100 sq. ft.	When both calcium and sulfur are needed and soil pH is high Helps loosen clay soils
Kelp meal, liquid seaweed	N 1% P 0% K 12% Trace minerals	Meal: Up to 1 lb. per 100 sq. ft. Liquid, dilute 25:1	Contains natural growth hormones Use sparingly Lasts 6 months
Sulfur	Sulfur 100%	1 lb. per 100 sq. ft. to lower pH 1 point As fungicide, 3 tablespoons per 1 gallon of water	Lowers pH in alkaline soils Increases crop protein Ties up excess magnesium

came home to find the bag empty and a black dog with a very white muzzle. She ate the *whole* thing! I was worried, of course, and called the veterinarian immediately. After he had a chuckle, he told me not to worry, that except for a minor digestive upset from eating so much, she would be fine. Keep this in mind when you're applying organic fertilizers that might appeal to hungry critters. You may want to keep pets out of the yard or cover newly laid fertilizers.

Chemical fertilizers. Chemical fertilizers come in liquid, powder, granule, and tablet forms. Those containing the three main elements, plus trace elements, are called complete fertilizers. All-purpose, slow-release fertilizers, which need to be applied only once or twice a year, are real labor savers.

Fertilizers list what percent of each major element is contained in the package. This is listed as N-P-K, in that order. The best combination varies for each type of plant. Ornamental plants without showy blossoms prefer a high nitrogen compound, while fruits and vegetables prefer a high potassium compound. Phosphorus feeds bulbs, fruits, flowers, and food crops.

The advantage of chemical fertilizers is that they contain all the nutrients needed by a particular plant. There are, for instance, acid mixes, rose mixes, and vegetable mixes. The containers are clearly labeled, so that choosing the correct fertilizer is easy. They are inexpensive and convenient, and if not overused, can be a real boon to the low-maintenance garden. Unfortunately, many chemical fertilizers can poison insects, birds, fish, and domestic animals, either directly or through run-off into streams and other water supplies. Special care must be taken to avoid breathing or splashing some of the more potent combinations. In addition, unlike organic fertilizers, synthetic additives do nothing to improve the basic structure of the soil.

How to Apply Fertilizer

Labels on packaged fertilizers give instructions for use and should be followed carefully. Even organic fertilizers can burn your plants, if used incorrectly. The easiest method of applying fertilizer is to broadcast it by hand. Spreaders that roll or spray the fertilizer achieve a more even distribution. A nearly effortless way to fertilize is by delivering liquid fertilizer through your sprinkler or drip-irrigation system as you water. Each device is a little different, so check your system requirements.

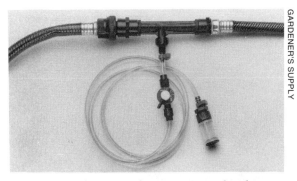

▲ *Devices that attach to your garden hose make delivering fertilizer quite simple.*

Good timing is important. Fertilize early in the growing season. To get young plants off to a good start, incorporate fertilizers into the seed bed when you're preparing the soil. Continue to feed plants every six weeks or so, until late in the growing season. Stop feeding perennial plants and shrubs toward the end of the growing season. Fertilizers stimulate new growth, and it's important for many plants to become dormant before the weather turns cold. It is equally important not to overfertilize. This can do more damage than not fertilizing at all; rampant growth, stimulated by too much fertilizer, causes plants to become susceptible to plant disease and insect attack. Follow label directions, and when in doubt, underfeed rather than overfeed.

Proper nutrition in the garden will reward you with an abundant harvest and a beautiful landscape!

GREEN MANURE: A FERTILIZER PLUS

It's possible to garden with very little added fertilizer. Certain plants add nutrients to the soil when they are turned under and allowed to break down. These plants are called *cover crops* or *green manure* plants. In addition to adding nutrients to the soil, green manures slow erosion, store nutrients, add organic matter, and aerate the soil. If you plant a part of your garden in green manure every year, you will greatly improve your soil with a minimum of work.

Beans and peas can be used as both crop plants and

★ Nitrogen promotes rapid "green" growth.

★ Phosphorus encourages root formation, flowers, and fruit.

★ Potassium aids in root growth and seed production.

★ Cover crops can reduce the need for extra fertilizer.

★ Apply fertilizer early in the season and about every six weeks thereafter; stop just before plants go dormant.

★ Do not fertilize when plants are stressed by drought or disease.

★ Follow product label directions carefully.

Good Cover Crops

Legumes

Field bean

Crimson clover

White clover

Lupine

Austrian winter pea

Vetch

Grasses

Alfalfa

Winter barley

Buckwheat

Oats

Annual ryegrass

Winter rye

---

green manure plants in the same season. After you harvest the vegetables, dig the plants under and let them degrade and replenish the soil.

Don't let cover crops get too tall, and don't let them go to seed. Clover, for instance, can grow long roots that make cultivation difficult if plants are allowed to grow too large. Young, succulent crops break down faster and add more nutrients to the soil. Most local and mail-order nurseries supply cover crop seeds.

COMPOST

Compost is essentially pure, homemade humus — that fine, dark brown or black material you find underneath the dead leaves on the forest floor. It is the ideal material to improve your soil and at the same time boost plant nutrition. According to some research, virtually all soil structure and nutrition problems can be solved with organic matter. Everyone can have access to rich, soil-building compost, and once you experience its benefits, you'll never get enough of it.

A few communities and neighborhoods have outlawed backyard composting. They cite odor, flies, raccoons, and other varmints as reasons for this ban. If you live in this sort of community, try a small "worm farm" to use your kitchen scraps and enrich your soil without offending your neighbors.

★ Composting offers a real solution to the problem of ever-growing sanitary landfills.

★ Compost provides good aeration and drainage, yet retains an enormous amount of water.

★ Compost builds nutrient-rich, friable (easily crumbled) soil.

★ Compost corrects the pH of soil. Soil that is too acid, as well as soil that is too alkaline, can make nutrients unavailable to the plants. Studies have shown that compost brings soil into the range of 6.5–7.5 pH, which is ideal for most crop-bearing plants.

★ Compost darkens the soil and thus increases its ability to absorb heat from sunlight; warmer soil means earlier crops.

★ Humus-rich soil, such as that produced by adding compost, holds water-soluble nutrients that are not easily washed away by rain or irrigation.

★ Compost attracts soil-building earthworms, controls nematodes and plant diseases, and adds trace minerals as well as growth-stimulating enzymes to the soil.

★ Last, but not least, compost is free. Apply nature's recycling methods and reap the benefits!

(See pages 89-92 for more on worm farms.) Admittedly, even a healthy compost pile has a distinctive odor at times, but composting odors can be controlled. Regulating the temperature and moisture of the compost helps to manage the odor. "Hot" heaps, which are decomposing quickly at high temperatures, have very little odor compared to moisture- and oxygen-poor "slow" heaps. Turning and mixing the materials encourages faster composting; even poking holes in the pile to aerate it will speed the process and cut down on odor problems. Enclosing the heap with wooden fencing or simply throwing black plastic over it will also reduce the pungent perfume of decay.

How Does Compost Work?

Microscopic organisms, such as bacteria, fungi, and yeasts, transform organic materials into a form that roots can absorb as food. When soil, moisture, and plant residues are mixed in a contained area, heat builds up as the materials break down, helped by the life activities of microorganisms. As mentioned, the "hotter" the pile, the faster the composting cycle.

Materials for Compost

Leaves. Although rich in minerals, leaves should be mixed with other plant residues and compost materials, both because they are not a complete fertilizer and because they do not break down quickly. Unmixed leaves pack down and impede the aeration that is important to the composting process.

Grass clippings. Grass clippings are high in nitrogen and heat up quickly. When you add them to your compost pile, they will speed up the decomposition of the entire heap. Since grass clippings tend to pack down, they should be mixed with lighter materials to ensure good aeration. Don't use clippings from grass that has been treated with "weed-and-feed" or other lawn-care chemicals.

New hay. Alfalfa or clover adds nitrogen and minerals that are beneficial to the overall fertility of the finished compost. New hay breaks down quickly. Old hay takes longer to break down, but it is good for aerating a compost pile and it makes a nice, fluffy product. Remember that hay may contain viable seeds. One of my worst gardening experiences took place after I imported some hay for compost and mulch. It took many seasons and a lot of pulling to rid my yard of unwanted alfalfa sprouts. Save yourself trouble — use straw (which has no seeds).

Straw. The stem of the plant only, straw has the same composting advantages as hay. There is less risk of unwanted

★ *Cat or dog feces.* Cat feces can harbor a parasite *(Toxoplasma gondii)* or a roundworm *(Toxocara cati),* both of which can infect human beings. These are a special risk to pregnant women, unborn babies, and children. Dog feces can contain a roundworm *(Toxocara canii)* that is dangerous to children. (Other animal manures are safe.)

★ *Grease or fat* attracts unwelcome animals and slows down the composting process.

★ *Coal, coal ashes, and charcoal briquets* contain high amounts of iron, sulfur, and other harmful substances.

★ *Diseased plant material* may infect the pile unless the compost is very hot, but why take the risk. If necessary, diseased material can be added if it is burned first.

★ *Polyester, plastic, and other synthetics* don't break down.

★ *Street sweepings in an urban area* may contain high residues of lead from fuel exhaust.

★ *Bulky materials* may be used if pulverized, chopped, or burned first; otherwise, they may slow the process.

★ *Sludge* is a questionable additive, as there is no way of knowing if it contains heavy metals or insecticides.

plants sprouting, although there will always be a few hardy seed escapees.

Kitchen wastes. When mixed with soil and some fibrous extender, such as hay or straw, kitchen wastes are an excellent — perhaps the best — source of compost material. All fruit and vegetable trimmings can be used. Citrus rinds break down very slowly, so don't use too many of these. Eggshells, also, are slow to decompose; finely crushed eggshells, however, loosen soil texture and improve drainage. You'll be surprised how much compostable material comes out of your kitchen. Don't use meat or fat. It spoils, attracts unwanted critters, feeds the wrong bacteria, and generally fouls the heap.

Garden residues. Weeds and other garden residue are great compost fodder. They are similar to kitchen waste in that there is hardly any plant material that is unsuitable for composting. Unless you have a very active (hot) heap, however, avoid adding large leaves or stems, or, if you do, chop or shred them, so that they will break down more quickly. *Do not use diseased plants,* which can spread unwanted microorganisms to your garden soil if they are not destroyed by the heat of composting

Nut shells, wood fibers, and peanut hulls. These all make fine compost materials.

Composting Methods

A compost pile can be simply that — an unrestrained pile — or it can be collected in a bin or other container. The most popular method of composting is the *pile* or *heap* method. The most efficient pile — that is, the one that "cooks" the fastest — is at least 3 feet wide and 3 feet high.

Composting happens slowly or quickly, depending on your method, the size of the heap, the compost materials, and the weather. To start your compost heap, whether framed or not, spread a 6-inch layer of plant waste on the ground. Add a 2-inch layer of manure and soil, then straw, hay, or other fibrous materials. Sprinkle the layers with lime, bonemeal, or wood ashes, and spray with water until it is just moist. These layers can be repeated until the desired height is reached. Don't trample the heap; it needs to be well aerated in order to work properly. In a few days, bacterial action will cause the heap to heat up. The temperature in an active heap can reach 160°F. If you keep the pile moist and turn it frequently, you can speed the composting process. Many gardeners keep three piles going at once: one to which they are currently adding fresh materials, one that is in the break-down process, and one that is completely composted and ready for use. Excellent designs appear in Jeff Ball's *60-Minute Garden* (Rodale Press, 1985) and Stu Campbell's *Let It Rot* (Garden Way Publishing, 1991).

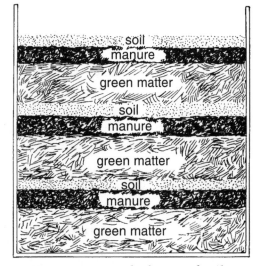

▲ *To compost, make layers of soil, manure, and fibrous materials. Sprinkle the layers with lime, bonemeal, or wood ashes, and keep the pile moist.*

✎ **If your chief gardening concern is to make things easy for yourself, you may not wish to tackle the often-recommended "hot" compost methods, which are the most difficult.** Only energetic gardeners with strong backs should undertake compost-making techniques that involve frequent mixing of the pile — it can be heavy work! Instead, experiment with methods like *bag composting*, ventilating stacks (such as a bundle of cornstalks or a cylinder of wire mesh placed upright in the pile) that automatically aerate the pile so that you don't have to turn it, or prefabricated compost barrels. Or you may be able to talk a neighbor or friend into giving your pile a turn once in awhile to lessen your composting chores.

Sheet-Composting Method

One of the easiest methods of composting is known as *sheet composting.* Spread raw organic materials on garden beds when they are fallow and leave them to compost naturally. The materials don't break down as quickly as in some other methods, but it's a way of improving garden soil without strenuous digging or turning. You can alternate growing beds so that one is composting while the others are producing.

Sheet composting can also be used in an actively growing garden area, so it's a space saver. Furthermore, because worms are surface feeders, they flock to your nicely layered kitchen scraps, churn the earth through their digestive systems, and further improve soil texture.

During the process of decomposition, bacteria consume

nitrogen that plants need for good nutrition. Later in the compost cycle, this nitrogen once again becomes available to the plants, but the temporary shortage can cause plant-growth problems. To get around this, add high-nitrogen plant materials, such as clover, peas, alfalfa, and used tea leaves, as well as other nitrogen-rich organic substances, such as cottonseed meal and blood meal. You can also sprinkle the soil with a complete fertilizer before using a composting-mulch.

Use organic material as mulch around growing plants to mulch and compost at the same time. This works pretty well if you choose the right material. Layering slow-acting, high-carbon wastes (straw, wood chips, cornstalks, dried leaves) with fast-acting, high-nitrogen plant refuse (kitchen waste) provides the essential ingredients for successful, although slow, soil improvement. This type of composting doesn't generate any heat, so it doesn't kill weed seeds.

Other Methods of Composting

Some gardeners put composting barrels on frames, where the barrels can be easily turned. Because the materials in these barrels are mixed with each rotation, they quickly break down. Boxes or bins confine and protect your compost from the elements. They are also more acceptable in the suburban yard, as they can conceal what some consider the unsightliness of compost heaps. Ready-made compost barrels and bins are available from most garden supply houses. They are generally lightweight, long-lasting, and attractive.

▲ *Ready-made composting barrels make it simple to turn the mixture.*

Building a Compost Bin

A contained pile keeps compost materials under control, and building a compost bin is easy. ☛ **If you're not up to building it yourself, get a friend to help.**

Size. Make the bin at least 3'x3'x3' to in-

If you have limited space, little compost material, or lack the time or energy to create and maintain a "formal" compost pile, make compost in plastic bags. *Anaerobic* (without oxygen) "bag composting" takes up minimal space and is quick and odor-free. Because plastic bags are lightweight and portable, it is easy to mix the compost. Problems arise, however, when the materials rot rather than compost. This happens when overwet materials are closed in a bag and tend to spoil rather than break down. To avoid this problem, add "fluffy" materials such as straw or hay to your compost bag and never add water after the first sprinkling. Put a few holes in the bag; although some organic material may escape, the holes will aerate and drain the "pile." Some garden supply catalogs feature plastic bags with holes pre-punched for this purpose. To turn and mix the compost materials, give the bag a shake or roll it around on the ground.

sure that there is sufficient mass both to heat up and to retain heat while the composting process is taking place. Smaller piles are possible, but they don't work as well.

Flooring. The bottom of the pile should be exposed to the earth, so that earthworms and natural microbes can help with the composting process.

Covering. The top of the pile, unless it is shaded by an evergreen tree, should be covered with either black plastic or a waterproof tarp to protect it from the weather. Rain can wash out the nutrients and pack down the pile so it can't work; extreme heat and sun can dry out the pile and stop the composting process.

Sides. The simplest contained compost pile can be made by enclosing an area with joined *fencing* or half-inch *chicken wire.* Wire compost "cages" provide good air circulation, can be built to almost any dimensions, are commonly available, and because they are lightweight, can be easily moved. They work well for small piles, but too easily bend out of shape to contain large piles. *Snow fencing* can be used to construct a cage for piles up to 5 feet in diameter. *Concrete blocks* or

Easy Composting

★ Keep your compost heap small.

★ Try bag composting.

★ Try sheet composting, the easiest method.

★ Try compost barrels that rotate on a frame.

★ Enlist a garden buddy to help you build, or turn, your compost heap.

★ Create a compost co-op with your neighbors; share compost materials and duties.

★ Start a worm farm.

bricks make fine compost bins. They are long lasting and good looking. Enlist the help of "hired muscle" for this style. *Wooden pallets,* such as those used on a fork-lift, can be strapped or hinged together to form long-lasting compost bins; you can often get these free from nurseries or home-improvement centers.

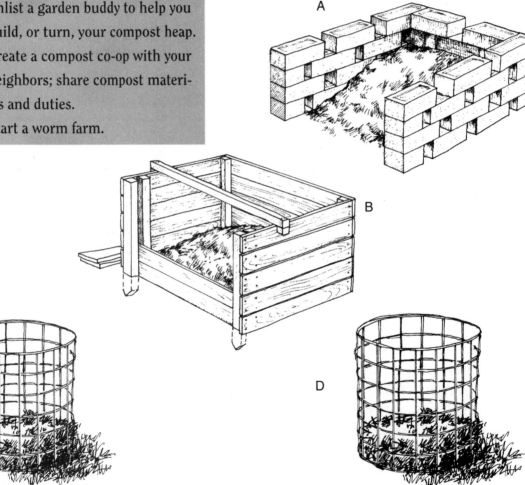

▲ *Compost bins come in all sizes and materials: (A) concrete blocks, (B) a sturdy box with a removable front and a bar across the top to prevent spreading, (C) fencing, (D) a frame made of 1" x 6"s and 1-inch wire mesh.*

A Special Kind of Composting:
The Earthworm Farm

The perfect garden helper is quiet and rarely seen; you never have to pay it a salary, and it eats garbage. This excellent assistant — the earthworm — will make compost for you.

The earthworm conditions the soil as it digests its food. Earthworm castings are far richer in minerals and nutrients than the soil it inhabits and eats. The worm's gizzards grind the soil and organic matter with secretions that increase plant nutrients such as nitrogen, phosphorus, potassium, calcium, and magnesium. These secretions also change the structure of the soil, creating small clumps that make the earth loose and crumbly. As it moves through the soil, the earthworm mixes, aerates, and improves the drainage and quality of the soil.

Phenomenal eaters and digesters, worms produce their own weight in castings every day. A good worm population can produce tons of organically enhanced soil each year! They can act as an alternative garbage-disposal system or as an adjunct to your compost pile. In the compost heap, they speed the breakdown of organic matter and help aerate the pile. Worms can be harmed by insecticides and herbicides, so if you want to encourage these garden helpers, don't spray with toxic chemicals.

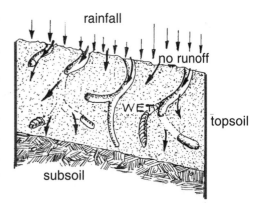

▲ *Earthworms mix, aerate, and improve drainage and quality of soil.*

Encourage worm activity by adding mulch to your garden. Mulch is a layer of material, often organic, that is placed on the soil surface. It moderates soil temperatures and moisture levels, thus making your soil more attractive to worms that are heat and moisture sensitive. The more worms in your garden, the better the soil quality.

If you want to do more than simply encourage an earthworm population by mulching, develop an earthworm farm. Creating good growing conditions for worms is easy. First, they need a place to live. A shallow box, a deep dishpan, or a wooden fruit crate are good "worm beds." For pampered worms, build a home of concrete blocks, which will keep the soil cool and moist. Situate your worm farm in the shade where it won't heat up or dry out too fast.

Worm beds don't need to be very large. About 1 square foot of space for every pound of organic material to be digested is recommended. With a 2'x3' box, you will get 6 square feet of surface area. A box this size can handle about a pound of kitchen waste, including coffee grounds, daily. If you don't produce that much waste, add bran or some other acceptable worm food to keep your earthworms happy.

Shredded paper, peat moss, soil, and leaf mold all make good bedding material. Commercial, bagged soil mixes may be used if you have a small worm farm and don't mind the expense. Worms need air, and some of them feed on the surface, so don't make bedding too deep — 1 foot is about right.

You can order worms by mail from many suppliers of organic garden materials. Addresses are listed in appendix 5, as well as in the classified ads of most gardening journals. You can also dig your own, although it may take you awhile to collect the 1–2 pounds of worms that are recommended for the size box we have discussed.

After your worms arrive, mix the bedding material in a large container, soak it thoroughly, and squeeze out the excess water. Put the moistened bedding in the box and spread the worms on top. They will burrow out of the light pretty quickly. Cover the box to retain moisture and to keep the light out (they will come to the surface to feed when it's dark.) It's unlikely that your worms will make a break for it, so there's no need to cover the box tightly.

Place the box in a protected area. The worms prefer a moderate temperature range — about 50°–75°F, although they can tolerate temperatures a little out of this range. Keep your worms in the house if you like, although most people find this rather odd. Perhaps a place in the shade, just outside the kitchen door, is best. Garages or basements make nice worm farm areas if you don't mind going there to deliver their dinner.

To feed the worms, simply spread collected kitchen waste on top of the bedding. To alleviate insect problems, you can dig a small hole, dump in the feed, and lightly cover it with bedding material. Almost any kitchen waste is acceptable. Only meat and/or fat should be avoided; it gums up the soil and attracts nuisance animals. Commercial worm producers often feed their worms cornmeal mush, but buying special food for your worms defeats the purpose of using them as "garbage grinding machines."

Make sure the bedding stays moist, for worms suffer very quickly if they dry out, and you may lose your whole population if you neglect this aspect of their care. Water the bedding with collected rainwater, if possible; chlorinated or treated tap water can harm the worms. If tap water is your only source, before sprinkling it on the bedding, let it sit for twenty-four hours so that chlorine and other harmful gases can escape. It's very important not to use "softened" water; it is high in sodium and may burn the fragile worms.

Worms are said to live up to four years. As they will be reproducing in your box, you will be able to keep your farm indefinitely. When any worms do die, remove them from the top of the bedding to prevent disease.

Tips for a Successful Earthworm Farm

★ Keep them cool. Earthworms are temperature sensitive, so find them a place out of the sun.

★ Keep them moist. Earthworms dry out very quickly, so cover the bed to decrease evaporation.

★ Keep them well fed. One pound of earthworms will eat 1 pound of scraps daily.

★ Give them air. Shallow beds and loose bedding material will be well aerated.

★ Keep them safe. Don't use poisons or treated water in the worm beds, as worms are very sensitive to chemical injury.

★ Give them room. Remove dead worms and castings to the garden to give new worms room to grow.

If you're raising the worms for castings, stop feeding them after they have become established, and they will eventually digest all the organic matter in the bedding box and die off, leaving you with mostly castings. To harvest the castings, simply turn the box over, allow the remaining worms a few minutes to burrow out of the light, and scoop up this great soil enhancer. This can be sifted and added to potting soil or to the garden beds.

If you want to keep your worm bin active, divide the farms every six months. Remove some of the castings and worms and replace some of the bedding material. Don't water the bedding the week that you plan to divide the box. Slightly dry bedding makes the worms easier to handle. Do your dividing outside in the bright sun or under a strong light so that the worms burrow down and cluster at the bottom of the box. The removed castings and worms may be put out in the garden to encourage a natural population in your outdoor beds, or you can start more worm farms. (A great gift idea for another gardening friend!)

Every garden can use a worm farm to improve soil and do the work of composting.

CHAPTER 5

GETTING YOUR GARDEN OFF TO A GOOD START:

SOWING SEEDS INDOORS AND OUT

Planting the garden is the fun part. This is what all that planning and preparation were about. Get instant results from store-bought transplants, or if you're patient, start your own seeds and save money. There are tricks and tips that make each of these methods easier.

Garden nurseries have a good selection of plants in various stages of maturity, ready for transplanting. The advantages of buying your garden "ready-made" include quick results and the opportunity to see the color and form of the plant before you put it into the garden. Starting with nursery-grown plants is the easiest way for the beginning gardener. The disadvantages are that it's more expensive than growing your own plants from seed and you are limited to whatever plants are on hand at the nursery. Eventually, most gardeners like to start at least a few plants from seed. So, let's talk about sowing seeds.

SEEDS

Seeds need certain conditions — warmth, moisture, light, and soil — to germinate and grow. Some seeds are not particular about their growing conditions and will sprout almost any-

SURE-FIRE SEEDS

Vegetables	Flowers
Beans	African daisy *(Arctotis stoechadifolia)*
Beets	Alyssum *(Alyssum* spp.*)*
Carrots	Bachelor's-button *(Centaurea cyanus)*
Corn	Cosmos *(Cosmos* spp.*)*
Lettuce	Larkspur *(Delphinium* spp.*)*
Radish	Marigold *(Tagetes* spp.*)*
Squash	Salvia *(Salvia* spp.*)*
Swiss chard	Statice *(Limonium* spp.*)*
	Sunflower *(Helianthus* spp.*)*
	Sweet pea *(Lathyrus odoratus)*

where. Throw them on the ground, sprinkle them with water, and the next thing you know, the garden is filled with little plants. Many annual vegetable and flower seeds are large, easy to handle, and tolerant of many soil types and weather conditions. Beans, lettuce, and radishes, for example, can be planted directly in the ground where you want them to grow, or they can be started in containers and transplanted to permanent beds. Carrots, corn, and peas, although easy to grow, resent transplanting; they are better sown directly into the garden.

Some seeds are more particular and need a certain amount of light or dark, or a specific temperature to germinate. These "fussy" plants require a very patient gardener. Seeds of tomatoes, peppers, eggplants, and other warm-weather plants, for instance, need relatively high temperatures for germination. Some growing seasons are too short for them to mature without a headstart indoors. Transplant them to the garden when conditions are just right.

Most seed packets include descriptions of the plant and its growing requirements. Botanical encyclopedias, garden books, and seed catalogs are also good sources of germination information for those who like the challenge of trying difficult plants. For assured success, if you are inexperienced, buy seeds that are marked "easy" or that are recommended for children's gardens. (See list of "sure-fire" seeds, above.) All you'll have to do is scatter the seeds, lightly cover them, tamp the soil, and keep it moist — you'll have a colorful garden in no time!

When you choose seeds, buy the best you can find. Browse the seed racks at your local nursery or order by mail (see pages 24-26 and appendix 5). Even the best seeds are inexpensive, so don't skimp on this most important garden ingredient.

Heirloom Seeds

Many seeds on the market are *hybrids* — the result of crossing different species and varieties of plants. Hybridizing is done in order to strengthen disease resistance, increase yields, and make other improvements. In recent years, some gardeners have become interested in growing non-hybrid, old-time plants that they feel have a hardiness, flavor, or other attribute that hybrids do not. (You may have relished a to-mato or bean that your grandfather grew, for instance, but haven't been able to find one that tastes as good.) These plants are known as *heirloom plants.* Unlike most hybrids, heirlooms usually breed true from seed. Some of these old-time plants aren't grown commercially anymore, but they may be available by trading with other gardeners or through a number of seed exchange organizations that keep old and useful plants alive by continuing to grow them. You'll find addresses for some heirloom seed sources in appendix 5.

Quality can be a problem with saved and collected seeds, because amateur seed savers may not be able to duplicate the methods commercial growers use to maintain freshness and vigor. Seed saving is a satisfying and addictive pastime, how-ever, and you may want to try collecting seed after you have had some garden experience.

Sow and Save

For folks on a budget, starting plants from seed saves money. Here are a few tips to stretch your funds and your seeds:

★ Mix your seeds with sand, soil, or dried coffee grounds. Purchase an adjustable seed-sowing machine or make a shaker by punching holes in the tight-fitting plastic lid of a

CINDY MCFARLAND

▲ *Punch holes in the lid of a small can and use it as a shaker to sprinkle fine seeds over a flat.*

VEGETABLE SEED SHELF-LIFE

VEGETABLE	AVERAGE YEARS OF VIABILITY
Beans	3
Beets	4
Cabbage	4
Carrots	3
Cauliflower	4
Corn	3
Cucumber	5
Lettuce	6
Melon	5
Okra	1
Onion	2
Peas	3
Peppers	2
Radish	1
Spinach	3
Tomatoes	3

The following seeds are short-lived and should not be saved from year to year: angelica, asparagus, delphinium, gerbera, *Salvia splendens*, geranium, painted daisy.

can (such as a baking powder can). Sprinkle your seed mixture from the can over the planting area. This will distribute the seeds over a greater area more evenly.

★ Start seeds like corn, peas, and beans in individual paper cups. At planting time, tear off the bottoms and plant the container. Because the roots are hardly disturbed, plants that usually resent being moved won't mind this type of treatment.

★ Carrots, onions, and radishes can also be started in cups, because they can be grown in clumps. Sprinkle a few seeds on the surface of each soil-filled cup. As with corn and peas, tear off the bottom of the cup at planting time and plant the container full of seedlings. They may need some thinning, but they will withstand transplanting, if their roots are not disturbed.

★ If you have leftover seed, store it properly to preserve its viability. Put it in small, airtight containers, such as empty baby-food or spice jars, label them, and store them in the refrigerator. (See list of seed shelf-life, at the left.)

★ Before you plant it in the garden, test some of your stored seed to see if it will germinate. Take a few seeds from each container and place them between two sheets of moist paper toweling. Label them so you know which kind is which. Roll up the toweling, put it in a plastic bag to maintain the moisture, and keep it in a warm place. After a few days, check for germination. Remember that some seeds take longer than others, but, if alive, most seeds will sprout within ten days.

STARTING SEEDS INDOORS

For plants that need a long time to mature, start seeds indoors or in a cold frame to get a headstart on bloom and harvest. Who doesn't want to be the first in town to harvest a ripe, homegrown tomato? This is especially helpful in areas with a short growing season. Chair-bound gardeners will enjoy starting plants in a convenient location where they can watch the progress of the seedlings.

Recycled Containers

You can sow seed into almost any container that provides drainage. If you use recycled containers with no drainage holes in the bottom, punch in several small holes. Containers must be deep enough to allow for unrestricted root development — 2½-3 inches deep. The container must be clean and disease-free. If you plan to reuse containers, they should be washable. You probably have a variety of inexpensive containers in your home. Here are some suggestions:

Disposable aluminum trays (available in any grocery store or recycled from packaged foods) are the most convenient and inexpensive seed containers. Punch holes in the bottom of three or four at one time by stacking them together and pushing a large nail or other sharp object through all layers — one in each corner and a couple in the center should be adequate. The bread-pan size is the most useful. Its depth gives seedlings good root room, and its width is just the right size for windowsill gardening.

Styrofoam cups are perfect for one-to-a-pot plants like tomatoes, peppers, and squash. Styrofoam cups keep roots cool and moist, so plants need less attention. Label the plants by writing the name right on the cup with a **waterproof** pen.

Punch holes in the bottoms (stack them to do a few at a time).

Any plastic tray that is deep enough can be used for seed starting. Use a hot nail to melt drainage holes in the bottom. Heat the nail by holding it over a flame or placing it in an ovenproof pan in a 475°F oven. Protect your hands by using pliers and a hot pad to hold the nail.

Milk cartons cut down to size, *frozen-food containers*, and *paper cups* sturdy enough to hold up under watering all make good homemade seed containers.

Purchased Containers

You can also purchase seed containers in garden supply stores or by mail. Some are made of *fiber, such as peat moss or degradable paper pulp.* These offer good drainage, but they dry out quickly and therefore need frequent watering and careful watching. *Peat pots, peat strips, and peat pellets* (which expand when soaked in water) are convenient, especially for planting large seeds. Once the seedling is ready for the garden, sink the whole container into the prepared bed. Some growers think peat pellets don't degrade fast enough to allow unrestricted root growth. To overcome this problem, tease the bottom open at transplanting time. Be sure to plant the pot below soil level, so that moisture doesn't wick out through the top edges.

Plastic containers with individual cells for each plant are strong and reusable, but the cost is high, unless you buy in large quantities. Each seedling is separate from the others and can be easily tipped out at transplanting time. Plants can grow for a long time in these containers, with little chance of root injury when they are removed. You can reuse the containers year after year to save money, but cleaning them costs time and effort. For the best results and easiest cleaning, spray leftover soil out of the

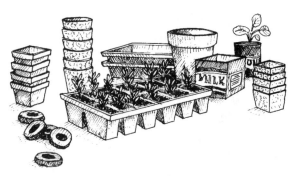

▲ *An assortment of purchased or recycled containers useful for starting seeds indoors*

containers right after you remove the plants. Then soak in a 10 percent bleach solution to sterilize them.

For convenience — and a real boon to gardeners who have difficulty handling seeds — nothing beats *preplanted seed starters.* These plastic or Styrofoam containers are filled with soil and already planted with seeds when you purchase them. All you have to do is add the water and wait! Many have plastic covers to preserve moisture and aid germination. Set these "mini-greenhouses" on the windowsill or under a grow light. A good variety of flowers and vegetables are available this way. When you consider the cost of the container, the planting mix, and the seeds, the prices are fair. (See appendix 5 for sources of preplanted seed containers.)

▲ *Small, plastic windowsill greenhouses keep germinating seeds moist and warm.*

Soil Mixes for Indoor Sowing

A purchased, sterile planting mix is safer to use than outdoor garden soil, which may contain diseases or insects. Ready-made mixtures that suit most plants are available from the garden-supply sources, or make your own germination mixture with equal parts of peat moss, vermiculite, and perlite. This combination is light, sterile, and airy. It retains moisture, but not too much. Adjust your mix to meet the needs of different plants. If you are planting seeds that require a lot of moisture, add a little more vermiculite, for its water-conserving properties. If you are planting seeds that rot easily, such as cactus or other succulents, use more perlite, or add sand for even better drainage and aeration.

For best results, premoisten the planting medium. Before filling the containers, thoroughly wet the mix with warm water (warm water speeds the process), and squeeze out the extra moisture.

A more time-consuming method — but useful if your hands are not strong enough to squeeze out the excess

EFFICIENT SEED-SOWING

KATHY YEOMANS

1. Have all your supplies at hand, including a handmade label for each plant variety.
2. Fill the containers with soil mix.
3. Sow the seeds, labeling as you go.

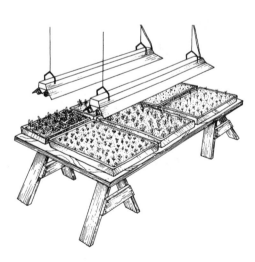

▲ *Fluorescent lights hung over a table full of seed flats provide even light for developing plants. Keep lights about 6 inches above plants.*

water — is to fill the containers with dry mix and then water from the top or put the container in a pan of water and let it soak in from the bottom.

After the soil is moist, pat it down firmly, especially in the corners, and level it. A block of wood, the size of the seed tray, will make this job go faster.

Sowing the Seeds

Scatter the seeds over the top of the soil, and then cover them lightly with planting mix or milled peat moss according to package directions. If you prefer, plant in rows, but it's extra work and unnecessary. Plant twice as many seeds as you want since some seeds won't germinate, and plants will be lost in thinning and transplanting. Tamp down the soil, and *be sure to label the container.*

Caring for Seed Flats

Germinating seeds need to be kept moist and warm. Cover the tray with plastic wrap or put it in a clear plastic bag. Put the seedling tray on a windowsill, but watch out for the hot sun — it can burn new seedlings very quickly. An east or north window is the safest. A fluorescent light hung a few inches over the trays provides both light and warmth. You can purchase special grow lights, which are designed to provide the proper light spectrum for growing plants, but I've also had good luck with inexpensive, shop light fluorescents.

Check trays daily for germination, but don't get discouraged! If the temperature or light requirements are not met, seeds may

★ Buy ready-made soil mix for germination trays.

★ Use seed tapes to plant straight rows quickly and easily. These are especially useful for those who have trouble handling seeds.

★ Mix tiny seeds with sand and shake them out of a salt shaker.

★ To see tiny seeds, use a large magnifier that you can hang around your neck. These are available in needlework departments and craft stores (or see appendix 5).

★ A magnifier light — a combination magnifying glass and light fixture on a heavy base — or a shop light that has a magnifying glass surrounded by a fluorescent light is a real boon when handling very tiny seeds. The latter easily attaches to a table with a clamp. These, too, are available at craft shops or by mail (see appendix 5).

★ Sometimes it's hard to see or you can't remember what areas of a seed flat have already been seeded. As you plant each section, sift light-colored sand over the top so that you can tell at a glance where seeds are planted.

★ Water several containers full of seedlings at once by soaking them in a large watering tray.

★ Thin seedlings by clipping extras away with nail scissors.

take longer to germinate than indicated on the seed packet. During this stage, watch your plants closely. Fragile seedlings can overheat, dry out, and wither in a very short time.

As soon as the seedlings germinate, remove the plastic cover to allow fresh air to reach the plants. Keep the new seedlings in bright light, but out of direct sunlight. Seedlings growing in a window have a tendency to lean toward the light, so turn them occasionally to encourage them to grow straight.

Water seedlings carefully. Overwa- tering is just as detrimental as under– watering. Some fungal diseases are encouraged by overmoist soil and wet leaves. Instead of sprinkling from overhead, water seed trays from the bottom by

▲ *Water seed gently so that you don't wash the soil mix away.*

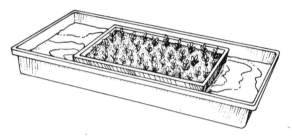

▲ *To water seed trays the easy way, bottom water by placing flat in a larger pan containing water.*

putting the seed tray in a slightly larger container. Fill the outer container with water until it reaches about halfway up the sides of the trays. Soak the trays for an hour or so: Water will move through the soil, from the bottom of the tray toward the top. When the soil surface is moist, remove the seed trays and let them drain. Usually, bottom-watering will keep the seedlings supplied with adequate moisture for at least a week, but check the soil frequently and repeat watering as necessary.

Keep the plants growing vigorously by applying quarter-strength fertilizer every two weeks.

Watch your new seedlings for problems that can be fatal. Newly sprouted seedlings may fall victim to a disease called *damping-off*, which is caused by a soil-borne fungus. Curb damping-off disease by using a sterile planting medium, providing good air circulation, and avoiding overwatering. Damping-off seems to be most prominent in warm temperatures (between 68° and 86°F), so keep seedlings on the cool side, when possible.

Crowded seedlings should be thinned and transplanted after they have developed four *true leaves*. The first two leaves that appear upon germination are called *cotyledons,* or seed leaves. These are food storage tissues and do not look anything like the leaves that will be on the mature plant. The true leaves are those that follow and are recognizable as belonging to a distinct plant family. Many garden books include pictures of common seedlings to help you identify them. Eventually, most gardeners learn to recognize familiar plants, even in the seedling stage.

Move plants out of their starter trays before they become rootbound. Plants that are rootbound are more sensitive to the trauma of transplanting and rarely attain full size. Studies have shown that smaller plants with uncramped roots catch up with, and even surpass, older, larger transplants in the garden. (Keep this in mind, too, when you buy plants from the nursery. Choose the younger, smaller plants, and pass up those that are already blooming — they are probably past their prime. Don't forfeit a healthy garden for instant beauty that is likely to fade.)

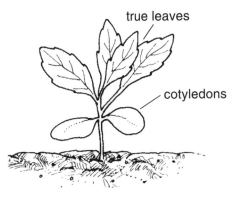

true leaves

cotyledons

▲ *Thin and transplant seedlings once they have four true leaves.*

If weather conditions are right when your seedlings are ready to be moved from the starter trays, plant them directly in the garden. Hardier plants, like spring-blooming annuals and cold-tolerant vegetables, can usually be transplanted to their permanent outdoor growing bed. If weather and soil conditions are not ideal, plants, especially heat-loving plants like tomatoes, peppers, eggplants, and many flowers, should be moved into larger containers and protected until weather conditions are just right.

Transplanting into Larger Pots

On the day before you transplant, soak the seedlings thoroughly to prevent stress, dried rootlings, and transplant shock. Also moisten the growing medium in the container where you will be moving them. You'll probably find that you have many more seedlings than you expected. That's good, because you'll lose some.

Use a butter knife, palette knife, ice-cream stick, or small spoon to pry the seedlings gently out of the seed flat. Separate them carefully, so you don't break stems or roots. Handle each seedling by the leaves to prevent injury to the vital stem area. If a leaf is broken off, a new one will grow; but if the stem is bent or pinched, the plant may never recover.

Make a hole in the soil with a pencil or a dowel — or use

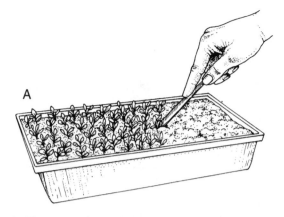

▲ *To transplant, (A) gently pry tiny seedlings out of the flat with a butter knife;*

▲ *(B) hold seedlings by the leaves to avoid damaging stems or roots, and place in prepared hole.*

a *dibble*, a stick with a pointed or rounded end that is made especially for this purpose. Lower the seedling into the hole, and place it *slightly* deeper than it was growing in the germination flat. Gently press the soil around the seedling's roots with a thin, flat tool, like a palette knife. Insert the knife next to the seedling and press the soil from the side. This gets the soil in good contact with the roots so they won't dry out.

Gently water the newly transplanted seedlings. Some gardeners use a vitamin-B solution on new transplants. Whether this actually gives them a boost or not is controversial. I've used vitamin-B solutions at times and plain water at other times, and I can't say there was a difference, but you may wish to try it.

New transplants may droop or wilt at first, especially if their roots have been damaged during the move. Don't worry — they recover quickly if they are kept moist and given good light.

If transplants no longer fit on the windowsill, move them to a cold frame or put them under fluorescent lights. Good light is important at this stage. Fast-growing seedlings get tall, scraggly, and weak in a few days, if the light is insufficient. Weakened plants are susceptible to pest infestation and disease, and will grow poorly when finally transplanted to the garden.

It's also important to keep your transplants evenly moist. Don't allow them to dry out, but remember that too much water can damage them, too. Put your finger on the surface of the soil; if it feels cool and some of the soil sticks to your finger, it's probably wet enough. You can judge water need by the weight of the pot — if the container feels very light, it's time to water. With some experience, most gardeners get a feel for this, and many depend on the "heft test" alone to determine water need.

PLANTING SEEDS OUTDOORS

The advantage of planting seeds outdoors is that you don't have to transplant seedlings. If air and soil temperatures are warm and your growing season long, save yourself time and energy by planting your flowers and vegetables right in the garden bed.

Preparing the Bed for Planting

Your garden soil should be moist and fertile. If it is light and fluffy enough to dig with your hands, it is just right for starting even the most particular seeds. Dig or rototill your seed beds a week or so before planting to let the soil settle. Add compost or other soil amendments as described on pages 75-88. This is a good time to incorporate dry and time-release fertilizers. For seed starting, in addition to general garden soil preparation (see Chapter 4), you may want to add sand, bark dust, soil mixes, gypsum, or a combination of these to lighten the soil. There are disadvantages to adding either peat moss or vermiculite to seed beds. When peat moss dries out, it is very difficult to rewet. Vermiculite is composed of air- and water-holding granules that aid germination and fluff soil; it is not a good additive in clay soils, however, because its water-retaining capacity can waterlog the soil and drown plants. A good additive is perlite, a volcanic ash that does not absorb

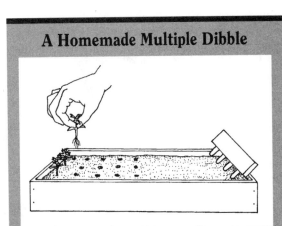

A Homemade Multiple Dibble

A multiple dibble makes evenly spaced transplant holes quickly and easily. It is well worth constructing if you plan to do a lot of transplanting. Evenly space dowels with rounded ends on a board about the size of your transplant flats (or a size that is convenient to work with), and nail them in place. At transplanting time, push the dibbles into the prepared, moistened soil.

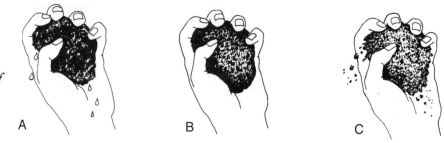

▶ *Judging soil readiness: (A) too wet if water can be squeezed from it; (B) still not ready if it remains compressed in a ball; but (C) ready if it crumbles in your hand.*

A   B   C

moisture but holds it on its surface. Perlite is light, aerates the soil, and stays cool — a plus for those plants that won't germinate at high temperatures.

After you've dug and amended the soil, break up soil clumps and rake the seed bed smooth. For the smoothest surface, use the back of the rake on your final pass. **If raking is difficult for you, use a board to flatten and smooth the seed bed.** For other tips on how to overcome problems associated with digging and cultivating, see Ruth Stout's "no-dig gardening" hints on pages 143-145. See also Chapter 2 for information about special tools that make these jobs easier.

Mark straight rows with string. Hold a hoe or rake edgewise and drag it across the bed to define deep, narrow furrows. Consult seed packets for proper planting depth. The general rule is to cover the seed with soil to a depth once or twice the thickness of the seed.

Wide-Row Planting

Instead of planting in rows, you can also use a system known as *wide-row planting*. Why fuss about placing seeds one by one in straight, narrow rows when they grow just as well, and perhaps better, scattered in wide rows? Many more vegetables can be harvested from a wide row than from a conventional single-row planting. Seed-sowing is easy, and the slight crowding

▲ *Drag the edge of a hoe along the row to make a furrow of the proper depth for the seeds.*

in wide rows discourages weeds, while the closely grown plants support each other, reducing the need for stakes and supports. Thickly growing plants also shade the soil, thus conserving moisture. Wide rows are real work savers.

Some people don't like the wide-row method of planting because it doesn't look as tidy as the conventional method. Instead of soldier-like plants marching single file down a nar-

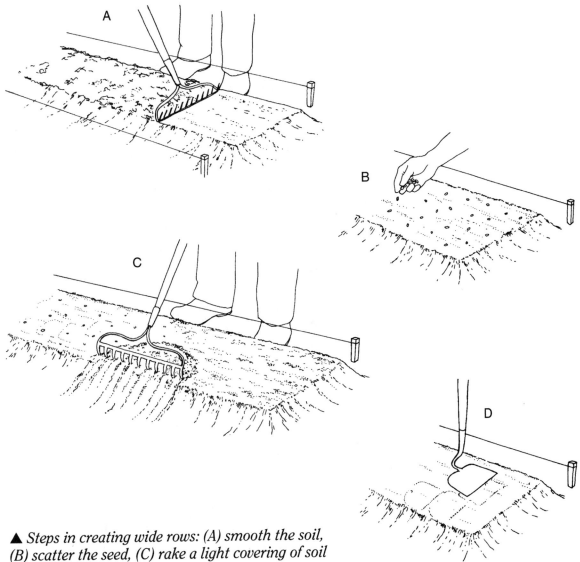

▲ *Steps in creating wide rows: (A) smooth the soil, (B) scatter the seed, (C) rake a light covering of soil over the seeds, and (D) tamp the seed bed.*

row garden row, plants grow willy-nilly in a completely filled band. But, for me, the advantages greatly outweigh this concern. The method works with flowers as well as with vegetables. There's nothing prettier than a wide row of bright yellow marigolds growing next to a wide row of blue lobelia or bachelor's-button — and it's so easy!

Here's how it's done: Prepare your bed as usual. Then, drag the back of a rake over the soil to define a wide row — the width of a common garden rake is a good width for a row of vegetables. Broadcast the seeds over the raked area. (See pages 95-97 and 109 for tips on handling seed.) Cover the seeds lightly with soil by raking or broadcasting more fine soil over them. It's difficult to cover each seed to the exact depth suggested on the seed packet, but it's my experience that, unless buried too deeply, most seeds don't mind a little variation. Tamp the row down lightly with the back of the rake, or place a board over the newly seeded row and step on it lightly to firm the soil. Water gently. Some seeds will be exposed and others will be properly covered, but don't worry about it. There is some loss of seed in this method of planting, but the ease and convenience make up for the slight waste.

Seeds in the wide row germinate much more thickly than you want them to grow. Thin them by pulling out some of the seedlings by hand, snipping them out with scissors, or dragging a rake through the area. The dragging method is quickest and easiest, though imprecise. Use thinnings of tender vegetables in salads.

Label Your Plantings

After you plant the seeds, *label the rows*. I can't stress this too much — it's easy to forget what you've planted where. Unlabeled rows often fall victim to indiscriminate "weeding" — a mistake I know from experience!

When you label the rows, jot down the planting date. Records of planting, germinating, and harvesting dates are helpful for future reference. You'll know which plants did well and which ones to skip next time. These records can be help-

★ *Use a seed-sowing board.* Drill ⅛–¼-inch holes in a piece of masonite, painted a light color to make the holes more visible. Place the board on the soil and simply drop seeds into the holes. Lift the masonite and sift soil over the seeds.

★ *Make a planting stick.* To avoid bending while sowing seeds, use a lightweight, homemade planting stick. Cut a piece of plastic pipe to waist or chest height, and attach a funnel to the top of it. Sharpen a dowel, and tape it securely to the outside of the bottom of the pipe, allowing it to protrude about 3 inches beyond the bottom. Use the sharpened dowel to make a small hole in the soil of the proper depth for the seeds you are planting. Place the bottom opening of the planting stick over the hole, and drop a seed into the funnel, letting it fall into the hole. This innovative tool was designed by Albert Pippi, of Baltimore, Maryland, who submitted it to *Organic Magazine*'s "Reader's Forum."

★ *Make a cane/planting stick.* Another version of a planting stick was created by a gardener who frequently uses a cane. She taped a plastic pipe, with a funnel on top, to her cane, letting the cane extend about 3 inches beyond the bottom of the pipe. When she sows seed, she makes a planting hole with the end of her cane, and then drops the seed into the funnel. You have to get used to positioning the cane so the seed drops correctly into the hole, but once you get the hang of it, it's easy. She uses the end of the cane to cover the seed with soil, and then steps on it lightly to firm it in place. She not only has a helpful planting tool, but also her cane is right at hand to give her support as she walks through the garden.

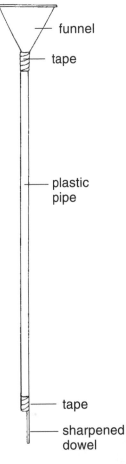

funnel

tape

plastic pipe

tape

sharpened dowel

ful, too, if you plan to rotate garden beds from year to year for insect and disease prevention. (For information about crop rotation, see page 183.) Whatever you do, don't rely on your memory.

Protect Your Plantings

Row covers, both plastic and spun-fiber covers, work in many ways to protect your young plantings.

To boost germination, cover the seeded rows with *clear plastic.* Plastic is easy to find and inexpensive. It also raises the soil temperature and thus increases the germination of warmth-loving seeds. This can be useful if you are trying for a headstart by planting early in the spring. Watch carefully, however, as temperatures can get too high underneath plastic. Remove the plastic, or prop it up, as soon as the seeds have germinated, so that fresh air can circulate. On a bright, sunny day, it doesn't take long for seedlings to "cook." In addition, the plastic traps moisture and inhibits air circulation, which encourages disease and rotting.

Spun-fiber row covers not only encourage germination, they also extend the growing season, keep plants clean, conserve moisture, prevent insect-borne disease, and protect both young seedlings and maturing fruits and vegetables from insects and birds. Both water and air can penetrate, so there's less chance of either cooking or drowning your plants, and row covers can be left in place almost indefinitely. Spun-fiber covers raise the soil temperature only minimally, so they don't protect early plants from a hard freeze, but in warm weather, they give heat-loving plants an extra boost, to encourage faster growth. (In very hot weather, however, they can raise temperatures too much, so you may have to remove them in high summer.)

CINDY MCFARLAND

▲ *Spun-fiber row covers protect young seedlings from pests.*

They have some minor disadvantages. Some are made of scratchy materials that can injure sensitive young plants. If this is a problem, prop the covers up and off tender plant leaves. Another problem with keeping your plants under cover all season is that the bees and other pollinating insects can't get to them. Unless you are willing to tackle the major task of hand-pollinating them, remove the covers when the plants bloom.

It is easiest to lay out a row cover as soon as the garden bed is planted or at least when the seedlings are small. Anchor it with bricks or staple it or tie it to the edge of a raised bed, so the wind doesn't blow it away. Do not stretch it tightly over the bed; apply it loosely to leave the plants growing room.

Row covers are sold in wide pieces and in narrow rolls. Narrow covers range from 5 to 8 feet, and wide covers, from 20 to 50 feet. The narrower rolls are easier to use. I prefer the softest, lightest kind, but there are a number of brands to choose from and all have advantages. Synthetic row covers are not inexpensive, but can be used year after year. I have not replaced mine for five years, although I use them only in the spring. If you are unable to obtain row covers from your local nursery, many mail-order firms carry them. Although you may not like their appearance — your garden looks like it's wearing a hairnet — row covers are a fine investment.

Spun-Fiber Row Covers: A Serendipitous Discovery

The material used for synthetic covers was first developed for use as fabric stiffeners, disposable diaper liners, and bandage fabrics. Then, a chemical company received a request for a protective covering for tobacco plants. Although the company did not have a product specifically developed for this use, it sent a bolt of upholstery backing. This fabric was longer-lasting, less expensive, and more permeable than the covers that the growers were using at the time. The tobacco growers loved it. In no time, other companies were trying lightweight fabrics as plant covers. Now, such coverings are used commonly by both commercial growers and home gardeners.

They're Here!

Keep new seedlings moist, but don't overwater — puddles

out in the garden are a sign of too much water. Quarter-strength fertilizer applied every two weeks will keep young plants growing vigorously.

Potential Problems with Seedlings

Seeds started outdoors are susceptible to some of the same problems as those planted indoors. Although damping-off disease is less common outdoors, it can occur. Tender seedlings can also quickly die if they receive too much sun and/or too little water. If your seed fails to germinate at all, any of the following may be the cause:

★ *The seed was too old.* Onion seeds, for instance, aren't reliable after one year, and parsley seeds are viable for only two years, while others may germinate after three years. Some flower seeds must be planted right after they are harvested. Most seed packets are dated. For best results, use fresh seeds. (See page 96 for average viability of some common seeds.)

★ *The seed may have been incorrectly stored.* Dampness and heat can harm seeds — keep them cool and dry.

★ *Soil temperature is too low.* This is a frequent problem, especially when you are sowing directly in the garden. Beans, for instance, are very intolerant of cool soil temperatures and won't sprout if the soil is too cold. Use a soil thermometer to help you decide if temperatures are right. Most seeds germinate best at 55°–75°F. Exact temperatures for specific plants are usually listed on the seed packet or in a garden encyclopedia.

★ **Soil may be too dry or too wet.** Soak the seed bed before planting, let it rest for a day or two, and then cultivate it to aerate the soil. Cover the seed bed with mulch or a row cover to retain moisture; it should not be allowed to dry out. Water deeply only after the seeds have germinated.

★ **Seedlings may not sprout in pure, unfinished compost.** This is because decaying organic matter releases carbon dioxide and other chemicals that can inhibit germination. Cucumbers are especially sensitive to these chemicals.

★ **Seed is planted too deep.** Very fine seed may not need any cover at all or a plastic or spun-fiber cover (not touching the seeds) may suffice. Broadcast or lightly rake soil over newly planted seeds; don't throw on shovelfuls of dirt.

★ **Light may be incorrect.** Some seeds require darkness to germinate, while others require light. Consult the seed packet or an up-to-date gardening encyclopedia for specific information.

★ **Birds, snails, and other thieves may carry off seed.** Newly germinated seeds are gourmet fare to sport-loving birds and creeping snails. I once lost a whole bed of carrots within minutes when a flock of sparrows invaded the garden. There wasn't a trace of green when they left, and if I hadn't seen their thievery, I never would have known the carrots had ever germinated.

★ **Difficult plants can also cause seed-starting disappointments.** Some plants require freezing or even fire in order to germinate. Other seeds sprout only when certain chemicals are present in the surrounding soil, such as those released during a wildfire or other natural event. Very small seeds or seeds with extra hard coatings give even the expert gardener trouble. Check your garden encyclopedia for specific seed-starting directions if you are consistently having problems with a particular plant or plant family.

TRANSPLANTING TO GARDEN BEDS

Once the weather has moderated, purchased seedlings or those you started indoors may be transplanted into the garden. Transplanting is a great shock to plants, so treat them gently. Fertilize with half-strength solutions for the first two weeks after transplanting.

The First Step: Hardening Off

Many tender plants that are begun in the house need to be put through a toughening up process called *hardening off* before they are shifted to the garden. Introduce them to outside conditions gradually by moving the trays or potted plants to a sheltered, shady area, such as a porch or under a tree. Begin by giving them an eastern exposure, where they receive morning sun but are shielded from the hot afternoon sun. After a few days, move them to a less protected area, where they receive sun all day long. Remember to check their water needs frequently; wind and sun can dry out the soil quickly. After a few days in a protected location, plant the seedlings in their permanent location.

Cold Frames

A good place to harden off seedlings is in a *cold frame* — a protected growing area outdoors, usually covered with glass or plastic. Cold frames are unheated except for the heat they get from the sun, but because they are enclosed, the air inside is warmer than outdoor temperatures. A cold frame should be at least 4'x4' to retain a sufficient amount of heat to protect the plants. Some gardeners like a narrower, longer frame that is easy to reach into from the front.

You can build your own cold frame or buy a ready-made one. Cold frame kits come in various sizes and are lightweight and easy to assemble. Most are easy to break down for winter storage. They last for years. Some have automatic opening devices that lift the top to vent the cold frame when the air inside reaches a certain temperature. This prevents seed-

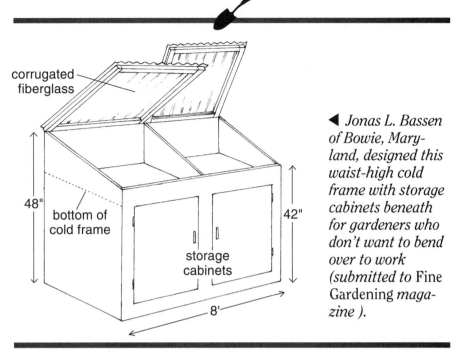

corrugated fiberglass

48"

bottom of cold frame

storage cabinets

42"

8'

◀ *Jonas L. Bassen of Bowie, Maryland, designed this waist-high cold frame with storage cabinets beneath for gardeners who don't want to bend over to work (submitted to* Fine Gardening *magazine).*

lings from being toasted on an exceptionally warm day. Such a device is a nice work saver for you, too. These simple devices can be bought separately and attached to your homemade cold frame (see appendix 5 for suppliers).

To take advantage of the warm sun, situate the cold frame so that the low end is facing south. It will be more sheltered if you place one side against the wall of the house. To add heat to a free-standing cold frame, put a few bricks, stones, or plastic gallon jugs of water in the cold frame during the day. They will heat up in the sun and release the heat slowly throughout the night to keep sensitive plants warm. If a freeze is expected throw an old blanket over the whole frame. Don't forget to remove the blanket, and "wake them up" in the morning!

If you are using your cold frame to harden off new transplants, keep the top closed for the first two or three days, unless the weather is very warm. After the plants have become acclimated to cooler outdoor temperatures, open the top during the day, but close it at night. If night temperatures are above freezing, keep the top propped open a little at night after a week. Eventually, open the top all the way, so that the plants are exposed to normal outside temperatures.

In late spring and early summer, the temperature inside the cold frame may get too high. Lower the interior temperature by raising the top a few inches to vent the hot air. You can also move the cold frame under a tree or toss a shade cloth over it.

HOW TO MAKE YOUR OWN COLD FRAME

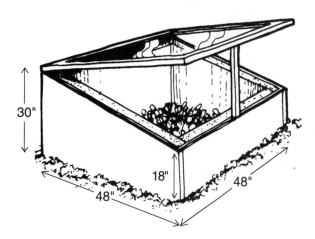

A simple cold frame can be assembled with a few pieces of lumber and a section of fiberglass. Make the back wall higher than the front wall to allow rain and/or snow to run off. The cold frame shown is lined with rigid insulation panels.

1. Cut a 4'x8' piece of $^3/_4$-inch outdoor-quality (CDX) plywood in half, crosswise, forming two 4'x4' pieces. From one of these pieces, cut the irregular-shaped sides, as shown. From the other, cut two rectangles: one 18"x48" for the front and one 30"x48" for the back, as shown. If you aren't able to do the cutting yourself, many lumberyards will cut wood for you for a minimal charge.

2. Nail or bolt the sides together, or use right angle metal braces attached to each side with wood screws. Nail wood blocks into the corners for added strength, if you wish. Alternatively, you can hinge the sides, so you can fold the frame for easy storage.

3. Using 1"x2" lumber, nail together a 4-foot-square frame for the top. Staple fiberglass, row cover fabric, shade cloth, or transparent plastic to the frame. Row cover fabric or shade cloth allows air to circulate, but the cold frame will not be as warm as one covered with a nonpermeable material. This can be an advantage if you don't want to bother venting the top on hot days. Nail a strip of wood at the rear top of the frame if you want to attach the cover with hinges, or just set it on top.

When to Transplant Outdoors

After the last frost is the usual time for transplanting outdoors. Some plants, like lettuce, carrots, peas and spinach, are tolerant of cold weather. Others, like tomatoes, peppers, squash, and eggplants, detest the cold. Wait until the nights, as well as the days, have warmed up before planting them outdoors. Many warm weather plants won't grow when night temperatures are below 50°F. Some gardeners get a headstart by covering the garden with clear plastic or mulching with a heat-absorbing material, such as black plastic. This will raise the temperature of the soil, but it's a lot of trouble for a harvest that may come only a few days earlier than if you had simply waited for warmer weather before planting.

Gray, overcast, and drizzly days are perfect for transplanting; hot sun and dry winds stress new transplants. If you must transplant on a sunny day, wait until late afternoon, when the sun's heat has diminished.

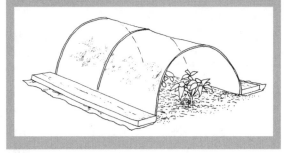

How to Transplant

Transplanting to the garden is much like transplanting to seed flats. Use your garden trowel or dibble to dig a hole somewhat larger than the root ball.

Position the plant in the hole, and then backfill with soil. Settle most plants about as deep as they have been growing. A few, however, benefit from being planted deeper. Tomatoes, for instance, will grow new roots on the portion of the stem that is below ground level, and the increased size of the root ball produces stronger, stouter plants. Press the soil firmly

Tip: A common beach umbrella makes an easy, portable shelter for transplants.

To transplant, (A) carefully remove plant from container with soil intact, (B) dig a hole slightly larger than the root ball, and (C) set the plant in the hole at the same level as (or for some plants slightly lower than) it has been growing.

Easy Transplanting

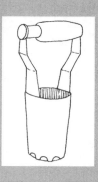

If you have trouble holding a trowel, use a bulb-planting tool to make the planting hole. A bulb planter looks like an empty tin can with a handle over the top. The "can" portion is pushed into the earth and twisted to remove a plug of soil. Bulbs (or transplants, in this case) are then dropped into the hole and the soil in the cylinder is used to refill the hole. Bulb planters come in various sizes and shapes. There is even one that releases the extracted soil plug with a squeeze of the handle — the way an ice-cream scoop drops ice cream.

around the roots, but don't pack the soil too tightly, or you may damage the roots.

Give transplants plenty of growing room. If this will be the plant's final growing place, pay attention to spacing recommendations. A good rule of thumb is to space plants as far apart as their width when mature. For example, a marigold plant that grows to be 6 inches in circumference, should be planted 6 inches from another marigold. Tomatoes and peppers usually need a minimum of 18 inches. Sprawling plants, like squash, melons, and cucumbers, require lots of room, unless you grow them vertically on trellises.

Water garden transplants deeply, unless your soil has poor drainage. Use a mulch to conserve soil moisture. If you allow plants to dry out at this early stage, you can irreparably damage the plant.

Use a dilute solution of fertilizer or *compost tea* to get plants off to a good start. Make compost tea by soaking a burlap bag full of compost in a large container of water. After about two weeks this solution becomes a fertile, although smelly, "tea" that plants love.

Insert stakes and set up growing cages

at transplanting time, while the plant roots are still contained; there is less chance they will be damaged when you pound in the stakes. If you wait too long, transplants quickly grow beyond the point where staking and tying is easily accomplished, and you risk broken stems and root damage. For more information on staking and supporting plants, see pages 150-155.

Protect new transplants from full sunlight for a few days by screening them with shade cloth, cheesecloth, or a lath screen. Turning a bushel basket over transplants is a traditional method of protecting them from the hot sun and drying winds; prop one side up with a stake to admit light and air. Berry baskets and overturned plastic flats also work well as temporary covers for newly planted seedlings. Gradually increase the light intensity to sheltered transplants by removing the protective covering for a few hours during the day; start in the morning and work toward the brighter afternoon hours. Watch the plants carefully; pale leaves are a sign of too much light. Plants don't get a tan — they get sunburned! On the other hand, if plants look tall and spindly, they are not getting enough light.

Wind is even more stressful to transplants than sun, because it dries moisture out of the leaves faster than their new roots can supply it. If it's windy, mist the plants daily for the first few days. If necessary, build a wind-

Quick Furrow Transplanting

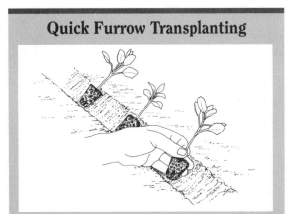

Instead of digging a hole for each transplant, use a small tool to make a furrow in the soil. Place the transplants along the furrow, and then backfill with soil.

Frost Protectors

★ Make individual greenhouses for your plants by cutting the bottom out of plastic water jugs and soda containers. Take the tops off to allow for air flow, and push them into the ground around each plant.

★ Place jugs filled with water next to transplants. The water will accumulate heat from the sun during the day and release it at night to raise nearby temperatures a little.

Successful Transplanting

★ Transplant after true leaves have formed.

★ Handle seedlings by the leaves. Handling by the stem may cause irreparable damage.

★ Transplants may droop at first, but they should recover quickly if kept moist. Do not overwater.

★ Transplants need bright light, but not direct sunlight. Pale leaves are a sign of "sunburn."

★ Acclimate your transplants. Hardening off is an important step in successful transplanting. Gradual changes in light and temperature allow new plants to become accustomed to the outdoors.

★ Label. Don't lose your transplants.

break with row-cover fabric or shade cloth attached to 4-foot stakes.

A late frost can sneak into your garden and wipe out your transplants overnight. Use the same devices that shelter your plants from sun and wind to protect them from frost. Row covers, bushel baskets, and windbreaks work to keep the temperatures above freezing. Don't count on them for extended protection, however. If the weather is consistently freezing, you have planted too early. Make a note of the date, and plant later next year. In the garden, timing is everything.

Watch out for snails and slugs that often hide under mulch and look for succulent new plants to nibble. These creatures can destroy your plants, leaving nothing but a slime trail and chewed stems. Look for snails and slugs in the dark, cool corners of the cold frame, under the flats and containers, or under rocks and wood in the garden. Protect the perimeter of beds with sand, ash, or cinders, which snails seem to avoid.

🍴 EASY TRANSPLANTS

★ Pace yourself. You don't have to transplant everything at once.

★ Bring a stool out to the garden to sit on.

★ Use a multiple dibble to save time and effort (see page 105).

★ Wait for a cloudy day. It's easier on both you and the plants.

★ Install a drip system and an automatic timer. You'll be able to give transplants adequate water without having to carry heavy hoses or watering containers (see pages 127-131).

CHAPTER 6

ABLE GARDENING:
CARING FOR THE GARDENER
AND FOR THE GARDEN

The seeds that were planted outdoors have germinated, and the transplants have been moved to the garden — what do you do next? Plants need continuing care to grow well and to produce colorful flowers, tasty vegetables, and mouth-watering fruit. Before we discuss what your plants need, however, let's look at some ways you can care for yourself while you care for your garden.

GROUND RULES FOR ABLE GARDENING

Avoiding Fatigue

It's easy to overdo when you are out in the garden enjoying yourself and trying to finish a specific task. Gardening activities often seem to expand as you work. What started out to be a quick and simple job of cutting a few dead flower heads can turn into a major pruning unless you learn to limit yourself. Sit down and rest at frequent intervals; fatigue is one of the major causes of accidents. Here are some other commonsense ways of managing your gardening tasks:

★ Balance activity with rest. Allow time for breaks.

★ Sit to work. It's less tiring than standing or bending.

★ Plan ahead — and stick to your plan. Organize so that you do the hardest tasks early in the day when you are fresh and strong. Avoid two heavy chores on the same day.

★ Prioritize. Do what is most important and leave the rest for another day.

★ Pace yourself. Alternate light and heavy tasks, and take a rest in between jobs.

★ Avoid staying in one position for a long time. Change positions frequently and stretch occasionally to avoid stiffness.

★ Avoid deforming postures or positions. Poor posture and unnatural body positions lead to fatigue, pain, and injuries.

★ Recognize the onset of fatigue; stop before you become over-tired.

★ Ask for help when you need it. An injury will keep you out of the garden for a long time.

★ Carry a whistle to summon help if you become overtired, faint, or injured in the garden.

★ Respect pain. Your body knows when to stop — listen to it.

Hints for Lifting and Carrying

Garden work often requires moving tools, soil, or plants. Certain techniques can save you an injury and keep you active in the garden. The best plan is to avoid heavy lifting and carrying whenever possible. If you must lift a heavy item, however, be sure to use good body mechanics. Here are some guidelines:

★ Avoid lifting altogether if you have a serious back injury.

★ Do not lift objects that are awkward or too heavy.

★ Face the object you are about to lift and stand close to it.

▲ *Learn proper lifting and carrying techniques.*

★ Shift your feet when you turn; don't twist your back.

★ Wear proper shoes and have a firm footing before you lift.

★ Securely grip the load, but be ready to release it promptly if you find it is too heavy for you.

★ Bend both your knees, not your back. Your back should always be straight.

★ Use your large leg muscles, not your more vulnerable back muscles, to help you lift.

★ Lift smoothly; don't jerk.

★ Keep the weight you are carrying close to your body, so that the larger joints of the arms and the shoulders do the work. Stand as straight as possible.

★ Lift and carry using not only your hands but your arms as well.

★ Use the strongest/largest joints and muscles for the job (your arms and legs, for instance), and avoid direct pressure on your smallest joints (your hands and fingers) and weakest muscles. For example, lift heavy items with the palms of your hands instead of your fingers; carry bags on your forearms or over your shoulder rather than with your hands.

▲ *Use large muscles — of the arms rather than the hands, for example — to do the heavy work.*

★ Push and pull. Slide heavy objects instead of lifting them. Use carts or wheelbarrows as much as possible.

★ Carry many smaller loads rather than one large load. It may take longer, but it may save you a trip to the hospital!

★ Keep a sharp eye out. Don't block your view by carrying stacks of objects or piles of debris that you can't see over. Look behind before you back up.

Other Garden Safety Rules

★ Beware of wet surfaces. Both pavement and grass are slippery when wet. Wear shoes with nonskid soles.

▲ *Use carts or wheelbarrows to do the carrying for you.*

★ Use sun protection. Wear a hat and sunscreen to protect yourself from harmful rays. Take an occasional rest in the shade to avoid overheating and sunstroke.

★ Replace fluids. Gardening is hard work. Drink an 8-ounce container of water or other fluid every hour you are out in the garden. Plastic fluid containers are safer and easier to carry than glass.

★ Dress for comfort and safety. Wear clothing that allows freedom of movement but is not so loose that it might get caught in gardening equipment.

★ Pace yourself. Allow plenty of time to accomplish your work and don't hurry. Accidents often happen when you're moving too fast.

★ Keep your mind on the job. Distraction and inattention are safety's enemies. Stay alert to avoid gardening accidents.

★ "The good goes up and the bad goes down." If you have one leg that is stronger than the other, lead with your strong leg when you climb hills or steps and with your weak leg when you descend.

★ Use assistive devices and/or splints if you need them. Assistive devices make a task easier by reducing the force placed on joints and weakened limbs.

★ Relax your standards — you don't need to have a perfect garden.

Keeping these general rules of garden work in mind, let's look at some of the tasks that need to be done, and find the easiest way to do them.

WATER WISELY

Water is a plant's "blood." Without water, the plant dies of thirst. Given too much water, the plant drowns. The successful gardener must provide just the right amount of water. Deciding just how much is "right" can be a problem.

How Much Water and How Often?

Water deeply about once a week, if it doesn't rain. Shallow watering encourages shallow roots, which are more likely to suffer damage from drought and injury. Depending on the temperature, wind, and soil, an inch of water each week is recommended for most plants, including vegetables, fruits, and many flowers. Cacti, succulents, and other "dry" plants need less. Know your plants' needs and your soil type before you set up a watering schedule.

To check how much moisture your plants are getting with each watering, set out a flat-bottomed, straight-sided container, such as a coffee can, when you turn on the sprinklers. An inch of water in the can means an inch of water has fallen on your garden. Of course, this won't work with drip irrigation. If you have a drip system, you can estimate the amount of water your garden is getting if you know how much water flows through each emitter per hour. Some formulas state that if each emitter allows 1 gallon of water per hour, the application rate is about ½ inch an hour. Most drip systems come with directions that help you estimate how long to leave the system on. A simpler way to tell is to inspect the soil after you've irrigated for an hour. Dig down an inch or two. Is the soil wet? Does it feel moist? You can probably tell if your plants need more water just by "eyeballing" the garden.

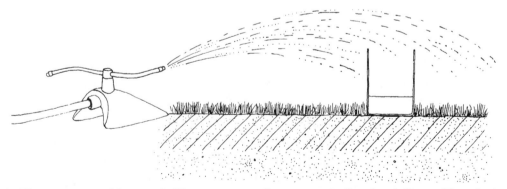

▲ *If you water with a sprinkler, measure the amount of water delivered by placing a can beside the plants or on the lawn.*

If the weather is very hot or windy, or if your soil is very sandy, you may have to water more frequently than once a week. Plants that are not getting enough water look pale, a good indicator that you should increase the amount of water or water more frequently. For most plants wilting is another symptom of thirst. Don't let squash and melon plants fool you, however. They will naturally wilt on very hot days; if they recover in the evening, they don't need more water. If the rest of your garden is getting enough water, your squash plants are, too.

Plants under water stress are more susceptible to insect attack and disease. Studies have shown that keeping a constant moisture level in the soil is better than the flooding and drought cycle that occurs if you depend on Nature to water for you. Uneven watering causes knobby potatoes, woody carrots, fibrous beets, and other problems that affect vegetable taste and flower blossom quality.

Tips for Solving the Challenge of Watering

Even the strongest gardener gets worn out when water sources are far away and the delivery system is an unwieldy hose or a heavy watering can, and watering presents the physically limited gardener with some real challenges. Just getting to the source of water may be a problem if you use a cane, walker, or wheelchair. You may not want or need an automated system, however. Here are some relatively simple watering suggestions.

★If you are gardening in pots near the house, choose small, lightweight, plastic watering containers. Water is heavier than you think. As the old saying goes, "A pint's a pound, the world around!" That means a full 2-gallon watering can weighs 16 pounds, plus the weight of the container. Lugging that much weight around for any length of time is tiring and can cause back strain. In addition, because the heavy weight throws you off balance, you are at greater risk of tripping or falling.

* Choose the lightest hoses you can find. Flat, self-draining hoses and portable hose reels are a great help.
* Elevate your faucets so you don't have to stoop to turn the water on and off.
* Install multiple water faucets throughout the garden.
* Leave extra hoses out in distant garden areas so you can simply attach them to the main hose instead of dragging them back and forth.
* Snap-on hose connectors are easier on hands and fingers than conventional twist connections.
* Attach on/off valves to each hose so that you don't have to return to the main faucet each time you connect or disconnect hoses.
* Place rain barrels or other water-holding tanks in each garden area. Install hose connections and stop valves on the tanks. Periodically fill these tanks and leave them open to collect rain.

Automating Your Watering System

Three factors determine how difficult watering chores will be: distance (how far the water needs to travel), the kind of water delivery system (hoses, watering containers, and/or automated systems), and the number of systems.

A combination of water delivery systems works best for most gardeners. Hand watering containers makes more sense for just a few pots than setting up a complicated drip system, but if you decide to automate your watering, which system you choose depends in part on the nature of your garden. You can choose among sprinklers, soaker hoses, and drip irrigation systems.

Sprinklers. The "rainstorm" effect of sprinklers is ideal for lawns and seed beds and cool-season plants like lettuce and carrots, as well as for plants that require high humidity, like begonias. Overhead watering has some disadvantages, however: It tends to splash dirt and disease-causing organisms around the garden and it can damage some hot-weather crops, like melons, squash, and other vine crops. Some sprinklers deliver water in a circular pattern, some oscillate back and forth, and some allow you to change the water pattern to suit the garden shape. Traveling sprinklers move about the yard on their own, so they save you hours of dragging sprinklers from one place to another. They work best on a lawn, where they can travel unimpeded. Impulse sprinklers cover large garden areas: Some can be installed in the ground so they pop up only when they are in use.

Set up various types of sprinklers to meet the different needs of each garden area and leave them in place to save time and work. Don't wait until late in the day to sprinkle. If plant leaves don't have time to dry before nightfall, mildew and fungus diseases are likely to occur.

Soaker hoses. Soaker hoses and in-line emitters work nicely in most flower beds and vegetable gardens. Also called *porous hoses*, soaker hoses deliver a low volume of water directly to plants. The best have dual-chambers (sometimes called *piggyback hose*). In dual-chambered hoses, water is routed through double tubing, equalizing water pressure along the length of the hose and eliminating the problem that some soaker hoses have of allowing a great deal of water to escape before reaching the terminal end. Soaker hoses are sturdy, flexible, and easy to use. Buried under soil, they deliver water to the root zone of plants, thus decreasing evaporation loss as well as protecting the hose from the sun, which can eventually destroy hose materials. They have some disadvantages: They are relatively expensive. They are large and bulky and therefore awkward to install. Because the flow of water is slow, algae can accumulate and block the pores inside the tubing. In addition, they deliver evenly only on flat ground.

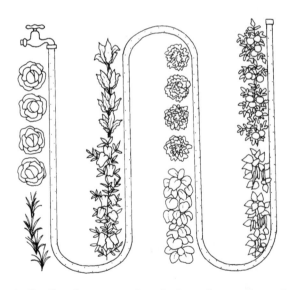

▲ *Soaker hoses, set just below the surface of the soil along the length of each garden bed, deliver water efficiently to the root zones where it is needed.*

It's a good idea to check water flow occasionally by digging into the ground at several places along the hose when it is operating to see if it's as moist as you expect it to be.

Drip irrigation. Drip-irrigation systems with spaghetti tubes and emitters deliver water efficiently when you have large plants, such as tomatoes, peppers, and melons, spread out over a big area, with no need to water the areas in between. Individual drip emitters can be used in pots and window boxes. Spaghetti lines with emitters can even be fixed along the roof line to deliver water to hanging plants or over the bird bath to save refilling chores.

A drip-irrigation system usually consists of a network of plastic tubes that deliver water drop by drop to the roots of plants. Drip systems have many advantages over conventional watering methods. They reduce water usage by 50 to 70 percent because less water is lost to evaporation and waste, and the consistent supply of water to the root zone promotes better, larger crops. Since water is applied only to the immediate root area of chosen plants, a side benefit of drip irrigation is that surrounding areas remain dry and thus fewer weed seeds germinate. And, drip irrigation is the *easiest* way to water your plants. Once the irrigation network is set up, it needs only occasional maintenance. Watering becomes the simple chore of turning a valve on or off. If you have an automatic timer, you don't even need to worry about that.

Although drip-irrigation systems take some planning, have a higher initial cost than hoses, and take some time and energy to install, the benefits far outweigh the disadvantages. For easy gardening, a drip system can't be beaten!

Selecting a Drip System

Drip irrigation kits include all the necessary parts to set up a small drip system. Most systems consist of a large plastic tube — *the delivery hose* — approximately 1 inch in diameter, that carries the water to various parts of the garden. This is a very stiff hose. Attached to the delivery hose are smaller *spaghetti tubes* that bring the water to the root zone. These

Do-It-Yourself Drip System

Here's an inexpensive, low-tech way to deliver water slowly and evenly to the root zone area of tomatoes, peppers, or other large plants: Create a simple drip-type water delivery system with plastic water jugs. Punch one small hole in the bottom of each gallon-size jug, and install a water emitter in the hole. Fill the jugs with water. Place one jug next to each plant. This method saves time if you have no regular drip system and you would

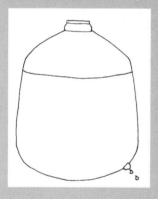

otherwise be hand-watering. Refilling the jugs is less of an effort if you leave them in place, and fill each one with a hose.

tubes have *emitters* at the end that allow water to pass at certain rates, measured in gallons or fractions of gallons per hour. Each plant can be supplied by an emitter, although this can be complicated and time-consuming to set up. Individual emitters are best for container gardens or for gardens with a small number of specimen plants.

In-line emitters are another type of irrigation system. Consisting of a plastic line or hose with water emitters spaced along it at regular intervals, these are less complicated to set up than the spaghetti-tube arrangement, but they don't deliver the water as precisely. In-line emitters dispense water at rates of either ½ or 1 gallon per hour. Watering time can be adjusted to deliver more or less water, as needed.

Installing a Drip System

Designing the drip system is easy if you have a copy of your general garden layout on paper (see pages 7-11). With garden beds and water sources located, you can estimate the kind and amount of irrigation material you'll need. All the major drip irrigation makers supply pamphlets that describe the equipment and make design suggestions. Some include sample layouts that are quite helpful. Keep your system as simple as possible. Add on to it later, if you need to.

Avoiding Problems with Soaker Hoses and Drip Systems

The problem with drip systems is that emitters sometimes get clogged with grit and hard-water minerals, and in both soaker hoses and drip systems, algae may breed in the moist tubes and plug the lines. Most drip-irrigation kits come with screen filters that fit between the faucet and the hose. These are helpful, but they may not be adequate. Some companies design their drip equipment with anti-clogging devices that send jets of water for the first few seconds after the water is turned on in order to flush the system. If your system doesn't have this feature, remove the end plugs of the lines and let water run freely for about five minutes; do this every month or so.

Anti-siphon or backflow prevention valves are also part of most irrigation kits and are required by law in some areas. These devices prevent water from siphoning back into the household water supply when the irrigation system is turned off. This is especially important if you have installed a fertilizer attachment to your system.

Timers for Truly Carefree Watering

Watering timers are great work savers. Set the time intervals and watering hours and walk away. No more traipsing out to the garden to turn the water on and off. Timers are especially useful with a drip-irrigation system, but they work well with sprinklers too. They will take care of your garden while you're gone, and deliver water at precisely set intervals. Get one for each water outlet and automate your whole garden.

The pressure regulator is an important feature that protects your system from excessive water pressure. A slow, even trickle of water is essential to the workings of a drip-irrigation system. If water is blasted into the system at too high a pressure, your lines may burst, or your emitters may get blown into the neighbor's yard.

THE EASIEST WAYS TO FERTILIZE

"Feed the soil, not the plant" is a basic garden principle. Fertilizers do not produce fertility, good soil does. Proper soil management, including the use of compost, mulch, and green manures, builds soil and minimizes the amount of fertilizer that needs to be added. The result is that you save work, time, and money. (The basics of fertilizing and soil amendment are discussed in chapter 4.) Plants use up nutrients, however, and eventually even the best soil needs a boost. Well-fed plants suffer from fewer diseases and are better able to resist insect attack, so regular fertilizing actually saves time and work in the garden.

Timing is important. When plants start to blossom, they need extra food to develop blooms, fruits, and seed pods. If you feed the plant too early, it uses that nutritional boost to grow lush leaves and roots at the expense of flowers. Don't fertilize until you see the "whites of the flowers' eyes." After the plants are well established, however, add fertilizer by side dressing, by pouring a liquid solution around each plant, by foliar feeding, or by broadcasting dry fertilizer. Heavy feeders, like sunflowers and corn, or slow-maturing plants, like tomatoes and peppers, benefit from a supplemental feeding. You can prolong the blooming period of most flowers by giving them a dose of fertilizer just after they start blooming. Quick-maturing vegetables, like beans, lettuce, peas, and radishes, do not need an extra feeding.

▲ *You may be able to rent a push-type spreader, which broadcasts fertilizer evenly over an area.*

Fertilizer comes in both liquid and dry forms. If you have a large area to fertilize, dry fertilizer may be most convenient. Liquid fertilizers, such as fish emulsion or seaweed solutions, are good mid-season fertilizers for most plants; the enriched water reaches right to the roots. Always water thoroughly before adding fertilizer to the garden bed. If you apply liquid fertilizer to dry soil, for example, it may not seep to the root area; and if it does, it may burn drought-stressed root hairs.

Broadcasting. Dry fertilizers may be broadcast by scattering it by hand, or by placing it in a push-type spreader or in a hand-held device with turning paddles that whirl the granules out and distribute it more evenly. Follow package directions to calculate how much fertilizer is needed for a given area.

Side dressing. Following label directions as to how much to apply, pour fertilizer next to or around the plants, and then cover it with soil. Many different kinds of fertilizer can be applied by this method. In *The Joy of Gardening*, Dick Raymond recommends the following homemade, organic, 5-10-5 fertilizer suitable for side dressing each plant:

> 2 handfuls of good compost
> 2 handfuls of dehydrated manure
> *or*
> 1–2 tablespoons of alfalfa meal

Foliar feeding. This method applies liquid fertilizer directly to a plant's leaves, which are its food factory — the production point for most of the things that a plant needs for growth. Foliar fertilizers are thus highly efficient, because they are absorbed right where they will be used. Some studies have shown that plants are able to use more of the nutrients supplied by foliar feeding than they are when fertilizer is poured into the surrounding soil. Be sure to use a product that has been formulated for foliar feeding. Some fertilizers are too strong for the foliage, and others don't have the proper substances to make the food cling to the leaf surface. Plants absorb foliar nutrients best in the early morning and mid-afternoon when the sun is out and the leaf systems are active.

▲ *To side dress plants, make a shallow furrow along the row and sprinkle fertlizer along its length.*

Alfalfa Tea

Soak alfalfa sprouts or hay in water, and use this "tea" as a fertilizer. Alfalfa is not only high in nitrogen, it contains a "plant booster" enzyme. In *The Joy of Gardening*, Dick Raymond suggests using certain cat litter box materials that are made of alfalfa pellets. As with any fertilizer, too much is often as bad as too little. Alfalfa is known to contain a chemical that actually deters plant growth when applied overzealously, so use it in moderation ($\frac{1}{2}$ cup of alfalfa sprouts soaked in 1 gallon of water overnight is fine).

★ Commercial fertilizers should never come into direct contact with seeds at the time that they are sown; strong chemicals in these fertilizers dehydrate or inactivate newly sown seeds.

★ Always apply commercial fertilizers to the side of a plant or seed bed; they can harm the sensitive stems and leaves of trees, shrubs, and other plants.

WAR ON WEEDS

Weeds compete with your plants for space, food, light, and water. The crowding and poor air circulation that occur when weeds run rampant encourage pest and disease problems. Weeds are host plants to a number of insect pests that infest and infect your garden. It's important to keep your garden as free of weeds as possible, but weeding can be a time-consuming, back-breaking job. In the battle against garden weeds, use your head instead of your back! **Here are some tips that make weeding easier:**

★ Bone-dry soil makes weeding and cultivating harder. Deep water the day before you intend to weed, and you'll have less trouble pulling weeds out. To avoid spreading disease, however, wait until the plant leaves dry.

★ To eliminate weeds before you plant a garden bed, try "cooking" weed seeds out. After wetting the ground, cover it tightly with black plastic. The heat of the sun will roast the weeds and their seeds, hindering germination. (A similar technique, called *solarization*, will rid a garden bed of disease as well as weed seeds [see pages 187-188]).

★ Weeding is one of those "stitch-in-time-saves-nine" jobs. The longer you wait, the more there is to do. Keep up with the weeding chores so that they don't become overwhelming. Pulling a few small weeds every few days is easier than clearing out a whole bed of established giants.

★ Sit down when you weed. Bending over causes back strain

and poor balance, increasing your chances of injury. You can sit right on the ground, but a low stool or chair will be more comfortable. Choose one that doesn't tip over easily. Some weeding stools are built with raised handles to help you push yourself up off the ground. (See more on kneeling and sitting stools on page 32.)

▲ *To avoid back strain, sit in a low beach chair to weed your garden.*

★ Knee pads and gardening pants with built-in knee pads protect you from injury. Even with knee pads, however, don't spend so much time on your knees that you strain your knee joints. It's better to sit, but if you must kneel, change your position often.

★ Wear gloves while weeding to protect your hands. Blisters are quite painful and prone to infection.

★ Drag along a wagon or other cart to collect the weeds. This saves clean-up time when the job is finished. Empty the weed wagon occasionally — it's a good way to change positions. Don't let the wagon get so full that it's too heavy to handle. You can use a child's toy wagon, a reinforced plastic tarp with handles, or a plastic trash container with wheels, as well as plastic buckets, baskets, or nearly anything with handles. Lightweight tarps are available from many of the garden supply houses (see appendix 5).

Certain gardening techniques, such as raised beds (pages 43-47), wide rows (pages 106-108), and watering systems that deliver water to the plants and leave the surrounding areas dry (pages 127-131), reduce the need for weeding. Of course, you can also ignore the weeds. There are many gardeners who don't give a hoot about weeds in the garden. Some theorists state that certain weeds even help other plants grow. Ruth Stout, the author of *How to Have a Green Thumb Without an Aching Back* and a former weed-puller, was disgruntled to note that a friend who allowed weeds to grow in his garden sometimes had a better harvest than she did.

Mulch: The Practical Weed Preventer

Mulch — a layer of material placed on the soil surface — not only keeps the weeds down, but also keeps the ground cool and preserves moisture in the garden. In addition, if you use organic mulch, you will also be adding nutrients and improving soil texture. Mulch helps keep sprawling plants clean, off the ground, and disease-free. Depending on the type of mulch you use, it can also neaten the appearance of your garden. Mulching protects plants from freezing during the winter and maintains a more consistent soil temperature all year-around.

Always apply mulch after the ground has warmed up. If it is applied too early in the season, it keeps the soil too cool for germination. Generally, dark material, such as black plastic, will warm the soil, while light-colored materials will reflect heat and keep the soil cool.

To prevent the growth of weeds, apply a thick layer of mulch — usually 2 or 3 inches. Finely shredded material does a better job of weed prevention than unshredded material.

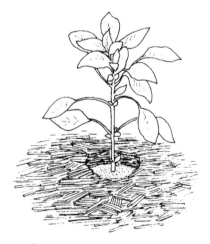

▲ *Leave an opening in the mulch at the base of the plant.*

Don't apply the mulch too close to the plant stem because it might cause stem rot.

For best results, wait until the seedlings have appeared and grown about 4 inches before mulching. If you must mulch a seed bed, mulch materials should be loose enough to allow the seedlings to poke through.

Mulching has a few disadvantages. One is the danger of rot when mulch is applied too close to the crown of some perennial plants. Another is that mulch makes a nice home for snails, slugs, and sow bugs. This becomes a real problem in wet, shady areas of a garden. Light, loose mulches discourage these pests. Some fungal diseases that are caused by high humidity, such as damping off of seedlings, may be encouraged if mulch is applied too soon after germination. Wait until seedlings are at least 4 inches high before using mulch.

Mulch Materials

Practically any organic and many synthetic materials can be used as mulch. Mulch materials can be obtained at garden centers, sawmills, feed stores, farms, and some landscaping supply houses, or use yard waste.

Black plastic is a popular mulch material. It's inexpensive, easy to use, and looks neat in the garden. Its heat-absorbing quality benefits such warmth-loving plants as tomatoes, peppers, and melons. One problem with the plastic, aside from the fact that it doesn't improve the composition of the soil in any way, is that the soil may stay too wet underneath it, increasing the risk of root rot and other diseases brought on by dampness. On the other hand, to allow for adequate irrigation (unless you have a drip system), you may need to cut holes in the plastic. Recent tests show that *white plastic*, more than black, increases the yield of some plants, such as potatoes.

Permeable polypropylene or polyester fabrics are synthetic materials made just for mulch. These fabrics admit water and air, but block light. Although broad-leaved weeds can't penetrate them, certain aggressive grasses are still a problem, as some can grow underneath this fabric. Weed seed germination is definitely reduced, however. When used as mulch, these fabrics reduce evaporation, erosion, and weeds, and they also make a tidy ground cover.

Organic materials are good for mulch because they improve the nutrition and structure of the soil as they break

Mulch Dos and Don'ts

★ Use dark-colored mulch if you want to warm the soil.

★ Use light-colored mulch if you want to keep the soil cool.

★ Use mulch to keep sprawling fruits and vegetables clean.

★ Keep mulch away from the plant crowns.

★ Don't mulch when the ground is too wet; good aeration is necessary for healthy plants and healthy soil.

★ Wait until seedlings are 4 inches high to mulch.

★ Use mulch in containers as well as in the garden to conserve water and keep plant roots cool.

MULCH MATERIALS

TYPE	DURATION	ADVANTAGES
BARK	1–2 years, depending on size and type	Slow to decompose Stays in place Ornamental appearance Not attractive to termites
TREE TRIMMINGS	1–2 years	Inexpensive and readily available, although should be shredded first
SAWDUST	Less than one season	Good conditioner when worked into the soil
PINE NEEDLES	2 years or more	Slow to decompose Excellent weed suppressant Moisture retentive Lightweight
STRAW	1 season	Insulator Lightweight Easy to remove
GRASS CLIPPINGS	1 season or less	Readily available
LEAVES	1 season	Insulator Lightweight
NEWSPAPER	1 season	Completely blocks light, preventing weed germination and growth Absorbant
RICE HULLS	Up to 2 years	Absorbant and cushiony Slow to decompose Good conditioner when turned into soil

DISADVANTAGES	BEST USES
Larger pieces can be difficult to work around	Landscape, around ornamentals
Could introduce disease High cellulose content could harbor termites	Pathways around ornamentals, if composted
Decomposes quickly Temporarily depletes nitrogen at soil surface Flammable Compacts so tightly that it may shut out rain and waterings	Pathways around vegetables, small fruits, or ornamentals, but might require nitrogen supplementation
Flammable Contains chemical that might stunt the growth of some plants	Acid-loving ornamentals or small fruits
Not ornamental Blows around	Around vegetables after soil has warmed Over vegetable or perennial beds in winter after dormancy
Quickly decomposes Could temporarily deplete nitrogen at soil surface Could contain herbicides Heats up so much that it can damage plants	Around vegetables Best to compost or age before using
Can blow away if not shredded or composted Raw leaves are toxic to brassicas	For winter cover, apply after dormancy; remove or till into soil in early spring To cool soil in summer, apply after soil has warmed
Blows around unless wet or covered with top mulch Blocks air, unless shredded	In rows between vegetables, after soil warms Pathways
Needs top mulch to hold in place Can contain weed seeds Can cake and slow drainage, causing root rot	Vegetable or ornamental beds; best if composted first

TYPE	DURATION	ADVANTAGES
NUT AND GRAIN SHELLS	Up to 2 years	Uncrushed shells decompose slowly (oily shells decompose more quickly) Attractive
SEAWEED	1 season	Rich in trace elements and other nutrients
HAY	1 season	Readily available Same as straw, except for possibility of weed seeds
COMPOST	1 season	Perfect
BLACK PLASTIC	3–4 seasons, maybe longer	Very moisture retentive Warms soil Speeds maturity increasing yield of heat-loving plants Suppresses most weeds Inexpensive
WHITE PLASTIC	3–4 seasons, maybe longer	Same as black plastic, except cools soil Intensifies light around plant
PERFORATED PLASTIC (including Miracle Mulch and Super-Mulch)	3–4 seasons, maybe longer	Same as for other plastic mulches Water and air can penetrate
LANDSCAPE FABRIC (including Earth Blanket, Typar, Weed-X, Weed Barrier, Weed Block, Magic Mat)	Long-lasting	Durable Air and water permeable Preserves life of top mulch Suppresses most weeds below mulch
DEGRADABLE FILM (including Plastigone, Agplast-Leco)	1–2 seasons	Commercial crop production

DISADVANTAGES	BEST USES
Sharp edges may inhibit earthworm activity Oat hulls may inhibit plant growth as well as weed growth; peanut hulls not recommended, because they could contain nematodes	Uncrushed shells for ornamentals and walkways Crushed shells also for vegetables (hulls not recommended)
Decomposes quickly if shredded Needs to be rinsed before put in garden Best composted first	Composted, around vegetables and fruits
May contain seeds that will sprout Highly flammable	Same as straw
None	Around fruits and vegetables
Nondegradable; not air or water permeable	Around heat-loving plants, to warm soil in spring Weed control
Same as black plastic	To cool soil in summer
Nondegradable Weeds can sprout through	Like black plastic in the vegetable garden With top mulch, in landscape or ornamental beds
Grasslike weeds still penetrate Some weeds can grow in top mulch	Landscapes, perennial beds or borders In strips between fruit trees or bushes Under walkways Patios
None	All uses

down. Almost any fibrous material — such as *shredded leaves, straw, ground corn husks, peat moss, grass clippings, and even newspapers* — can be used. Some of these materials do present problems. *Grass clippings* can pack down and ferment, rather than compost, causing a slippery mess and robbing the soil of nitrogen. Prevent this by combining the grass clippings with other fluffier material and sprinkle a high-nitrogen fertilizer on the soil before spreading the mulch.

Newspapers have been used successfully as mulch, and shredded newspaper, in particular, breaks down quickly and allows air to circulate to the soil. Some studies have shown, however, that the inks are harmful to plants and people. Most newspapers today claim to use nontoxic inks in the print sections of the newspaper, but the colored cartoon and magazine sections may still contain harmful elements. Newspapers do blow around the yard in windy weather and need to be held down with gravel or bark. Damp, folded papers aren't as likely to blow away, but they are slippery and unattractive.

Tip:
Mulch container gardens to decrease evaporation and keep plant roots cool.

Peat moss is an excellent dry mulch for heavy or overly wet soils. It lowers the pH of alkaline soils and is one of the most attractive organic mulches. One problem with peat moss is that it is difficult to re-wet once it dries out, and water runs right off it rather than soaking into the soil underneath. Peat moss breaks down quickly and can blow or wash away, so it must be replenished at regular intervals.

Alfalfa hay is often suggested as a mulch material, and in terms of texture and nutrient potential, it's tops. However, I can tell you from personal experience that alfalfa seeds are quite vigorous, and you may end up with a yard full of alfalfa seedlings sired by your mulch. Although the alfalfa is not hard to pull up when it is small, why add to your gardening chores? Composting the alfalfa is a better option; the seeds will "cook" in a hot compost heap and you will still reap the benefit of this excellent material as a soil additive.

TAKING MULCH A STEP FURTHER: GLEANINGS FROM RUTH STOUT

Ruth Stout might be called "the mother of no-dig gardening." A devoted gardener who refused to give up her beloved pastime when her strength diminished, she developed techniques to make gardening easier. She was over 70 years old when she wrote *How to Have a Green Thumb Without an Aching Back* to share her discoveries with other gardeners who faced similar life changes. Much of her advice is based on the theory of no-dig gardening: "Young or old, my friends, if for any reason you would like to grow things, throw away your spade and hoe and make your garden your compost pile. You will not be sorry, I promise you." Here are some of Ruth Stout's principles:

★ Apply 6 to 8 inches of organic material to the garden surface; the soil underneath will stay so soft, loose, and moist that you won't have to spade it before planting. Use nutrient-rich material such as kitchen scraps and garden refuse, which will break down to feed the soil and improve its texture. "When you throw these things in the garden, they are simply returning home, where they belong." This mulch also kills weed seeds.

★ Leave vegetable waste, such as cornstalks and pea vines, in the garden. Spread mulch over it, and leave it to decompose.

★ To plant in a mulched garden, pull the mulch back, mark a row with a little lime, drop the seeds, cover them with a strip of cardboard, and pull the mulch back over. Seeds seem to sprout faster this way and the cardboard can be removed as soon as they do. Note that in hardiness zones below zone 4, mulch may keep the soil too cool, which may inhibit or prevent seed germination.

★ Let tomatoes "roam" on top of mulch instead of staking and pruning the plants.

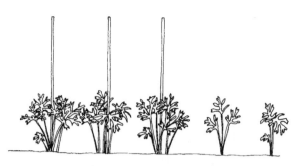

▲ *Carrot seedlings planted in clusters marked by sticks are easily thinned to one plant per cluster.*

▲ *Rake leaves onto an old blanket, and then pull the corners together so that you can drag the bundle of leaves to the garden to be spread over the beds.*

★ If you don't have the strength to set bean poles, dig a small hole, make it deeper with a crowbar, set the pole in place, shovel back some earth and firm it down. *Or,* use giant sunflowers for bean poles; let the sunflowers get a head start, then plant beans around them.

★ For easy potato planting and harvest, make a furrow, drop pieces of seed potatoes in, and cover thoroughly with hay. Water as usual. When potato plants die down, rake off the hay and there are your new potatoes!

★ For easy thinning, put sticks in the ground, as far apart as the recommended planting distance for the seeds you are sowing, and plant a few seeds around each stick. Thin the seedlings gradually until there's only one plant for each stick.

★ Get help when harvesting fruit trees. "I don't believe in climbing ladders after your bones get brittle. The only way to make absolutely sure you won't fall off a ladder is not to get up on one."

★ To make raking leaves easier, "lay an old blanket on the ground, rake the leaves onto it, take the four corners and hold them together, then drag the blanket into the garden" and distribute the leaves for mulch.

★ Don't overdo: "There are only 24 hours in each day and you have to use a few of them for sleeping."

★ To conserve energy, "never work after two o'clock in the afternoon and never do anything unless you feel enthusiastic about it."

★ "Work slow and steady, never hurry." Miss Stout learned this from farmers, whom, she noticed, said, "Take it easy," rather than "Goodbye" when they parted company.
★ "Planning a garden is like planning a way of life, arrange it to please yourself."

KEEP THEM TRIM: PRUNING

Keeping plants "lean and mean" is another garden work saver. Plants get out of hand quickly. Thoughtful pruning will keep them under control and growing vigorously.

There are many reasons for pruning. Perhaps most obviously, pruning controls the size and shape of plants, and keeps your garden attractive. A reason more basic to the plants' health, however, is that pruning removes nonessential growth, so the plant will be better able to get air and sunlight. Pruning also removes injured or diseased plant parts to save the rest of the plant. Removing dead flowers and aging stems reserves water and plant nutrients for the healthy, growing parts. Did you realize that whenever you pick a flower or cut some roses, you are pruning?

Pruning is also done when you transplant large trees or shrubs or plant bare-root specimens. Because root growth and top growth are related, there must be a compensatory reduction of top-growth when the root system of a plant is reduced. Otherwise, the plant will not receive enough water and nutrients from the soil. A good rule of thumb is to prune back one-third of the top growth so that the roots are not overburdened.

Be careful not to over-prune. Most plants need a certain amount of green material to use the sunlight and metabolize nutrients. Never remove more than one third of an actively growing plant. Plants that are dormant can be pruned more radically, but check a gardening encyclopedia for specifics. Some fruit trees produce well only when pruned in a particular manner and at a particular time of the year.

I admit that I don't follow every pruning rule. When a tree

or shrub looks scraggly, I use the pruning shears. Fruit trees are an exception. Because crop production depends on proper pruning, consult pruning books to give each kind of fruit the trim it likes best. Ornamentals, however, will tolerate a little pruning variation.

You will feel more confident about pruning if you understand how pruning affects your plants' growth patterns. Usually, pruning during dormant periods stimulates growth, and summer pruning slows growth. Here is how it works: In winter, roots contain stored food that was produced by the leaves during the past summer. When you prune the branches, there is less plant material to use all that stored food, so the fewer branches that are left receive more energy and grow rapidly. On the other hand, cutting branches during the summer reduces the number of food-producing leaves, so growth is slowed and there is less food to store in the roots for the winter. If you prune too early, you may stimulate too much new sprouting; if you prune too late, new growth may not have enough time to harden off before winter comes. It's impossible to give hard and fast pruning dates for each part of the country. Consult garden encyclopedias and local nurseries for specific information for your zone. A few mistakes won't kill a well-grown tree or shrub; just try again next year!

Traditional Pruning Rules

Deciduous spring-flowering shrubs and trees, such as forsythia, mock orange, lilac, spirea, flowering almond, peach, and crab, are best pruned right after blooming. Some types of rambler and climbing roses also benefit from post-bloom pruning. This is because the flowers are borne on last year's growth of wood. By pruning early in the growing sea-

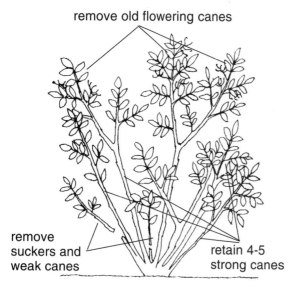

remove old flowering canes

remove suckers and weak canes

retain 4-5 strong canes

▲ *Pruning a climbing rose.*

son, you are encouraging the plant to grow new wood for next year's buds. Cut back all the spent flowering wood to lateral shoots or new buds. Remove any suckers and weak or misdirected shoots. Cut to a bud on the outside of a branch whenever possible. This will encourage new growth to go outward and keep the plant open and airy.

Deciduous flowering shrubs that bloom in the summer or fall on the current season's growth should be pruned in the late fall or early spring. Hydrangea, hibiscus, and crape-myrtle are plants that fit into this category. All the old shoots that have flowered should be cut back as far as possible, in order to promote new flowering branches.

Broad-leaved evergreens, such as azaleas, rhododendrons, and camellias need very little pruning. These are, therefore, great plants for low-maintenance gardening. Simply remove the faded flowers and seed pods. Be sure to leave the side shoots below the blossom when you are picking off the faded blooms, because this is where next year's flowers will be produced. Some fast-growing, broad-leaved evergreens, such as acacia and broom, should be pruned in the summer right after blooming. Light but continuous pruning encourages bushy growth without stressing the plant. Prune away branches that have flowered.

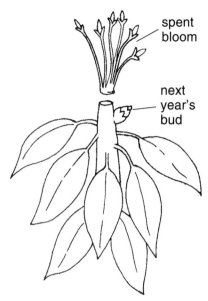

spent bloom

next year's bud

▲ *To prune rhododendrons, remove spent bloom, taking care not to disturb next year's bud.*

How to Prune

Be aware of the natural shape and growing pattern of each plant you prune. Most plants look better if you thin out whole branches rather than give them a "butch cut." You destroy their characteristic shape if you lop the tops off shrubs that have grown out of bounds. Avoid creating a garden full of green lollipops. Pruning to conform with and conserve the typical shape of individual plants is less trouble than trying to force plants into unnatural forms.

To make a clean cut on smaller branches, hold the prun-

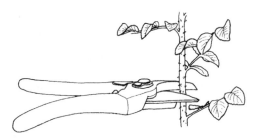

▲ *To make a clean cut, place pruner blade next to the part of the branch that is to remain on the plant.*

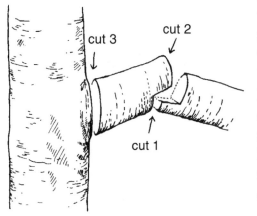

cut 3

cut 2

cut 1

▲ *To remove a large branch, make three cuts in the order shown.*

ing shears with the blade next to the portion of the twig or branch that is to remain on the plant. Because a ragged cut doesn't heal quickly, insects and diseases have time to attack.

To remove a large branch, cut it off in pieces. The full weight of a large limb is hard to handle and can tear tree bark as it falls, or suddenly come crashing down on your head. To avoid getting hit by a falling branch, throw a sturdy rope over a higher limb, then tie one end to the branch that is to be cut. Anchor the other end to keep the rope within reach. This allows you to ease the branch to the ground with the rope after it is cut loose from the tree. Make two cuts, one from the underside first, about halfway through the branch, and then one from the top. This will keep the bark intact. Finally, cut the stump off close to the trunk but leave the small raised area where the branch joins the trunk. Recent studies have shown that this "collar" must be left intact; this is where the healing callus tissue forms to cover the prune wound.

Get help for any branch that is more than a foot over your head or more than 3 inches in diameter. If you have to climb a

PRUNING BASICS

★ Prune at the proper time.

★ Always remove dead, injured, or diseased growth (this can be done any time).

★ Preserve the natural growing pattern of the plant; avoid "butch cuts."

★ Woody plants need only light pruning; plants with soft, fast-growing stems can take more severe pruning.

★ When in doubt, check a garden encyclopedia before pruning.

ladder to reach a branch, don't do it — hire a professional.

Paint fresh pruning cuts over 1 inch across with a protective compound or cover them with electrical or adhesive tape until they heal. These precautions discourage bacterial infection.

Pruning Tools

Good tools are tough and will last a lifetime. Look for tools made of *drop-forged, heat-treated* steel. The simplest tools, with a minimum of moving parts, last the longest. Find ones that can be taken apart easily for cleaning, sharpening, and replacement of parts. Cutting tools, especially pruning shears, should have a locking mechanism for safe pocket-carrying. Top-quality pruning shears, loppers, and hedge shears should have rubber, neoprene, or spring bumpers to absorb the shock when a cut is made. Choose pruning tools that fit your hands, arms and strength. There are tools made with narrow grips for smaller hands; others have contoured handles for comfort. Usually, small tools work just as well as large tools, and you can use them longer with less fatigue. Don't buy tools that you have to stretch to grip.

Pruning shears. For cutting wood up to ½ inch in diameter, use pruning shears to harvest and prune grapes, snip flowers, clip twigs, thin and prune shrubs, and cut back small tree branches. Pruning shears come in many sizes and weights; find a pair that fits your hand. If necessary, build up the handles with foam or adhesive tape so that you can get a good grip on them. Ratchet-action shears require less hand strength to use. Bypass-type pruning shears are recommended over the anvil-type; they make an easier, cleaner cut because there is less friction and less resistance.

▲ *Bypass pruners*

Loppers. Like overgrown pruning shears, loppers have long handles, and powerful cutting jaws provide better leverage and allow you

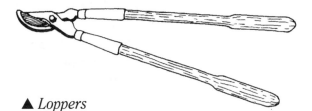

▲ *Loppers*

to prune in awkward places and cut larger branches. Some loppers cut branches up to 2 inches in diameter. Maintain good posture when you're using loppers; some gardeners have a tendency to "bend into" heavy work, a habit that throws off your balance. Instead, get as close as possible to the branch you are cutting, stand straight, and use your shoulders and arms to work the handles, not your elbows and wrists.

Hedge shears. Designed for keeping the tender new growing tips of hedges trimmed and shaped, hedge shears should *not* be used for a hedge that has gotten out of hand and needs reshaping or radical pruning. Use pruning shears or loppers, instead. Electric or gas-driven hedge shears are designed for heavier work and can also be used to reshape a hedge, if the branches are no larger than ½ inch in diameter.

▲ *Hedge shears*

▲ *Pruning saw*

Pruning saws. Designed to cut wood up to 3 or 4 inches in diameter, pruning saws are fast, because the teeth are set to cut in both directions.

KEEP IT UP: STAKES AND TRELLISES

Keeping your garden looking neat can be a lot of trouble. It seems just about the time you want to sit back and have a glass of lemonade, the plants flop over. Whatever form of support you use, install it early, when plant stems are flexible and roots are less likely to be injured. Here are some ideas to give you more time for lemonade-sipping.

Many plants need staking to encourage tall, rather than sprawling, growth. An unstaked plant, rambling unchecked, can soon take over your garden and walkways. A tomato plant staked early is manageable; later it will be too big to handle. Vertically grown plants are easier to care for and easier to reach. Raising plants up off the soil keeps them out of the way of ground-dwelling pests like slugs, snails, and in some areas, turtles. Supported plants decrease stem breakage from high winds or heavy fruit sets. You will also make more efficient use of limited garden space if you train plants to grow vertically.

Materials

Plants that bear fruits and vegetables become heavy, so use strong materials to support them. Wooden stakes are available in many sizes. For the largest plants, like tomatoes, squash, or cucumbers, choose stakes that are 2"x2" in width or larger. Drive them at least 12 to 18 inches into the ground. This can be difficult for any but the strongest back — I usually need help with this task. Stakes go into moist soil more readily than into dry soil, so water the day before you plan to put them in. Use a post-hole digger or crow bar to make a starter hole. Set the stake into this hole and backfill with soil.

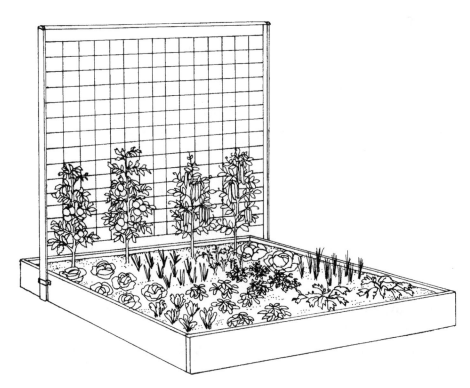

◀ *If you have a raised bed, you can bolt trellis supports to the sides with pipe brackets and attach netting to the uprights.*

If you can leave the stakes in place for a number of years, it saves redoing this difficult job too frequently. Wood, even cedar or redwood, although readily available and easy to work with, is not the best material for long-lasting plant supports. Not only does it decay, but wood tends to bend and weaken under the weight of heavy plant material.

Both metal and plastic pipe are strong and last indefinitely, but metal pipe is sturdier and easier to drive into the ground than plastic. If you have raised beds, bolt pipes to the sides with pipe brackets. Connect a horizontal top bar to the uprights with elbow connectors to make a sturdy frame for netting or tying strings. A frame like this at each end of a raised bed will also support fabrics or plastic to extend the planting season or protect plants from insects.

Metal fence posts are another alternative to wooden stakes. They come in lengths up to 8 feet and will last for years. The sharpened end makes these metal fence posts easy to drive into the ground.

Supports That Keep Your Garden within Reach

Tripod ("teepee"). One of the strongest and easiest vertical supports, a homemade tripod takes more room than a vertical stake, but because it doesn't have to be driven into the ground, it takes less strength to erect. Bamboo makes a sturdy, long-lasting tripod; the older, dried stalks are the strongest. You can also use straight saplings or purchase wood poles. To make a tripod, lay three 8-foot poles side by side, and tie a length of twine to one about 6 feet from one end. Then, weave the twine over and under and around the three poles several times, allowing a little give between the poles. Set up the poles in a teepee position and tighten the twine by wrapping it firmly around the top of the positioned poles. I have successfully grown beans on teepees; covered with grow-netting, they also work nicely for peas, melons, squash, and other climbers.

Another style teepee is made of string. Drive a 6- or 8-foot wood pole into the ground, and put a nail at the top —

A

B

▲ *To make a tripod for climbing plants, (A) weave twine over and under three 8-foot poles about 2 feet from one end, and (B) set up the poles, wrapping the twine around all three to anchor them securely.*

don't hammer the nail all the way in. Surround the pole with 18-inch stakes placed about 2 or 3 feet away from its base. Attach strings to the stakes and wind them around the nail at the top of the pole. This simple tripod can be broken down by clipping the strings, making end-of-the-season cleanup easy. Beans and peas wind happily up the strings. Morning glories, sweet peas, and other vining plants are lovely growing on a string teepee. When the plants are full grown, the leaves and blossoms hide the structure. Children love playing under these flowering tents.

Wire cages. Typically used for tomato plants, wire cages keep almost any vertically growing plant off the ground and within reach. Cucumber

▲ *String teepees are easily constructed by driving a long pole into the garden and running a number of strings from the top of the pole to 18-inch stakes placed 2 to 3 feet from the base.*

STRING TEEPEES IN WOODEN CONTAINERS

If you are an armchair gardener, you may enjoy arranging for a container-grown climbing plant. Insert a stake, with an eyebolt or nail in the top, into the middle of a container. Screw eyebolts into the top of the container at evenly spaced intervals. Thread a piece of twine through an eyebolt on the container and then up to the top of the stake. Continue around the container until the string teepee is finished. You can also staple the twine to the

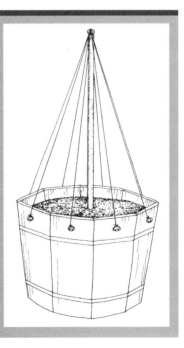

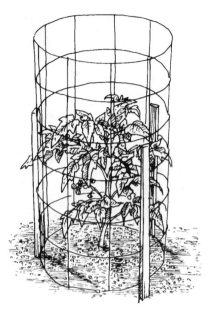

▲ *A simple tomato cage formed by a cylinder of fencing tied to stakes driven in the ground around the plant.*

vine can be tied to the sides of cages, and beans and peas will climb freely up them. Only a few vinelike plants, like melons, may be too heavy for the standard wire cage. Cages are long-lasting, reusable, and easy to install; once installed, they don't need any further attention.

Cages are made by joining a length of concrete-reinforcing wire or galvanized pig fencing to form a circle. Chicken wire is fine as a support for sloppy flowers, but it's too weak for tomatoes. Use lengths of 4–7½ feet for cage diameters of 18–30 inches. For tomatoes and larger plants, an adequate cage should be at least 4 feet tall and 2 feet in diameter. Attach the ends with wire, twist ties, or twine. For safety's sake, clip any wire ends that are sticking out. Set the cage over the plant and drive a tall stake into the ground on either side of it. Tie the cage to the stakes to keep it from toppling in the wind.

Lattice, netting, or metal trellises. Use lattice, netting, or metal trellises to bring your garden up to eye level. Cucumbers can be elevated on wire or even string; squash and melons need a stronger support. For easy harvesting, place the trellis where you can reach both sides of any vertical support. You will need to help some plants climb. Because plant stems are sensitive and easily injured by narrow or tight ties, use strips of cloth, old nylon stockings, or wide, ready-made plant ties to tie stems to the support. Make a loose figure-eight with the tie material, weaving it around the plant stem and the stake; this gives the stem some growing room. Be sure not to tie them too tightly.

Horizontally laid lattice also works well to keep melons, squash, tomatoes, and cucumbers off the ground. Lay a lattice screen between concrete blocks over the garden bed. As sprawling plants grow, weave their stems up through the lattice.

Brush or twigs. The traditional support for peas, sweet

peas, morning glories, and other vining flowers is a "planting" of brush or twigs. In the perennial border, floppy flowers are supported by a few branching twigs, which are soon hidden by plant foliage.

String-and-wire. A sturdy string-and-wire support for tall-growing peas can be made by inserting 8-foot-long steel fence posts no further than 10 feet apart. String a length of plastic-coated steel or aluminum wire (the kind used for clotheslines) tightly between the tops of the poles, and another strand along the bottom. Then, weave jute or other strong twine back and forth between the two strands of clothesline at 4-inch intervals. After harvest, cut the twine and leave the posts in place.

▲ *A simple A-frame trellis made of light-weight wooden supports laced vertically and horizontally with twine.*

Ready-made plant supports. A variety of ready-made wire supports, cones, and cages can be ordered from garden catalogs.

Fruit Tree Trellising Techniques

Espalier is a technique that limits plants, such as fruit trees, to a few main branches that are trained horizontally along wires or against a wall. This not only keeps the plant and its fruits within reach, but fruit produced on espaliered trees is frequently bigger and of better quality than that produced on trees growing more naturally. For more information about espalier, see pages 223-224.

CHAPTER 7

GARDEN PESTS AND PALS

Insects are those ubiquitous six-legged creatures that fly, crawl, or wriggle around our homes, gardens, and landscape. Only about 1 percent of insects are considered harmful, but this 1 percent can consume 10 percent of our crops, parasitize our animals, and cause diseases. On the other hand, insects pollinate most of our fruits, vegetables, and flowers; they produce honey; and they provide food for birds, fish, amphibians, and mammals. Although we think of insects as voracious destroyers, they play an important role in nature. For these reasons, it is important to think in terms of insect *control* rather than insect *extermination.*

WHAT TO DO

The struggle against insect damage and insect-borne disease began when gardeners planted the first seeds. Since then, we've picked, swatted, sprayed, and prayed to overcome them. Chemical weapons seemed to be the answer, but every day brings news of long-lasting toxic damage to the earth from the use of synthetic insecticides. Careful and conscientious gardeners feel obliged to look for nontoxic alternatives —alternatives that won't blast the "good guys" along with the "bad guys," and put gardeners themselves at risk when they spray their plants or eat their harvest.

Control vs. Elimination

Toxic chemicals have been used for decades, with the intent of annihilating certain insects, yet these insects continue to exist; many, in fact, have become resistant to some of the strongest chemicals. Instead of poisoning the world around us in an attempt to overcome these tiny enemies, it makes more sense to restrict pest numbers and minimize damage. A few pests in the garden are part of the normal scheme of things. You can limit pest populations through prevention and control: *prevention* of garden pests by maintaining good garden hygiene and vigorously growing plants, and *control* by using natural and nontoxic methods. Here are some of the controls that can be effective.

Resistant varieties. One of the most effective solutions, resistant varieties are plants that have been developed specifically *not* to appeal to the usual insect pests.

Row covers. Spun-fiber row covers protect plants against both pests and diseases introduced by insects. (See pages 110-111.)

Interplanting. Some crops, such as marigolds, are not as well-liked by destructive insects. If you place these alternately in a row with your main crop, you may be able to confuse or repel insect pests.

Bacillus thuringiensis (Bt). Especially effective against some pests on broccoli, cabbage, and other Brassicas, *Bt* is a bacteria that is harmless to plants, wildlife, and humans but causes a usually fatal, flu-like illness in insect pests. Keep in mind, though, that this disease attacks the larvae of ornamental butterflies as well as the pests. As with any insecticide, use sparingly.

Insecticidal soaps (commercial or homemade). Soaps contain fatty acids that break up the membranes in soft-bodied insects and cause dehydration and death. A tablespoon of liquid soap in a gallon of water will have a similar effect. You can strengthen the effectiveness of this solution by adding pulverized chile peppers and garlic to the solution. Apply weekly for four weeks; repeat if pests are seen later in the season. This solution tends to clog your sprayer; to alleviate this problem, filter it through cheesecloth a couple of times before spraying.

Traps. Some traps rely on both food and sex lures to attract many pest insects. Once attracted to the lure, they fall into collection containers from which they cannot emerge. Other traps rely on attractive colors (often yellow or red) covered with sticky mixtures like Tanglefoot or Stickem.

Trap crops. Plants especially favored by certain insect pests can be planted nearby to lure the little rascals away from your garden.

Paper collars. Tar-paper or cardboard tubes, or sections of milk cartons or juice containers can be placed around the base of newly transplanted seedlings to protect them from cutworms.

Sand, wood ash, and diatomaceous earth. These materials sprinkled around plants keep slugs and snails away. Diatomaceous earth is a fine, powdery material made up of the shells of tiny prehistoric sea creatures called *diatoms*. The shells are very sharp and cut the soft bodies of insects and pests that crawl over the dust. A diatomaceous barrier may work against aphids, cabbage loopers, codling moths, potato beetles, cucumber beetles, cutworms, bean beetles, and tomato hornworms, as well as slugs and snails.

▲ *A paper tube placed around new transplants protects against cutworm damage.*

Organic pesticides. Pesticides made from plants with insecticidal qualities are safer than synthetic chemicals, but I use even them as a last resort. Like synthetic chemicals, these natural insecticides are not selective, and garden friends will be destroyed along with garden foes. *Pyrethrum, sabadilla dust, and ryania* are a few of these plant-based pesticides.

Follow label directions carefully.

Some synthetic chemicals. Although some synthetic chemicals are said to break down quickly in the environment, I prefer not to use them, because I encourage birds and beneficial insects to share my garden with me. Furthermore, I like to grab a tomato right off the vine and eat it without washing it. I suggest using chemicals only if you're really under siege. Since preserving and maintaining a natural balance in your garden is vital, strong insecticides should be considered a last resort.

Beneficial insects. Also called *predatory insects*, beneficial insects are among the safest and easiest of pest control methods.

THE BENEFICIAL INSECTS

Some insects actually help us in the battle with garden pests. Most people are aware of the ladybug's appetite for aphids, and the ground beetle's taste for caterpillars, but there are other, less well-known, insect helpers.

Assassin bugs *(Reduviidae).* Assassin bugs deliver "the kiss of death" with their powerful beaks. Unfortunately, their poisonous bite is not reserved for harmful insects. A certain number of butterflies, bees, and other flower visitors may also be victims. Some assassin bugs have been known to bite humans as well, so watch out — this helpful insect can also harm.

Damsel bugs *(Nabidae).* Small, drab-colored flying insects with front legs much like those of the praying mantis, damsel bugs hide in flowers to prey upon aphids, leafhoppers, treehoppers, and caterpillars.

Green lacewings *(Chrysopa* spp.). Most useful in their larval stage, green lacewings patrol plants in search of aphids, red mites, leafhoppers, thrips, moth eggs, and other pests. It is said that a lacewing larva eats up to sixty aphids an hour, so import some of these little gluttons to your garden. You can obtain

▲ *Assassin bug*

▲ *Damsel bug*

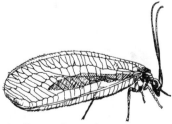
▲ *Green lacewing*

▲ *Hoverfly*

▲ *Ladybug*

▲ *Praying mantis*

▲ *Trichogramma wasp*

green lacewings in the egg stage or in larval form. The larval form is easiest to handle. Release them as quickly as possible, for they get hungry and will eat each other if there is no other food. Green lacewings cannot live in cold temperatures, so wait until the air warms up before ordering your supply.

Hoverflies (*Syrphidae*). Hoverflies resemble small wasps, although unlike wasps, they don't sting. This mimicry protects hoverflies from predators. Hoverflies feed on nectar and are beneficial as pollinators. Immature hoverflies devour as many aphids and thrips as the ladybugs do.

Ladybugs (*Hippodamia convergens*). Best-known and most popular of beneficial insects, a single ladybug consumes over fifty aphids a day. With the help of a good crowd of ladybugs, the aphid population may be so reduced as to eliminate the need for spraying. They also have a taste for mealybugs and scale.

Praying mantises (*Mantis religiosa*). Praying mantises get their name from the pious attitude they assume while waiting for their insect dinner. They eat as many helpful insects as harmful.

Rove beetles (*Staphylinidae*). These slender, unbeetle-like scavengers prey upon or parasitize harmful insects. Rove beetles eat cabbage maggots, mites, beetle larvae, and aphids.

Spiders. Although considered by some as loathsome, spiders are among our most worthy garden friends. Since they make no distinction between good and bad insects when they select their meals, spiders deplete the total insect population. Many spiders trap their prey in webs or nets, patiently waiting for the unfortunate meal to get stuck; others hunt down their quarry and actually run them to ground. Hunting spiders eat caterpillars and larval forms of insects and are therefore more of a threat to garden pests than the web-building ones. So, leave those spiders alone; they are good soldiers in your battle with insect pests!

Trichogramma wasps (*Trichogramma minutum*).

These wasps attack the eggs of most destructive moths and butterflies. Some important victims of the trichogramma wasp are the European corn borer and the tomato hornworm. Trichogramma wasps are especially recommended for protection of fruit crops.

Yellow jackets, hornets, and potter wasps *(Vespidae).* Although not usually considered helpful, in spite of their sting wasps do pollinate fruits and flowers and so must be considered in this category. Personally, I dislike yellow jackets because I think they are ill-tempered creatures that get hostile for no reason at all. If your garden is plagued by yellow jackets, and you don't feel they're much help, trap them in a jar of malt vinegar; they are attracted to it, fall in, and drown.

▲ *Yellow jacket*

How to Establish Imported Beneficials

Most beneficial insects are available commercially, and you can obtain them through the mail (see appendix 5 for sources). Some of the more familiar beneficials — ladybugs and praying mantises, for example — can be found in many local nurseries.

It's easy to introduce these helpful predators and parasites into your garden. Praying mantises are introduced as egg cases that are simply tied to a branch or pole, where they soon hatch and fill your garden with tiny mantids. Although newborn mantids are tasty snacks for spiders, birds, and even each other, if you're lucky, a few will be left at the end of the season to breed and start the cycle over again.

Imported ladybugs have been collected out in the field by the suppliers, rather than bred. Unfortunately (in this case), ladybugs are homebodies — they like to stay where they were born. When you release them in your yard, they may immediately fly off in search of their former habitat. Furthermore, if there are not enough aphids for them to eat, they'll move along to "greener pastures." Release them in an area that is infested with aphids at dusk or nighttime when they are less active. Some gardeners cover them with netting for a few days until they become familiar with their new home.

BENEFICIAL INSECTS

HELPER	PREFERRED HABITAT	FOOD
ANT LIONS	Sandy soil	Ants and other small insects
ASSASSIN BUGS	Beehives and flowers	Aphids, Colorado potato beetles, leafhoppers, and Mexican bean beetles
CHALCID WASPS	Flower blossoms	Aphids, scale, and cabbageworms
DRAGONFLIES & DAMSEL BUGS	Wading pools and water	Mosquitoes
GREEN LACEWINGS	Fences, woodlots, and floodlights	Aphids and scale
GROUND BEETLES	Drainage ditches, rocks, and wood pallets	Aphids, flea beetles, and leafhoppers
HONEYBEES	Beehives and flowers	Hives provide home for useful predators
HOVER FLIES	Herbs and flowers	Aphids, mealybugs, scales, and leafhoppers
ICHEUMONIA WASPS	Woodlots and flowers	Caterpillars and borers
LADYBUGS	Grassy paths, humus, and crates	Aphids, Colorado potato beetle eggs, and spider mites
PRAYING MANTIS	Kochia stems, wood, grass strips, and fences	Aphids, beetles, leafhoppers, caterpillars, and wasps
SPIDERS	Beehives, pallets, fences, and flower stalks	All insects
TACHINID FLIES	Herbs and flowers	Cutworms, Japanese beetles, corn borers, and grasshoppers

Green lacewings usually stay in the area of their release and, because they reproduce every four weeks, the population builds quickly. Water must be available to the new lace–wings or they'll dry out. Adults can be enticed to remain in the area if they are provided with nectar and pollen, or a homemade solution of 1 part sugar and 1 part brewer's yeast dissolved in water.

Attracting and Keeping Beneficials

The best way to lure beneficial insects to your yard is to landscape with plants that are attractive to them. These plants provide nectar for some of the adults and harbor their insect prey. Lacewings flock to members of the Carrot Family (*Apiaceae)*, such as Queen-Anne's lace, carrots, and celery. They are also attracted to oleander (*Nerium oleander)*. Ladybugs are often found swarming on alfalfa, angelica, goldenrod, morning-glory, and yarrow. Parasitic wasps are also attracted by members of the Carrot Family, as well as by goldenrod, strawberries, and oleander. Members of the Daisy Family (*Asteraceae)* attract many beneficial insects. Include some plants that attract garden pests, like nasturtiums, calendulas, and cosmos, and you'll be providing a good food supply for the beneficials. Since these pest-attractors are easy, fast-growing annuals, it won't seem so hard to sacrifice a few as aphid bait.

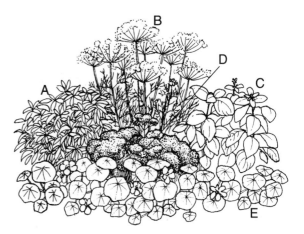

▲ *To lure beneficial insects to your yard, grow plants that attract them, such as (A) sage, (B) dill, (C) basil, (D) parsley, and (E) nasturtiums.*

Other useful plants include many of the perennial and annual herbs, such as basil, sage, fennel, dill, caraway, and parsley. The flowers of these herbs provide nectar for many adult beneficial insects whose larvae feed on aphids, mealybugs, and cutworms. Harvest these herbs for use in the kitchen and reap a double benefit.

Beneficials need shelter and water as well as food, so set aside an undisturbed area of fast-growing plants, such as comfrey, burning bush (*kochia*), or sunflowers that provide leaf cover for the lacewing family. A water source will attract damselflies and dragonflies, both mosquito eaters. Insect-eating birds will also congregate near a water supply.

If grasses and weedlike plants such as dandelions are allowed to grow, many beneficial insects will lay their eggs. Leave some of the ground undisturbed so that beneficial insects can pupate and overwinter in the garden. Mulch will also encourage ladybugs and ground beetles to reproduce. Although it may not be the prettiest part of your garden, a sheltered spot where you can plant an "Insect Garden," will keep insect pests under control (see pages 202-203).

COMPANION PLANTS

The theory behind using herbs and other plants as companion plants or deterrents is one of deception, and it works this way: Insects are attracted to a specific plant by its odor and taste. If plants taste or smell "wrong," insects will be confused and avoid them. In addition, some plants act as decoys, at-

▬ GOOD COMPANIONS ▬

PLANT	COMPANION	INSECT/DISEASE
ASPARAGUS	Tomato	Asparagus beetle
BEAN	Marigold	Mexican bean beetle
CABBAGE	Chamomile, mint, rosemary, sage	Cabbage maggot, damping-off disease
CARROT	Rosemary, sage, wormwood	Carrot fly
POTATO	Garlic, horseradish	Potato beetle, blight
RADISH	Mint, wormwood	Black flea beetle
STRAWBERRY	Chrysanthemum	Insects in general
TOMATO	Garlic	Blight

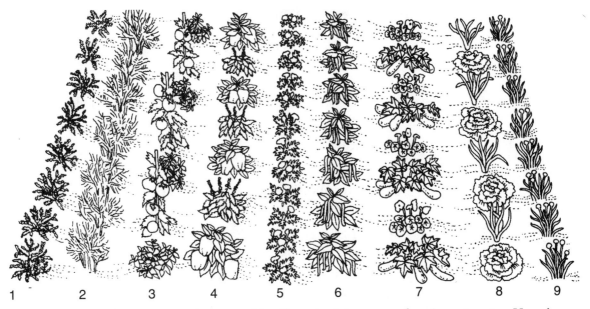

▲ *Companion planting uses plant combinations to deter or confuse insect pests. Here is one garden design: (1) Summer savory, (2) asparagus, (3) tomatoes and basil, (4) peppers and sage, (5) marigolds, (6) green beans, (7) summer squash and nasturtiums, (8) lettuce and onions, (9) chives*

tracting insects away from crop plants.

A variety of plants can be used to protect your plants from damage. These include garlic, marigolds, nasturtiums, onions, rosemary, sage, and tansy. Basil and chives are especially beneficial to tomato plants, because the herbs improve their taste as well as protecting them from insects. Either plant companion plants in the garden among the favored plants or make a tea by steeping their leaves in water and spray it on the plants to confuse the insect pests.

Coriander (Coriandrum sativum) and *anise (Illicuim verum)* are said to repel aphids. Coriander is also effective as a carrot fly deterrent.

Rue (Ruta graveolens), once used to ward off pestilence, repels fleas and Japanese beetles. Plant this in your garden near susceptible plants or make a strong rue tea for a spray.

Tansy (Tanacetum vulgare) is one of the most potent herbs for keeping insects at a distance. It was used as a strew-

PEST	PLANTS THAT REPEL
ANTS	Pennyroyal, spearmint, tansy
APHIDS	Anise, garlic, chives, coriander, pennyroyal, spearmint, tansy
ASPARAGUS BEETLE	Tomato
BORER	Garlic, onion, tansy
CABBAGE MAGGOT	Mint, rosemary, sage
CARROT FLY	Coriander, rosemary, sage
CUCUMBER BEETLE	Radish, tansy
CUTWORM	Tansy
EELWORM, NEMATODE	Marigold
FLEA BEETLE	Catnip, mint, wormwood
JAPANESE BEETLE	Garlic, rue, tansy
PLUM CURCULIO	Garlic
POTATO BEETLE	Catnip, coriander, horseradish, tansy
TOMATO HORNWORM	Basil, borage, marigold

ing herb in former times because of its reputation for keeping flies away.

Thyme and rosemary, with their strong-smelling volatile oils, are excellent insect repellents.

Garlic, onions, peppers, and bay leaves will cause damaging insects to move along.

PESTICIDES FROM PLANTS

Pesticides derived from certain plants damage or kill insects rather than repel them. These natural pesticides have been used since ancient times and, in this day of growing environmental awareness, are regaining popularity. Because beneficial insects are also affected by whatever you use even the relatively safe herbal remedies should be used only when insect damage has become critical.

Just because these insecticides are of natural origin, they should not be considered harmless. Many contain active ingredients that are potential poisons. Nicotiana can cause convulsions; and citronella, camphor, and eucalyptus can produce serious gastrointestinal symptoms. Horseradish and hot peppers cause severe eye, skin, or mucous membrane injury if used improperly. Used with care, however, these natural ingredients offer a less toxic alternative to chemical insect control.

A combination of these may be the most effective plant protector; experiment and learn what works best in your garden. Start with the safest and move on to the more toxic only if insect damage has become intolerable. Here are some of the most common:

Nicotine, obtained from plants in the genus *Nicotiana,* is one of the oldest insecticides. Its effectiveness has been recognized by chemists, and it is used even in commercial mixes. Nicotine is an alkaloid that poisons insects, but it is also toxic to humans and domestic animals. Use it only on intractable

━━━━━━ ENVIRONMENTALLY FRIENDLY PEST CONTROL ━━━━━━

★ Use nontoxic controls if possible. There are both helpful and harmful insects, and chemical controls destroy garden helpers along with harmful pests.

★ Cover your plants. Floating row covers prevent insect infestation, and protect plants from pest-carried diseases as well.

★ Plant resistant varieties.

★ Encourage helpful insects.

★ Introduce natural controls such as *Bacillus thuringiensis,* a bacteria that attacks certain pests but is harmless to animals and people.

★ Try nontraditional methods of pest control, such as insecticidal soap, bug juice, chile/garlic solutions, and vanilla-scented sprays.

★ Barriers and water sprays may deter wandering cats and dogs.

★ Be realistic! Think in terms of pest *control* rather than *elimination.*

insect infestations.

Pyrethrum, used in insecticidal sprays and powders, is derived from the flower heads of *Chrysanthemum coccineum.* Generally effective against soft-bodied insects, it paralyzes its victims. Pyrethrum is nontoxic to humans and domestic animals and has been widely used for fly and mosquito control. *Rethrins*, the active chemicals in pyrethrum, deteriorate relatively rapidly. Mixing pyrethrum with longer-acting herbs, such as thyme, reduces the need for frequent application.

Sabadilla seeds contain alkaloids that destroy insects. This is another plant-based commercial insecticide that can have harmful effects on humans and domestic animals. Although it is far less toxic than some synthetic insecticides, it should be used carefully and sparingly.

Azadirachta indica is a new botanical insecticide, produced from the seeds of a tropical tree and marketed under the brand names Neemisis and Bioneem. The active ingredient, azadirachtin, acts as an insect growth regulator, disrupting the normal insect life cycle, and also as a repellent, preventing many insects from making themselves comfortable in your garden. It is reported to have a low toxicity to people and animals, and should not harm earthworms and other beneficials. Since this new insecticide has not been on the market very long, it's effectiveness is not guaranteed, and it is registered for use on ornamental plants only. Further testing will prove its worth and safety.

INSECT PESTS

"Know your enemy" is one of the first rules in the fight against insect damage, since treatment varies depending on the identity of the invader. For instance, the defense against snails and slugs is very different from that against flea beetles. Learn to recognize common insect pests or their damage. Instituting the right treatment for the right pest offers the greatest chance of winning the battle.

Although there are many insect pests, you will probably experience only a few of them in your garden. Here are some of the most common:

Corn earworms. The larvae of a gray-brown to olive-green moth, corn earworms are about 2 inches long and green or brown with lengthwise stripes. They attack the buds and feed on new leaves. In addition to corn, they also burrow into the fruits of tomatoes, and into beans, cabbage, broccoli, lettuce, peppers, and tobacco crops. Cotton bolls and even artichokes are destroyed from the inside out.

▲ *Corn earworm*

Bt spray will control the larvae. Mineral oil applied to each corn ear when the silks have withered (but before they turn brown) may prevent ear infestation. Deep-digging your garden in the fall exposes the buried pupae to predators, such as birds, and the elements.

Cucumber beetles. Adult cucumber beetles are olive-green with both stripes and spots. They feed on squash, corn, melon, and bean seedlings and blossoms. The eggs, which are laid at the base of the plants, hatch in about ten days. The larvae feed on the roots of the seedlings, and although this can slow the growth of the plant, most of the destruction is done by adults.

Since the cucumber beetle emerges when temperatures reach 60°F, planting early minimizes damage. Cover seedlings and transplants to keep adult beetles from laying their eggs on the plants. Pyrethrum sprays can be used to control a heavy infestation, but only as a last resort.

▲ *Cucumber beetle*

Studies have shown that the cucumber beetle is attracted to a certain bitter-tasting chemical called *cucurbitacin,* and plants that lack this chemical are of little interest to the beetle. Some gardeners spray squash plants with a vanilla-flavored solution to confuse them; it might be worth a try if cucumber beetles are a problem in your garden. Some people make beetle traps by leaving out poisoned cucumber peelings, but these might actually lure the beetles to your yard. Resistant cucumber varieties include Saticoy; resistant melons, Planter's Jumbo, Hale's Best, Early Dawn, and Goldstar; and resistant squashes, Patty Green Tint, Table King, and Early Butternut.

Mexican bean beetles. Although Mexican bean beetles attack the leaves and fruit of many plants, their favorite food is the bean plant. A relative of the helpful ladybug, it can be distinguished by its copper, rather than red or orange, color. It also has more spots (sixteen to the ladybug's twelve), although you probably won't stop to count. Suspect Mexican bean larvae are at work when your bean plants' leaves are lacy and skeletonized.

▲ *Mexican bean beetle*

When you first see evidence of the bean beetle, import *pedio wasps* into your garden. These wasps parasitize the pupal stage of the bean beetle. Do not use any toxic sprays if you are releasing wasps. Garden cleanup in the fall is a good preventative, because it destroys the bean beetle's wintering-over sites.

Squash vine borer. This destructive caterpillar tunnels into and feeds on the stems of squash, cucumbers, and melons, causing wilting and the eventual death of the plant. The borer, a larva of a clear-winged, wasplike moth, is a wrinkled, white, inch-long worm with a brown head. Control is difficult.

▲ *Squash vine borer*

Fabric row covers will prevent the moths from laying their eggs on the plants. Injecting *Bt* right into the affected stem might work. Or, slit the stem and remove the worm by hand. After this operation, the plant can sometimes be saved if you bury the cut stem under the soil, thereby encouraging it to start new roots. It's worth a try. Resistant varieties include Butternut, Striped Cushaw, and Golden Cushaw.

Tomato hornworm. Anyone who has grown tomatoes is probably familiar with this ugly, fat, green monster, which is the larva of a giant gray moth. The caterpillars feed mainly at night and, if unhindered, can strip a tomato plant of all its leaves in a day or two. They also eat the leaves of peppers, potatoes, and eggplants.

One recommended method of control is to hand-pick these brutes, but I've never had much stomach for that — they look too formidable. I usually collect them in plastic bags and drop them in the trash. A better idea is to encourage helpful birds in your garden. A friendly scrubjay keeps most of the hornworms out of my garden. Another solution is to use *Bt*.

▲ *Tomato hornworm*

Other common garden pests include *earwigs, ants, aphids, spider mites, mealybugs,* and *thrips.*

Special Report on Snails and Slugs

The snail belongs to a group of low-lifes called mollusks, which include oysters, clams, and octopi. Gourmands eat them; I hunt them down and step on them. This soft, slimy creature is a gardener's nightmare. Its rasping mouth destroys the leaves and stems of an incredible variety of plants. In a single night, it can wipe out whole beds of emerging carrots and lettuce seedlings.

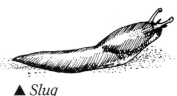
▲ *Slug*

Each snail lays its eggs in masses of twenty-five or more; eggs hatch in about twenty-eight days. Theoretically, this means that one snail produces 11,000,000 descendants within five years. If that doesn't send you out to the garden with your stomping boots on, nothing will. As you cultivate your garden, you may run into the eggs, usually white or gray mucilaginous masses buried in compost piles or under stones, flower pots, boards, or in other dark, damp places. Destroy these and you destroy generations of snails.

The snail's scientific name is *Gastropoda,* which means "belly-foot," an appropriate name for a creature that digests your garden as it travels. Its soft, unsegmented body is protected by a shell. This gives it a certain survival advantage, since it is never homeless. When threatened, it simply withdraws into this protective mobile home and waits for the enemy to get bored and go away. In adverse weather conditions, a snail can "close its door" by sealing off the opening with a mucous sheet that dries to a leathery texture. It has been

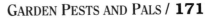

known to remain in this state, dormant but alive for five to six years.

It sports two pairs of tentacles, the large, upper pair bearing eyes at the tip, and the smaller pair below used for smelling. Its mouth is in the center of its head and below that is the slime gland. The slime gland produces the silvery trail that is left by the snail as it creeps through your garden. This material that smooths the way and allows the snail to climb up walls and cling upside down also protects its sensitive body as it crawls over rough surfaces.

A slug is but a snail without a shell. Both are nocturnal feeders and are most active in cool, damp weather. Discourage them by eliminating the dark, moist places in your garden, such as debris, old boards, or pots that they can hide under. Here are some other anti-slug and -snail tactics that may work:

★ Hand-pick and destroy them after dark or early in the morning. This is not a job for the squeamish!

★ Surround your garden or favorite plants with a barrier that irritates their sensitive bodies. Snails will not cross lime, wood ashes, crushed egg shells, diatomaceous earth, cinders, or sharp seed pods. Some gardeners protect their plants by surrounding them with fences of frayed window screens. The sharp wires stop the snails — but be careful you don't injure yourself, as well.

★ Horseradish is a favorite snail food and it is reported that they will eat this instead of other plants. Use the leaves as bait and collect the little gluttons as they feast.

★ Beer, too, successfully baits and drowns them. Instead of beer, make your own brew by fermenting 1 pound of brown sugar with a teaspoon of yeast in a gallon of water. Don't close the cap on the jug, the fermenting potion needs room to expand.

★ Spray plants with a mixture of hot pepper juice, ginger, and a drop or two of soap.

★ Make a spray of their blenderized brethren. One might suspect that this solution has some adverse psychological ef-

PEST	TARGET	NATURAL CONTROL
APHID	Most vegetables and ornamentals	Insecticidal soap, row covers, ladybugs
ASPARAGUS BEETLE	Asparagus	Hand-picking, row covers, ladybugs, birds
CABBAGE LOOPER	All vegetables	Hand-picking, *Bt* for serious problems, birds, row covers
CABBAGE WORM	Brussels sprouts, cabbage, cauliflower, kohlrabi	Row covers, hand picking, *Bt*
CORN BORER	Beans, corn, peppers, spinach, Swiss chard, potatoes, tomatoes	Hand-pick, split plant stalks and remove borer, soap-and-pepper spray
CORN EARWORM	Beans, corn, tomatoes, cotton, peppers, squash	Half a dropper of mineral oil applied to corn silk, *Bt*
CUTWORM	Most vegetables, especially seedlings	Paper collars, *Bt*, wood ash barrier, diatomaceous earth
FLEA BEETLE	Cole crops, beans, eggplants, radishes, turnips	Lime, diatomaceous earth, row covers, sticky traps
HARLEQUIN BUG	Brussels sprouts, cabbage, horseradish, mustard, eggplant	Hand-picking, row covers, soap spray, fall cleanup
JAPANESE BEETLE	Lawns, fruit trees, ornamentals, asparagus, beans, corn	Beetle traps, *Bacillus popillae* (milky spore disease), hand-picking
LEAF MINER	Beans, beets, cabbage, lettuce peppers, potatoes, Swiss chard	Row covers, remove and destroy infested leaves
MEXICAN BEAN BEETLE	Beans, squash	Hand-picking, row covers, fall cleanup
POTATO BEETLE	Eggplants, peppers, potatoes, tomatoes	Hand-picking, row covers, birds
SQUASH BUG	Cucumbers, pumpkins, squash, melons	Hand-picking, row covers, fall cleanup
SQUASH VINE BORER	Cucumbers, squash, pumpkins	*Bt* injected into stems, hand-picking, cutting larvae out of stem
TOMATO HORNWORM	Eggplants, tomatoes, peppers, potatoes	Hand-pick, encourage birds, *Bt*

DEER-PROOF PLANTS

Trees

California bay (*Umbellularia californica*)

Maple (*Acer* spp.)

Oak (*Quercus* spp.)

Spruce (*Picea* spp.)

Sweet gum (*Liquidambar* spp.)

Shrubs and Vines

Carolina jessamine (*Gelsemium sempervirens*)

Clematis (*Clematis* spp.)

Holly (*Ilex* spp.)

Jasmine (*Jasminum officinale*)

Spindle tree (*Euonymus japonica*)

Ground Covers

Algerian ivy (*Hedera canariensis*)

Bearberry (*Arctostaphylos uva-ursi*)

Carpet bugle (*Ajuga reptans*)

St.-John's-wort (*Hypericum calycinum*)

Sea pink (*Armeria maritima*)

Small Plants

Ageratum (*Ageratum* spp.)

Black-eyed Susan (*Rudbeckia hirta*)

Any cactus with spines

Chain fern (*Woodwardia* spp.)

Marguerite (*Chrysanthemum frutescens*)

fect on the snails. In reality, it encourages certain bacteria and fungi that attack snails and slugs, and thus acts as a form of biological warfare. If you use this spray on vegetables, be sure to wash them well.

★ A pet duck is a capable snail-eating machine and well worth the price of a few heads of lettuce.

★ If you pour salt on them, they will fizz and bubble and melt away like the Wicked Witch of the North. This reaction to salt may be why snails avoid seaweed, which makes an effective mulch. If you use salt as a protective barrier, remember that it may damage nearby plants.

★ Snail baits containing the poisons Metaldehyde or Mesurol come in the form of pellets, meal, or emulsion. They are most effective during damp weather. Mesurol should not be used near fruits or vegetables. Protect pets and wildlife from the poisons by covering the bait with an overturned pot or "snail jail." Read directions carefully and use any chemicals with caution.

OTHER PESTS

Cats. Your own and your neighbors' cats are among the most difficult unwelcome garden visitors to control. If they aren't digging up the newly turned earth for their own hygienic reasons, they're munching on new, tender green sprouts. It is not considered good form to take pot shots at the neighbor's cats nor is a fence likely to stop them, since they can leap or crawl over anything. An unpleasant surprise works best with cats. If you are alert and prepared, send your furry visitors scrambling by turning on the hose or sprinkler next time they enter your "No-Kitty Zone."

Row covers or overturned plastic flats keep cats and other animals from destroying newly seeded beds. Chicken-wire covers are also a good defense, but costly and awkward to set up.

Dogs. If you've ever arrived home to find your favorite plants or your prize pumpkin dug up and spread all over the yard, you have had experience with the renegade dog. A dog can do more damage to a garden in five minutes than almost any other animal or natural disaster. Two dogs, romping and acting up in the garden, can destroy a year's harvest.

Fences usually keep dogs out of the garden, but if you have a really determined canine, you may need to install an electric fence. Farm stores and mail-order catalogs are good sources for these last-resort defenses. The electrical charge is meant to startle rather than harm. It is usually necessary to charge it only a few times, as most animals learn pretty quickly. The electric fence offers protection against opossums, rabbits, and raccoons, as well as dogs and cats.

Deer. Some gardeners spend a lot of time trying to outsmart deer, as they love to eat all the foods that we eat. The only way to keep deer from "shopping" in your garden is to erect a very tall, very strong fence. The most effective deterrent, an electric fence, is expensive and difficult to install. If this is out of the question, try double-fencing. Deer-country gardeners report that two 4-foot fences, erected 5 feet apart, will keep deer out of the garden.

▲ *Hang bars of soap among your tulips to discourage deer from nibbling them.*

You can also surround your garden with deer-proof plants — plants that deer either do not eat or will avoid walking through (see list on page 174). Unfortunately, this is not a foolproof solution to the deer problem, since deer in different areas have different tastes.

Garden lore abounds with "sure-fire" deer deterrents. Try some of these:

★ Hang small cloth bags filled with blood meal around the garden and among the plants.
★ Mix two raw eggs with 1 gallon of water, and spray this mixture on your plants and trees. Supposedly, the smell of decomposing eggs keeps the deer (and perhaps other visitors) away.
★ Hang bags made from nylon stockings and filled with human hair (the local hairdresser is a good source) throughout the garden.
★ Use chile-pepper-and-soap sprays.
★ Hang or scatter deodorant soap around the garden.
★ Hang strips of aluminum flashing or plastic flags so that they flap in the wind.

Kids. Keeping kids out of the garden is another story altogether. It may be best not to try. Offering them jobs and their own special place to garden works much better than chasing them off all the time. Children can help you collect garden pests like snails and tomato horn-worms, or assist you with your harvest. Offer them a small reward for each pest collected and you'll soon find your garden is pest-free. Including the youngsters is a good way to introduce them to the joys and benefits of gardening.

Gophers. These destructive creatures are hard to control. To rid yourself of gophers, you must locate and block off all the entrances to their tunnel systems, and then try flushing them out with water or smoking them out by dropping an emergency flare down the hole, or put ammonia-soaked sponges in all the entrances. Some sources suggest using chicken-wire baskets and underground fencing as barriers to limit gopher damage. Traps are available, and so are various types of poisoned bait. Use poison as a last resort. I fought the battle with gophers for a very long time; I even saw a gopher pull a full-grown artichoke plant into his hole. Then I acquired a good hunting cat. That cat got rid of every gopher in the yard and proceeded to take care of the neighbors' gophers too.

Groundhogs or woodchucks. A single woodchuck can devastate a garden in no time. Tunnel fumigation, traps, and barriers are commonly used to rid the area of groundhogs. You can also surround your garden with chicken-wire fencing; insert the fencing underground, as groundhogs will dig right under an unprotected fence. Since they love alfalfa and clover, plant a patch to lure them away from the main garden. Keep paths clear around the garden, so that they have no shelter from predators. Their natural predators are cats, dogs, and hawks.

plastic edging

▲ *Underground fencing can serve as a barrier against gophers, groundhogs, and other burrowing animal pests.*

Moles. Although moles don't eat your plants, the tunnels they make disturb your garden. Some ways to deter moles include trapping, digging up their runs, and pouring used cat litter into their burrows.

Raccoons. The night-raiders of the garden, these wily little bandits know just when to harvest your corn and munch your melons. They make such a mess that I sometimes suspect they are driving tractors around in the garden. Raccoons can get over or under most types of fencing, unless it's electrified. Some gardeners staple black plastic to wooden stakes to create a barrier that is too slippery for the raccoons to climb. Use 36-inch-wide plastic and leave about 6 inches of it resting on the ground. Chile-pepper sprays, black pepper sprinkled on ripening corn ears, and a radio playing in the garden are other suggestions to keep raccoons at bay. You can also try hanging flashing or swinging lights in the garden. Relatively inexpensive outdoor lights with motion-detectors that turn on automatically when a body moves in front of the sensory device might work out nicely in the garden.

CHAPTER 8

PLANT DISEASE:

PREVENTION AND TREATMENT

Plants, like humans, can get sick. They can be attacked by bacteria, fungi, and viruses. If your garden is hit by a case of "plant flu," don't panic. Although fighting plant disease is a work-intensive, time-consuming occupation, you can maximize garden enjoyment and minimize garden work by taking steps early to prevent diseases rather than trying later to cure them. Controlling plant disease is possible if you understand what causes it. Plant diseases are often encouraged by poor garden management and some of the methods that make gardening easier also ward off plant disease.

CAUSES OF PLANT DISEASE

Poor hygiene. It may surprise you to know that many vegetables are related to common weeds. When these weeds are diseased, they can spread the infection to related vegetables. For instance, the mosaic virus that affects cucumbers and muskmelons is often spread by milkweed, pokeweed, and ground cherry. Horsenettle, jimsonweed, and nightshade carry diseases that spread to other members of the Nightshade Family, which include peppers and tomatoes.

Too much or too little water. Overwatering can drown the roots of plants. Good drainage is essential for a disease-free garden. Most disease-causing organisms need moist conditions to thrive, and overwet soil encourages certain fungi. The spores that attack plants travel by wind and water. Water splashed from the ground or spread among wet plants carries these fungal diseases through the garden.

Not enough water is just as bad as too much. Hot, dry weather stresses plants and weakens their resistance to disease. Spider mites, which suck plant juices and spread disease, flourish in hot, dry conditions.

Poor nutrition. Healthy soil is your first line of defense against plant disease. Well-nourished plants can fight off infections. Many common disease-causing organisms are normally present in the soil, but disease-fighting organisms are there, too. Healthy soil creates a balance that allows the beneficial organisms to keep the pathogens in check. Good soil is good preventative medicine in your garden.

Insects. Sometimes called the Typhoid Marys of the plant world, insects cause plant disease in two ways. First, they weaken plants when they suck plant juices, chew roots, or attack leaves; and second, they spread disease when they move from one plant to another. Whiteflies and thrips are notorious for spreading viruses to tomato and pepper plants. They are so prolific, it seems they can infest and infect a whole garden overnight. Leafhoppers, aphids, and mealybugs are also efficient disease carriers. Keeping insect populations under control can help prevent plant disease. Enlist the help of birds, as well as spiders and other beneficial insects, in your war against garden plagues.

RECOGNIZE THE SYMPTOMS OF PLANT DISEASES

Early diagnosis and treatment can save your garden from devastation. Certain symptoms are common, and although it may be hard to diagnose the problem exactly, you will soon

DISEASE	DESCRIPTION	PLANTS ATTACKED	CONTROL
BACTERIAL BLIGHT	Small dead spots with yellow halos on leaves	Beans	Practice crop rotation. Don't work in a wet garden.
BACTERIAL WILT	Leaves wilt and plant dies	Cucumbers, melons	Control cucumber beetle, which spreads the disease.
DAMPING-OFF	Base of the stem near the soil pinched and bent over	Seeds and seedlings of most plants	Plant in well-drained soil. Use sterile soil mix for indoor plants.
DOWNY MILDEW	Irregular brown or yellow spots on upper leaf surface. Purple or white hairy mold covering lower leaf surface	Brassicas, cucumbers, muskmelons	Plant resistant varieties. Avoid wetting the top of plants when watering.
FUSARIUM WILT	Yellowed, curled, and wilted lower leaves	Cucumbers, peppers, potatoes, tomatoes	Plant resistant varieties. Solarize the soil. Destroy infected plants.
POWDERY MILDEW	Powdery white growth on the tops of leaves	Beans, cucumbers, lettuce, peas	Plant resistant varieties. Avoid overhead watering. Water early in day.
SEPTORIA LEAF SPOT	On older leaves, yellow spots that later turn dark brown with tiny black spots in the middle	Blackberries, celery, parsley, tomatoes	Plant resistant varieties. Solarize the soil. Control weeds that can carry the fungus.
VERTICILLIUM WILT	Lower leaves start yellowing and wilting, then die	Apricots, blackberries, eggplant, okra, peppers, potatoes, strawberries, tomatoes	Solarize soil. Destroy infected plants. Rotate crops.
VIRUSES	Mottling, streaking, yellowing, puckering, curling of leaves	All	Control insects that spread disease. Destroy infected plants. Solarize soil.

learn to recognize signs of impending trouble.

There are four main categories of plant disease: those diseases caused by poor growing conditions, and those caused by fungal, bacterial, and viral infections.

Poor growing conditions. Too much or too little water, inadequate soil or sunlight, or nutrient deficiencies result in unhealthy plants. The symptoms of environmental diseases include poor leaf color, weak-looking plants, slow growth, and wilting. Plants weakened by poor conditions can be attacked by more serious diseases introduced by viruses, fungi, and bacteria.

Fungal diseases. Fungi are microscopic plants that parasitize other plants. Some of the easily recognized plant diseases are caused by fungal attack. A dusty, white powderlike appearance on the leaves of affected plants, for example, is an indication of *powdery mildew* or *downy mildew*. *Rust diseases* are distinguished by rusty spots on the leaves. Many leaf spot diseases and blights are attacks of parasitic fungi. These diseases spread slowly through the garden and, if treated early, can be controlled or even eradicated.

Bacterial diseases. Bacterial infections cause rotting and wilting. Gray, mushy plants and wet-looking, bent-over stems signal bacterial disease, which cannot be cured. Immediate destruction and removal of infected plants is essential. In this case, prevention is the only defense.

Viral diseases. If your plants turn yellow or look small and sickly, a virus may have attacked your garden. Viruses destroy the chlorophyll in plant cells. The infection spreads very quickly through the garden, usually borne by insects. As with bacterial infection, there is no cure, and plants must be destroyed and removed.

METHODS FOR PREVENTING PLANT DISEASE

Keep your garden clean. Don't let diseased plants and weeds lie around the garden. Remove fallen fruit and plant debris. When you pull weeds, remove them from the gardening area. Decaying, diseased plants left in the garden cause or spread disease. Diseases (as well as insects) overwinter on plant material. To prevent the infection of next year's garden, clean up thoroughly at the end of the gardening season.

Rotate crops. Planting the same crop in the same place every season encourages disease. Pathogens accumulate in the soil and, over time, run rampant. Disease organisms prefer specific types of plants. For instance, tomatoes, potatoes, and peppers are highly susceptible to the same diseases. Moving the favored host plant to another area of the garden for a few seasons controls disease-causing populations.

Healthy soil. Keep garden soil in good condition. Adding compost and other nutrients helps plants to resist disease. Rich compost harbors large populations of beneficial microbes, so that it not only improves soil texture and adds nutrients, but it has specific antibiotic properties that work to keep your garden disease-free. Studies have shown that compost produces fatty acids that are toxic to certain fungal and bacterial diseases of plants. Encourage earthworms; they are soil-making helpers.

> ### Crop Rotation: Soil Builder and Disease Preventer
>
> Crop rotation is not only a good disease preventative, it also builds better soil. Rotate crops that need different soil nutrients as well as harbor different diseases. For instance, plant beans, and after the harvest, till the plants under to add nitrogen to the soil. The next season, plant lettuce or some other green vegetable that needs extra nitrogen. Alternate root vegetables, legumes (beans and peas), and vining plants (squash, melons).

Use healthy plants. Buy only from reputable nursery and supply houses that take good care of their plants. A plant that looks unhealthy at the nursery isn't going to get any better in your yard. It's so easy to introduce disease into your garden, and so hard to get rid of it.

Eliminate weeds. Weeds spread disease and rob your plants of water and nutrients.

Keep plant leaves dry. To avoid spreading disease, cultivate, weed, and harvest when leaves are dry. Water before noon to allow plants time to dry out before sundown. Diseases that thrive in damp, cool conditions are less likely to infect dry plants. Drip irrigation, which limits overhead splashing, decreases fungal movement through the garden.

Provide water when needed. Keep your plants evenly moist to guard against spider mite invasion. Mulching keeps roots cool and slows evaporation even in the hottest weather.

Use row covers. Row covers keep disease organisms and disease-spreading insects off plants. These are real work savers for those who can't spend a lot of time in the garden.

Destroy diseased plants. Don't even think about leaving diseased plants in your garden. Eliminate them immediately.

Choose resistant varieties. This is one of the easiest and most effective ways to prevent problems. Some plants are more resistant to disease than others. Some come by their immunity naturally, while others are bred for specific disease resistance. Evergreens and herbs are rarely attacked by diseases, for example, while mildew-resistant roses, blight-resistant ornamentals, and virus-resistant vegetables have been developed by commercial plant growers. Choose these superplants for the easiest-care garden. Read seed packets, catalogs, and plant descriptions in garden encyclopedias, and consult garden catalogs and local nurseries for specific information about disease-resistant plants. Plants that have a natural disease resistance are a boon to the gardener who has little time to spend being a "plant doctor."

Choose the right plants. Plants that are appropriate to your environment are better able to withstand disease attack. Consult local nurseries and garden encyclopedias to find plants that are especially suited to your area.

Good sanitation. Clean tools that have been used around diseased plants by soaking them in a 1:10 chlorine bleach solution for two hours, and then dry them. Gloves and clothing worn in the garden while cleaning up diseased plants should be washed before they are worn in the garden again.

Herbs as Plant-Disease Inhibitors: Medicines from the Garden

The bacteria and fungi that attack plants are simple micro-organisms that feed on organic material. Some plants contain natural chemicals that fight plant disease by inhibiting or killing microbes. The more we learn about these natural defenses, the more we can use them as nontoxic solutions to insect and disease problems. Prepare a spray of these potent herbs or plant a few throughout the garden to do double-duty by protecting your garden and adding flavor to your meals.

Garlic (*Allium sativum*). *Alliums* have been used in medicine longer than they have been used in cooking. A sulfur compound called *allicin* gives garlic its characteristic odor; it has also been found to be a potent antibiotic. In the past, garlic paste was used in wartime to treat wounds when other antibiotics were unavailable. It has also been used against influenza, tuberculosis, and other microbe-caused diseases.

Garlic is an effective preventative spray for garden disease. Its antibiotic properties control diseases, and its odor deters disease-spreading insects. Garlic can be used against powdery and downy mildew, potato blight, and apple scab.

To make an effective garlic spray, mash ten cloves of garlic and let them stand overnight in 1 gallon of water. Strain the liquid, and mix it with two or three drops of liquid soap to make it spread better. For best results, spray this solution on your plants weekly. (Adding hot chile powder or ginger to this solution discourages even the most persistent insects.)

Recipe for Herbal Plant Spray

1. Crush the plant material to release active oils. Use enough to make a very strong-scented solution.
2. Cover with cold water to preserve active ingredients.
3. Allow to steep at least twenty-four hours.
4. Strain the solution for easier spraying.
5. Add a few drops of liquid soap to help spread the spray.

German chamomile (*Matricaria recutita*) and Roman chamomile (*Chamaemelum nobile*). Chamomile has been called the "plant's physician." Some gardeners say that if another plant is sick or drooping, chamomile placed nearby helps it recover. Chamomile is useful against a number of plant diseases, but it is especially effective in the treatment of those fungal diseases caused by overwet conditions, such as damping-off disease. The whole plant can be utilized, but the flower heads are the most potent. The active principles are a volatile oil, tannic acid, and a glucoside.

To make a tea spray, soak dried flower heads in cold water for a day or two, and then spray on plants every ten days for best results. Dried chamomile flowers are available in most health-food stores.

Horseradish (*Armoracia rusticana*). The horseradish root contains oils and chemical compounds similar to those in garlic. The very pungent oil is an antibiotic, and its odor and taste keep insects away. Steep the scraped root in water for three days and use it as a preventative spray.

Thyme (*Thymus vulgaris*). The phenols in thyme have been shown to be effective against many types of bacteria. Because thyme is a relatively long-lasting antiseptic, it can be applied less frequently than other herbal remedies for plant disease. Growing thyme among the vegetables will also help protect them by inhibiting insect activity.

African and French marigolds (*Tagetes erecta* and *T. patula*). Both African and French marigolds are resistant to root-rot nematodes and can pass this nematode resistance to nearby plants. Marigolds used as a cover crop and then turned under the soil have been found to control nematodes just as well as some chemical fumigation treatments. They have also been used in companion plantings with cabbage, chile peppers, and eggplant to increase yields. In addition to killing nematodes, the marigold's strong odor repels other insects and reduces the spread of insect-borne disease.

Chives (*Allium schoenoprasum*). These small and tasty Alliums, like garlic, contain the pungent oil allicin.

Coriander (*Coriandrum sativum*). Useful in the treatment of human infections, coriander may prevent plant disease as well.

Mustard seed oil, rhubarb, wild ginger, and ***Echinacea.*** These plants all contain natural antibiotics.

SOLARIZATION

Solarization is a method of sterilizing infected soil without the use of chemicals. Solarization is valuable in gardens that are infested with disease year after year. Solarization, similar to pasteurization, is based on eliminating harmful organisms by raising their temperatures, or "cooking" them. Harmful bacteria, viruses, and fungi take up residence in the soil; they wait from season to season to attack your plants and continue their life cycles. If you cover the soil with clear plastic during a sunny season, you will trap heat and raise the soil temperature high enough to kill these microscopic enemies of a healthy garden. In the process, you are actually "pasteurizing" your soil.

More than twenty major plant diseases, as well as fourteen species of nematodes and many kinds of weeds can be controlled with solarization; weed seeds get cooked right along with the harmful bacteria. While harmful organisms are destroyed, beneficial, microscopic organisms survive to attack and subdue the weakened pathogens.

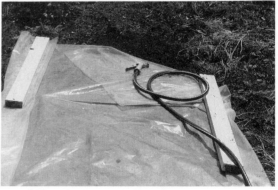

▲ *Solarization sterilizes infected soil by raising the soil temperature enough to eliminate harmful organisms.*

The best time to solarize is in the summer, when daytime temperatures are high and the sun is shining. Prepare the area to be solarized as if you were going to plant it: Remove weeds and crop residues, and smooth the surface. After thoroughly soaking the soil with water, cover the area with 3–6-mil-thick clear plastic. Anchor the edges of the plastic as tightly as possible, and pile dirt along the edges to seal in the heat and prevent the plastic from blowing away. Choose a manageable area to solarize. Don't try to do the whole garden at once. Remember that this part of the garden will be fallow while solarization is in process. Leave the plastic in place for four to six weeks; the longer it cooks, the more effective the treatment. Remove the plastic, and plant your garden as usual.

This is an excellent, low-cost, low-energy (the sun does all the work), nontoxic method to prevent and treat plant diseases. Repeat the process as often as necessary, since the bad guys do return after awhile.

CHEMICAL CONTROLS: A LAST RESORT

The chemical compounds are the "big guns" of disease control. Their powerful ingredients kill or control bacteria and fungi. The terms *bacteriostatic, antibiotic,* and *fungicide* define the chemicals that control infections and fungi. As with other synthetic gardening controls, they can be harmful to beneficial insects, birds, pets, and people, as well as to disease organisms. Apply them with caution and follow label directions.

Chemical controls come in a dust, powder, liquid, or granular form. Liquid spray is probably the easiest to apply, but it is the most dangerous. Wear eye protection and a mask to avoid contamination with these strong chemicals. The systemic granular forms are the safest to use, as long as you wear gloves to protect your skin. Sprinkle them *only* around ornamental plants, since their long-acting toxins should not come into contact with food crops.

Fungicides prevent infections from getting started. An established infection can't be cured, but it can be kept from spreading. Apply a fungicide at the first sign of disease and be prepared to apply it at repeated intervals as necessary. Some fungus diseases are eradicated by chemicals, although most plants never really recover from fungal attack.

Many antifungals are now being removed from the market. Some fungicides are suspected of causing cancer and birth deformities. For the safest garden, avoid strong chemicals. It is safer to sacrifice a few plants than to risk your health.

CHEMICAL SAFETY

★ Read the label. Observe precautions and mixing proportions. Stronger is not better.

★ Choose the appropriate compound. There is no one-shot-gets-all chemical control. Diagnose the problem and buy the correct compound.

★ Mix as directed.

★ Mix chemical controls outdoors. Ventilation is important. Clean up spills immediately. Wear a mask, eye protection, and gloves when mixing toxic solutions.

★ Avoid getting chemical controls on your skin, or in your eyes or mouth. Watch out for splashes. Don't eat or smoke in the mixing area. Keep clothing used while mixing and spraying separate from other laundry.

★ Spray in the evening when bees and birds are inactive. Chemical controls can be harmful to birds and bees.

★ Observe waiting periods to reapply; don't fall into the more-is-better trap. Equally important, follow directions regarding the safe period to apply before harvest, so that no harmful residues remain when you pick your crop.

★ Store all chemicals safely. Keep them out of the reach of children and away from food storage or preparation areas. Do not remove labels or pour into other containers. Store chemicals away from light, heat, or moisture.

★ Buy small amounts. Buy only as much as you need, and write the date on the container. Some pesticides lose their potency with time.

★ Dispose of empty containers properly. Most cities have toxic-waste disposal sites or special pick-ups. Do not throw bottles in normal trash.

CHAPTER 9

TWENTY SPECIAL GARDENS

Throughout history, gardens have been associated with pleasure. The original Garden of Eden was considered a "paradise on earth"; the luxurious Hanging Gardens of Babylon were a delight to the senses; the sacred groves of the druids inspired the celebration of Nature. The Zen gardens of the Japanese, created for contemplation and relaxation, sometimes don't even contain plants; instead, a few well-chosen stones and carefully raked gravel inspire serenity.

Although gardening takes time and effort, a well-designed garden can also be a place for relaxation and retreat. Each gardener seeks something different from his or her "paradise on earth." Some garden for exercise or to enjoy nature. For others, the ever-changing garden awakens feelings of renewal and growth.

Just as you strive to make your indoor environment pleasing to yourself, so too can you "decorate" and "furnish" your garden in the way you like. A garden can provide shelter and privacy, or sensory stimulation, amusement, and a place to entertain others. This chapter describes a variety of gardens appropriate for special needs and interests. Perhaps you will find one that suits your requirements, or you may be inspired to create a unique garden of your own design.

 GARDENS FOR ALL SENSES

The French painter Claude Monet loved flowers almost more than he loved painting. Although for years he suffered from advancing blindness, he did not give up his beloved garden at Giverny nor did he stop painting. Fading eyesight need not spoil the pleasures of the garden for you either. Do as Monet did — plant the largest and most opulent flowers, use the boldest of colors, and choose plants that stimulate your other senses. There's more to a garden than what meets the eye. Here are suggestions for gardens that satisfy your senses of smell, touch, hearing, and taste.

A Scented Garden

The sense of smell is considered our most provocative sense. Remember the gardenia you wore to the school dance? The first red roses you bought to give to your sweetheart or mother? The sweet, heavy scent of honeysuckle on a warm summer evening? The scent of a plant can evoke the most vivid of memories, and a garden's fragrance can be as delightful as its appearance. You don't need very many fragrant plants; some are so richly scented that they perfume the entire yard. If you plant subtly scented flowers, provide a seat nearby so that you can enjoy their fragrance while you relax.

Think about creating garden "rooms" that suit your mood. A "room" for relaxing might be located in the sun, where you can bask, surrounded by the soft scent of lilacs in the spring and roses in the summer. For the hottest summer days, create a cool, shady place planted with cool-scented mint, lily-of-the-valley, cyclamen, or violets to perk up your spirits.

Some heavy scents, like hon-

▲ *Place lilacs, roses, honeysuckle, or other plants with scents that tend to make one drowsy in a relaxing corner with the hammock.*

FRAGRANT PLANTS

COMMON NAME	BOTANIC NAME	ZONES*/PLANT TYPE
Shrubs and Trees		
Acacia	*Acacia* spp.	8–10
Butterfly bush	*Buddleia* spp.	5–10
Citrus	*Citrus* spp.	10
Daphne	*Daphne* spp.	4–7
Frangipani	*Plumeria* spp.	10
Gardenia	*Gardenia* spp.	8–10
Jasmine	*Jasminum* spp.	7–10
Lavender	*Lavandula* spp.	5–8
Lilac	*Syringa* spp.	3–7
Mock orange	*Philadelphus* spp.	4–7
Rose	*Rosa* spp.	3–8
Vines		
Easter-lily vine	*Beaumontia grandiflora*	9
Clematis	*Clematis* spp.	3–7
Climbing rose	*Rosa* spp.	3–5
Honeysuckle	*Lonicera* spp.	3–7
Jasmine	*Jasminum* spp.	7–10
Mandevilla	*Mandevilla* spp.	10
Passionflower	*Passiflora* spp.	7–8
Stephanotis	*Stephanotis* spp.	9
Sweet pea	*Lathyrus latifolius*	4
Wax plant	*Hoya carnosa*	9
Wisteria	*Wisteria* spp.	5
Annuals, Perennials, and Bulbs		
Gas plant	*Dictamnus albus*	3
Heliotrope	*Heliotropium* spp.	9–10
Hyacinth	*Hyacinthus* spp.	5
Lily	*Lilium* spp.	4–8
Lily-of-the-valley	*Convallaria majalis*	4
Mint	*Mentha* spp.	5
Beebalm	*Monarda didyma*	4
Peony	*Paeonia* spp.	5
Pinks	*Dianthus* spp.	4–6
Sage	*Salvia* spp.	4–8
Stock	*Matthiola* spp.	HA
Thyme	*Thymus* spp.	4–5
Violet	*Viola* spp.	5–8

COMMON NAME	BOTANIC NAME	ZONES*/PLANT TYPE
Ground Covers		
Chamomile (Roman)	*Chamaemelum nobile*	3
Corsican mint	*Mentha requienii*	7
Sweet woodruff	*Galium odoratum*	3
Thyme (creeping and woolly)	*Thymus* spp.	4–5

PLANT TYPE: HA = Hardy Annual

* Chart shows coldest hardiness zone tolerated by a species. Where a specific species is not named on the chart, look for a species appropriate to the hardiness range indicated.

eysuckle, jasmine, and wisteria, can make you feel sleepy. These are the ones to plant near the hammock or bedroom window. Dorothy, in *The Wizard of Oz*, fell asleep in a field of poppies: Your garden can be just as restful. A sunset stroll in a sweet-scented garden blooming with such plants as jasmine, Easter lily, hyacinth, sweet William, and nicotiana may help you get to sleep.

Herbs like lavender, rosemary, and lemon verbena, as well as rich, spicy citrus blossoms, are energizing; visit the part of the garden where they grow when you need a boost. The fragrance of culinary herbs like sage, thyme, and oregano often stimulate a lagging appetite; take a walk through the kitchen garden to both tempt your palate and inspire your cooking talents.

Some plants have scented leaves and stems that release their fragrance when they are touched or crushed. A pathway planted with chamomile, Corsican mint, or creeping thyme will treat your sense of smell with each footstep. Use these kinds of ground covers as fragrant "signposts." A path of mint can lead to a certain part of the yard, while a path of chamomile might lead in another direction. Scented geraniums and spicy herbs, planted along the edges of a walkway, will emit a pleasant aroma when brushed by the feet of garden strollers. A raised mound of soil, planted with a fragrant ground cover can serve as a sense-tickling seat to rest upon.

The Fragrant Indoor Garden

Many fragrant plants can be grown in the house. The alluring aroma of a jasmine plant, warm on the windowsill, perfumes a whole room. Sweet olive, jessamine, and heliotrope are easily grown indoors. Gardenias, one of the most richly scented plants, are more demanding but not impossible to grow inside. They usually benefit from an outdoor vacation in summer; bring them in when they are in bloom.

Choose flowers that have harmonizing scents, or your home may be overwhelmed by the clash of warring fragrances. Spicy-scented flowers, such as citrus and carnation, work well together, but generally its best to have just one strongly scented plant in bloom at a time. Very sweet fragrances, like jasmine and stephanotis, can be overpowering in a small room.

Bridal vine *(Stephanotis floribunda)*. A vigorous and slow-growing vine, bridal vine will tolerate a dry atmosphere and a missed watering, but it does require full sun and warmth. To bloom, it needs nighttime temperatures of 60°F. It also should be fertilized frequently during the summer.

Gardenia *(Gardenia jasminoides)*. The scent of these demanding plants brings back memories of summer dances and romantic evenings to many. They can be grown indoors only if the conditions are just right. They require acid soil, full sun, and warm nighttime temperatures that never fall below 60°F. A humid environment is critical. Most gardeners grow these finicky plants in a greenhouse or on a patio and bring them indoors when they are in bloom.

Heliotrope *(Heliotropium arborescens)*. One of my favorite scented plants, vanilla–scented heliotropes blossom all year-round but are most prolific during the spring and summer. They can be grown in hanging baskets or bushes, or they can be trained as standards. Heliotrope often looks a little ragged unless you keep it well trimmed. A south-facing window is the best placement for this sun–loving, sweetly scented plant. Heliotrope blooms best when its roots are cramped, so leave it in the same pot for as long as you can. Whitefly infestation is a problem for indoor heliotropes; keep a close watch for these pests.

Jasmine _(Jasminum_ spp._). Jasmines are easily grown in a sunny window. Bush-type jasmines, such as _J. sambac_ cv. Maid of Orleans and _J. nitidum,_ stay neat and require less pruning than their vining cousins; _J. sambac_ is considered one of the most deliciously scented jasmines. Both of these plants prefer warm nighttime temperatures of 50°–60°F. They do best in a south-facing window. Another good jasmine for indoors is _J. officinale_, the flower grown in France for perfume. _J. officinale_ is a rampant vine, and if it is happy, it may just take over your windowsill. Plant it in a hanging basket, or wrap the long branches on a trellis. For sweet scent in the winter, try _J. polyanthum._ This jasmine needs two months of chilly nights (40°F) to set buds, so keep it outdoors in the autumn if you want it to bloom.

Sweet olive _(Osmanthus fragrans)._ Sweet olive has one of the strongest fragrances of the plants that tolerate indoor conditions. The blossoms are not much to look at; in fact, you may not even see them unless you look closely. You'll certainly smell their candy-sweet scent, however. This plant can be grown in full sun or partial shade, and it thrives over a broad range of temperatures. A very dry room causes the leaf tips to turn brown; mist it occasionally to keep it from suffering.

Some of the many other fragrant plants that can be grown indoors include the following:

Angel's-trumpet _(Datura inoxia)_

Carolina jessamine _(Gelsemium sempervirens)_

Coffee _(Coffea arabica)_

Dwarf citrus _(Citrus_ spp._)_

Jasmine _(Jasminum_ spp._)_

Moonflower _(Calonyction aculeatum)_

Night-blooming jasmine _(Cestrum nocturnum)_

A Garden You Can Feel

Plants can appeal to touch as well as to sight and smell. Of all our senses, touch is one of the most pleasurable, and richly textured plants are a delight to the gardener with poor vision. How about a "Plant Petting Garden"? Children enjoy these gardens, too; it is a good way to introduce your young friends or family to the fun of gardening.

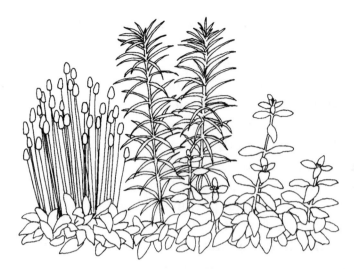

▲ *A garden bed with texture (from left to right): Lamb's-ears, hare's-tail grass, lily.*

Use some plants with soft, fuzzy leaves, like lamb's-ears (*Stachys byzantina*), woolly thyme (*Thymus serpyllum lanuginosus*), mullein (*Verbascum spp.*), and *Artemisia* spp. Pussy willow (*Salix* spp.) is another plant that invites petting. Hare's-tail grass (*Lagurus ovatus*) sports fluffy flower heads that feel as furry as the animal it was named after. The blossoms on some plants are silky to the touch; try hibiscus, gardenia, and most lilies. Statice blossoms (*Limonium* spp.) and globe amaranth (*Gomphrena globosa*) have a papery feel, as do the seed pods of honesty (*Lunaria annua*), which, in addition, make a wonderful rustling sound when the wind blows.

Place textured plants in a small, enclosed garden with comfortable garden seats or mossy places to sit. Garden beds raised to a height of 2 feet and constructed with edges to sit on bring touchable plants within reach. Soft plants like Corsican mint (*Mentha requienii*), which release a fragrance when sat upon, are a bonus in the touching garden. Choose only nonpoisonous and nonprickly plants for the petting garden.

A Garden You Can Hear

I love the sound of the wind blowing through tall pine trees and the flap of poplar leaves in a stiff breeze. The gar-

PLANTS TO TOUCH

COMMON NAME	BOTANIC NAME	ZONES*/PLANT TYPE
Feather grass	*Stipa pennata*	5
Gay-feather	*Liatris spicata*	4
Hare's-tail grass	*Lagurus ovatus*	HHA
Lamb's-ears	*Stachys byzantina*	5
Love-lies-bleeding	*Amaranthus caudatus*	HHA
Obedient plant	*Physostegia virginiana*	4
Poppy	*Papaver* spp.	1–7
Pussy willow	*Salix* spp.	3–6
Squirreltail grass	*Hordeum jubatum*	4
Statice	*Limonium latifolium*	4
Woolly thyme	*Thymus serpyllum lanuginosus*	3

PLANTS TO LISTEN TO

Small Plants

Animated oats	*Avena sterilis*	4
Balloon flower	*Platycodon grandiflorus*	4
Bamboos	(various species)	5–9
Chinese-lantern plant	*Physalis alkekengi*	5
Chives	*Allium schoenoprasum*	2
Honesty	*Lunaria annua*	HB
Hosta	*Hosta* spp.	3–5
Pampas grass	*Cortaderia selloana*	8
Pearl grass	*Briza maxima*	A

Shrubs

Flowering maple	*Abutilon hybridum*	10

Trees

Acacia	*Acacia* spp.	8–10
Birch	*Betula* spp.	3–5
Eucalyptus	*Eucalyptus* spp.	9
Pine	*Pinus* spp.	1–9
Poplar	*Populus* spp.	1–8
Silver-dollar tree	*Eucalyptus polyanthemos*	9
Weeping willow	*Salix babylonica*	5

PLANT TYPES: A = Annual, HB = Hardy Biennial, HHA = Half-hardy Annual

* Chart shows coldest hardiness zone tolerated by a species. Where a specific species is not named on the chart, look for a species appropriate to the hardiness range indicated.

Fruits for the Tasting Garden

Dwarf apple

Blackberry

Blueberry

Dwarf fig

Grape

Dwarf nectarine

Dwarf peach

Raspberry

Strawberry

den you can hear sets different and subtle moods: the whisper of willows and other "weeping" plants lends a sense of gentle calm; the clatter of quaking grass *(Briza media)* and the rustle of bamboo add activity and movement to an otherwise silent garden. Sit and listen to the changes in your garden as the seasons pass — the soft stirring of spring blossoms, the commotion of blowing leaves in a summer storm, the rattle of seed pods as autumn approaches, the sharp crack of shrinking wood in winter's silence.

A Garden You Can Taste

I can remember sitting under the cool shade of my grandfather's grapevines, plucking succulent grapes to pop into my mouth. Nothing tastes as good as fruits fresh-picked and eaten right in the garden. Red-ripe strawberries, warm from the sun, explode with flavor. You can almost taste the blue of blueberries just picked from the bush. Include a tasting garden in your landscape design — a place where you can sit, relax, and feast on the fruits of your labor. Most fruiting plants prefer a sunny spot, but you can provide shade for yourself by growing grapes on an overhead trellis. A garden umbrella will keep the hot sun off your head if there is no room for a grapevine. Keep your tasting garden small, so that all your ready-to-eat snacks are within reach. A hammock next to a dwarf peach or a garden bench placed among blueberry bushes makes munching convenient. Even if your garden is quite small, many fruits can be grown in containers; a strawberry jar planted with berries, for example, will keep your taste buds happy on a warm summer day.

If you use chemical fertilizers or pesticides in your garden, provide a container of water for washing the fruits before you eat them.

▲ *Plant strawberries in a terra cotta jar for a balcony or patio — a small, portable garden you can taste.*

THE NATURALIST'S GARDEN

So many wild things are vanishing from our earth, as asphalt and suburban sprawl replace the vast prairies and ponds that greeted the first settlers in America. Although there is beauty in architecture and safety in civilization, most human beings feel a certain peace when in natural surroundings. Preserve this sense of peace and at the same time provide sanctuary for the wild creatures that are losing their homes by designing your garden with a small corner for the natural community.

The Butterfly Garden

Butterflies are quiet, elegant visitors — painted jewels bringing to your garden a sense of serenity. They are also victims of insecticides and land development. It's easy to create a garden that provides color, fragrance, and habitat for these distressed creatures.

To establish a butterfly garden, first observe and identify, if you can, the butterflies that presently visit your garden. Most butterflies have food plant preferences, and if you

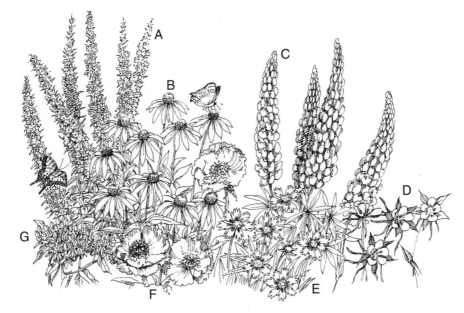

◀ Attract butterflies to your garden by growing plants with the colors, fragrances, and habitat that they love. This garden contains (A) lythrum, (B) purple coneflower, (C) lupine, (D) columbine, (E) coreopsis, (F) Oriental poppy, and (G) butterfly weed.

know which butterfly you are trying to attract, you can provide the plants that are the most alluring. Many butterflies choose weedy plants like thistles, milkweeds, and clovers for feeding and breeding. When they can't find their natural choices, some butterfly larvae will chew through your passion vines, violets, parsley, carrots, and anise.

Because adult butterflies often get their nourishment from different plants than their larvae, provide only nectar foods for the adults if you don't want caterpillars in your garden. Adult butterflies will sip the nectar of zinnias, lilies, sweet allysum, globe thistle, and coreopsis. Caterpillars, on the other hand, munch alfalfa leaves, butterfly weed and other *Asclepias*, cabbage leaves, dill, and nasturtiums. Watch your garden for a season or two, and you'll soon recognize which plants attract the adults and which are larval food plants. You may find it's as much fun to watch a tiny caterpillar chomp its way through an *Asclepias* or thistle plant as it is to watch an adult butterfly flit through the garden.

Butterflies seem to prefer purple flowers, but pink, white, and yellow also get their attention. Monarchs like orange butterfly weed *(Asclepias tuberosa)*. Choose flowers with flat surfaces that butterflies can perch on; upright flowers are easier to sip nectar from than drooping blossoms. Butterflies start appearing in the spring and continue into autumn, so plant a variety of flowers that will give continuous bloom, for all-season dining.

My favorite butterfly plant is *Asclepias tuberosa*, aptly known as butterfly weed. Its orange and yellow flowers bloom almost constantly, and the monarchs love it for nectar and larval food. It's true that the caterpillars eat the plants right to the ground, but the plants recover quickly for another round of blooms. Although *Asclepias* resents transplanting, it reseeds freely, so I always have plenty of it around the yard. For some reason, I've had problems starting hybrid *Asclepias* from seed. Sometimes the seeds germinate, only to wither and die before they reach the transplant stage. Other times, I've had trouble even getting them to sprout. So far, I've had to rely on nature to increase my collection of wild asclepias, and they are doing quite nicely.

A butterfly garden isn't always pretty. Some favorite butterfly plants are naturally ragged-looking and unattractive (or become so after the caterpillars start feeding). Locate your insect garden in an out-of the-way corner, if neatness is important to you. If you are a successful butterfly gardener, be prepared to see your butterfly plants come and go. Most butterfly favorites are either self-sowing or hardy perennials that recover quickly from the larvae's seasonal pruning, so don't worry about having to replant.

Butterflies need water and cover as well as food. Birdbaths, garden pools, and even sprinklers attract butterflies on a hot summer day. Leave a few brush piles around for the larvae to attach their cocoons and chrysalises to. In my garden, monarch larvae sometimes make these temporary homes on the underside of my lawn furniture. Look for them in any hidden niche. Some butterflies and moths have short life cycles and you may have two or three generations inhabiting your garden each year.

During fall clean-up, go easy on the butterfly area; rigorous cleaning may destroy hibernating pupae. Leave the defoliated milkweed plants to recover naturally. If you mow these down, monarch eggs might be lost.

BUTTERFLY FOODS

BUTTERFLY	LARVAL FOOD	NECTAR PLANT
Fritillaries	Violet	*Buddleia*
Monarch	Butterfly weed, milkweed, and other *Asclepias*	*Buddleia*, phlox, *Sedum*
Mourning Cloak	Poplar, willow	*Arabis, Aubrieta*, lavender, pussy willow
Orange Sulphur	Clover	*Buddleia, Gaillardia*, heliotrope, mignonette, *Scabiosa, Sedum*
Painted Ladies	Nettles, thistles	*Buddleia, Gaillardia*, heliotrope, mignonette
Red Admiral	Nettles, thistles	*Buddleia, Gaillardia*, heliotrope, mignonette, *Scabiosa, Sedum*
Swallowtail	Anise, carrot, fennel, parsley	*Asclepias*, beebalm, spicebush, sweet rocket

━━ OTHER PLANTS THAT ATTRACT BUTTERFLIES ━━

COMMON NAME	BOTANIC NAME	ZONES*/PLANT TYPE
Annuals		
Borage	*Borago officinalis*	HA
Candytuft	*Iberis* spp.	HHA
Mignonette	*Reseda odorata*	VHA
Sweet alyssum	*Alyssum maritima*	HA
Verbena	*Verbena* x *hybrida*	TA
Perennials		
Beebalm	*Monarda didyma*	4
Clary sage	*Salvia sclarea*	B
Coreopsis	*Coreopsis* spp.	4
Pinks	*Dianthus* spp.	4–6
Shasta daisy	*Chrysanthemum* x *superbum*	4

PLANT TYPE: B = Biennial, HA = Hardy Annual, HHA = Half-hardy annual, VHA = Very hardy annual, TA = Tender annual

* Chart shows coldest hardiness zone tolerated by a species. Where a specific species is not named on the chart, look for a species appropriate to the hardiness range indicated.

Avoid insecticides if you're trying to establish a butterfly garden. Instead, use row covers, crop rotation, and companion planting to protect your plants from garden pests.

Hug a Bug: The Insect Garden

Many gardeners would laugh, or even shudder, to consider creating a haven for insects, who are, after all, our sworn enemies when they ravage our gardens. But insects do many good deeds. Bees and other nectar-sippers pollinate fruits and vegetables. Spiders, ladybugs, and mantids dispose of insect pests. Some insects simply add a beauty of their own.

All insects need a source of food, a place to breed, and a place to overwinter. Most wild plants attract insects; simply preserving an uncultivated portion of the yard will give them what they need. You can add flowers for your own enjoyment, and water to entice the dragonflies and lacewings. Brush piles and damp leafy areas afford breeding places.

Beneficial insects that don't find enough food will move on to greener pastures. Plants alone don't provide food for insects that prey on other insects; to keep predators happy, you have to offer plants that lure the insect pests that are their food. For this food chain to be successful, include plants that can tolerate a certain amount of bug-abuse. If you are unwilling to put up with a little insect damage in the garden, insect-gardening is not for you. Whatever you do, don't use insecticides near the area where you want beneficial insects to live. Beneficial insects are affected by pesticides just as surely as insect pests, either by direct contact or because they lose their prey. Learn to resist the urge to reach for the sprayer every time you notice an insect attack. Hand-picking is the best method to control pest populations in an area where you would like to encourage beneficial insects.

Increase your helpful insect population by importing praying mantis egg cases, ladybugs, lacewings, and other garden helpers, and then get out the magnifying glass and have fun watching these "little beasties"! (For more information about attracting and supporting beneficial insects, see pages 159-164.)

Bird Gardens

Provide yourself with hours of enjoyment by inviting the birds to your garden. These winged visitors add grace and charm to even the smallest landscape. Sit quietly in the garden for awhile, and you'll find that the birds will soon join you. You don't need to be a serious birdwatcher to appreciate their antics as they swoop and dart through the garden, skirmishing like tiny warriors for the tastiest treats or the best territory. In my garden, their contests for "Featherweight Champion of the Yard" keep me constantly amused. Regular visitors become favorites, and I find myself rooting for certain contenders. Even on the dreariest day, these avian activities raise my spirits.

Your garden can provide the birds with a much needed sanctuary from the "paving" of North America, and at the same time provide you with amusing garden assistants, as they feed on garden insect pests. It's not hard to get birds to visit your garden. Putting up birdhouses and making food and water available are all that is needed to bring the birds flocking. If you add plants that provide them food and shelter you will get even better results.

Studies of natural habitats show that birds prefer the edges, such as a hedge, the border of a lawn, or tall trees next to a low stream bed. These edges attract a great variety of birds because they offer an assortment of foods, habitats, and shelters. Each type of habitat — shrubs, ground covers, trees — provides different fruits, insects, and nesting and roosting sites that appeal to many species of birds.

The vertical layers in a bird habitat are important, too. For instance, certain ground-feeding birds, such as wrens, towhees, and sparrows, congregate in areas where rocks, tree branches, or steep banks offer them a change of perspective. Evidently they want to be able to hop up and look around now and then while they are eating. Birds also have different preferences for feeding and nesting heights. A combination of tall hedges, medium-sized shrubs, and low plantings increases the bird appeal of a garden. Offer a variety of choices, and your garden will tempt a larger assortment of feathered residents.

Ground covers, rather than lawn, are preferred feeding places for most ground-feeding birds. Of course, lawns that are groomed and fed with chemical weed-and-feed mixes are harmful to birds. Even if you don't use synthetic controls, however, not only is there a greater insect population in ground cover than in a lawn, but some of these plants also produce fruits and berries for the birds to eat. Bearberry, crowberry, and creeping cotoneaster are highly recommended as bird-attracting ground cover.

Different kinds of birds choose different kinds of nesting places. If you have dead trees that can be safely left standing, birds will use them as homes. Woodpeckers, chickadees, and other "digging" birds excavate nesting cavities in decayed wood; their neighbors the kestrels, owls, titmice, tree swallows, and bluebirds then move in after the original occupants have moved out. Some of these birds will live in boxes if natural tree cavities are not available. Each type of bird prefers a particular home size. Check a bird book for the correct proportions of box-to-entrance-hole measurements.

A constant water supply is vital to a thriving bird garden. Ground-level pools, as well as elevated water baths, are used by many birds. Place the water in a spot where birds are safe from predators. Bushes and other cover are much appreciated by the birds but should be kept away from the immediate feeding and watering place. Cats can leap about 4 feet to catch a bird, so an area at least this size should be free of cat-concealing shrubbery. If you have no safe place to put a birdbath on the ground, hang one in a tree. Shallow plastic and ceramic containers with holes for hanging wires are available from garden and nursery suppliers. For the ultimate in convenience, set up a drip watering line to your birdbath, so that the bath is filled each time the water is turned on. If you can afford to use a little extra water, a continuous drip attracts many kinds of birds. Or, you can achieve the effect of moving water by hanging a water-filled bucket with a very small hole in its bottom over the birdbath. Of course, you must refill the bucket frequently, but this slow water drip is a proven way to lure birds.

Where space permits, an in-ground pool is a delightful addition to your garden. A bird bathing pool should be no more than 3 inches deep. Prefabricated plastic pool-liners are available in many sizes, or dig a hole the proper size and line it with heavy plastic. Create a natural-looking pool by concealing the edges with ornamental rocks and plants. Depending on weather conditions and the strength of the plastic liner, this pool will last for at least a few seasons.

Many birds enjoy a dust bath as much as they enjoy splashing in the water. It is thought that these dust baths rid birds of irritating parasites. A dust bath doesn't have to be large — a foot or more square is sufficient. Like the water

PLANTS THAT ATTRACT BIRDS

COMMON NAME	BOTANIC NAME	ZONES*/PLANT TYPE
Fruits Of		
Blackberry	*Rubus* spp.	3
Cherry	*Prunus* spp.	1–9
Currants, gooseberries	*Ribes* spp.	2–5
Fig	*Ficus* spp.	8–9
Firethorn	*Pyracantha* spp.	5–7
Grape	*Vitis* spp.	4–7
Ivy	*Hedera* spp.	6–9
Peach	*Prunus persica*	5
Persimmon	*Diospyros* spp.	5–6
Plum	*Prunus* spp.	4–6
Roses	*Rosa* spp.	3–8
Seeds Of		
Bachelor's-button	*Centaurea cyanus*	VHA
Birch	*Betula* spp.	3–5
Cosmos	*Cosmos* spp.	HHA
Elm	*Ulmus* spp.	2–5
Goldenrod	*Solidago* spp.	4
Most grasses		
Marigold	*Tagetes* spp.	HHA
Oak	*Quercus* spp.	3–8
Pine	*Pinus* spp.	1–9
Sunflower	*Helianthus* spp.	TA
Zinnia	*Zinnia* spp.	TA
Flowers Of		
Acacia	*Acacia* spp.	8–10
Beebalm	*Monarda didyma*	4
Butterfly bush	*Buddleia* spp.	5–10
Ceanothus	*Ceanothus* spp.	4–8
Citrus	*Citrus* spp.	10
Fuchsia	*Fuchsia* spp.	5–10
Honeysuckle	*Lonicera* spp.	4–5
Impatiens	*Impatiens* spp.	TA
Nicotiana	*Nicotiana* spp.	HHA
Penstemon	*Penstemon* spp.	3–7
Phlox	*Phlox* spp.	4–5

COMMON NAME	BOTANIC NAME	ZONES*/PLANT TYPE
Shelter In		
Abelia	*Abelia* spp.	5–8
Autumn olive	*Elaeagnus umbellata*	3
Bayberry	*Myrica pensylvanica*	4
Birch	*Betula* spp.	3–5
Blueberry	*Vaccinium* spp.	1–4
Bramble	*Rubus* spp.	3
Cedar	*Cedrus* spp.	6–7
Elderberry	*Sambucus* spp.	3–5
English ivy	*Hedera helix*	6
Grape	*Vitis* spp.	4–7
Holly	*Ilex* spp.	4–8
Honeysuckle	*Lonicera* spp.	4–5
Mulberry	*Morus* spp.	2–4
Oak	*Quercus* spp.	3–8
Privet	*Ligustrum* spp.	3–7
Trumpet vine	*Campsis radicans*	4
Viburnum	*Viburnum* spp.	4–8
Virginia creeper	*Parthenocissus quinquefolia*	4

PLANT TYPE: HHA = Half-hardy annual, TA = Tender annual, VHA = Very hardy annual

* Chart shows coldest hardiness zone tolerated by a species. Where a specific species is not named on the chart, look for a species appropriate to the hardiness range indicated.

---

bath, it should be out in the open where there are no hiding places for predators. A light soil, or a mixture of soil, sand, and ash, makes a good filler for the bathing area. You'll enjoy the antics that take place at the "dust bowl."

Create some food patches in your garden filled with flowers and plants that birds like, and watch them flock! Wildflowers with thistlelike seed heads appeal to many different birds, especially goldfinches. Other plants that birds like are sunflowers, asters, bachelor's-buttons, marigolds, and zinnias. In my garden, salvia has proven to be a good, all-round bird plant. Hummingbirds sip the nectar from the flowers, and goldfinches and titmice like the seeds.

For additional and year-round feedings, provide seed for the birds. Hang your feeders over paving or thick ground cover. Birds are messy eaters and many kinds of seeds are likely to sprout under the feeder. If you don't mind the weedy look of some of these seed plants, you can grow your own birdseed. Allow some of the spilled seed to grow to maturity, and then let the birds harvest it themselves. If your feeder is in a flower bed or the lawn where you do not want to introduce weed seeds, treat birdseed by placing it in the microwave or a hot oven for five minutes before you put it out for the birds. The quick cooking doesn't reduce the nutritional value of the seed, but it does decrease seed germination. Another way to avoid the sprouting problem is to feed only hulled sunflower seed, which won't sprout. Hulled sunflower seed is expensive, and many species of birds don't eat sunflower seeds, so there will be a limited variety of birds at your feeder.

It's fun to learn about the birds that visit. Get a good bird book, and make a place for yourself in the garden where you can sit quietly and observe the activities of your feathered guests.

Hummingbird Gardens

One of my favorite garden friends is a lively little feathered jewel that zips madly around the bushes as he chases his rivals. From his guard station in the lime tree, he has a good view of my garden, and alien hummingbirds are spotted immediately. Any that dare to venture near his feeder are met with a high-pitched twitter and an angry flash of bright wings. Hummingbirds are belligerent little beasts when they are defending their territory. About four individuals fight over the two feeders in my garden, and they are constantly buzzing back and forth, chasing each other around the garden. They do, however, tolerate certain intruders at their feeders, and I've spent many an hour watching this social interplay and trying to figure out if these are family members, cherished guests, or prospective mates. I often sit right between the two feeders in my yard for the best view of all the action. The hummingbirds have become so used to my presence that they will feed even as I am standing next to the feeder to refill it. And, if I let it run out, they hover near my head and squeak little hummingbird insults at me until I fill it again. Perhaps you, too, would be amused to be bullied by these tiny tyrants. If so, here are some suggestions for attracting them to your garden.

A hummingbird garden is perhaps the easiest bird garden to establish and the most fun. All you need is a hanging feeder filled with sugar water to attract these amazingly fast and fearless little visitors. If possible, you should also supply a variety of natural foods to meet the hummer's prodigious metabolic needs. A hummingbird feeds every 10 to 15 minutes from sunrise to sunset. He may need as much as 1,000 fucshia blossoms full of nectar daily to sustain him. As far as a hummingbird is concerned, you cannot have too many nectar-rich plants. Hummingbirds prefer red, orange, or pink solitary flowers that are large and droopy. Bright, tubular flowers that hold lots of nectar are quite popular. Plant for staggered bloom times, so that the food supply is constant. Salvias, fuchsias, nasturtiums, and four-o'clocks are some of the most popular blossoms. Fruit-tree blossoms and various herbs are also well-liked.

▲ *The author's hummingbird feeders provide hours of fascinating action.*

If you are using a hanging sugar-water feeder, find one that holds at least 2 cups; a quart container is even better. You'll be surprised how quickly these little gluttons can empty it. During hummingbird high season, I have found myself refilling the feeder daily. One-half cup of sugar to 3 cups of water seems to be a good mix. Boil the mixture on the stove or heat it in the microwave to dissolve the sugar, and then let it cool. Do not use honey instead of sugar; some studies have shown that honey grows a certain bacteria or fungus that may harm the birds. You can use food color to tint it, if you wish, but the birds don't seem to care once they know the food is there. I color mine because it's easier to see when it's time to make more syrup. Empty and clean the containers weekly to keep bacteria and diseases at bay.

To watch hummingbird antics put the feeder near the house. Cover windows that glare. Hummingbirds are espe-

HUMMINGBIRD PLANTS

COMMON NAME	BOTANIC NAME	ZONES*/PLANT TYPE
Annuals		
Larkspur	*Delphinium* spp.	HHA
Morning-glory	*Ipomoea purpurea*	TA
Scarlet runner bean	*Phaseolus coccineus*	TA
Scarlet sage	*Salvia splendens*	HHA
Zinnia	*Zinnia* spp.	TA
Perennials		
Beebalm	*Monarda didyma*	4
Clary sage	*Salvia sclarea*	B
Columbine	*Aquilegia* spp.	3
Delphinium	*Delphinium* spp.	4–7
Hollyhock	*Alcea rosea*	4
Shrubs		
Bottlebrush	*Callistemon citrinus*	9
Citrus	*Citrus* spp.	10
Fuchsia	*Fuchsia* spp.	5–10
Hibiscus	*Hibiscus* spp.	5–9
Lilac	*Syringa* spp.	3–7

PLANT TYPE: B = Biennial, HHA = Half-hardy Annual, TA = Tender annual

* Chart shows coldest hardiness zone tolerated by a species. Where a specific species is not named on the chart, look for a species appropriate to the hardiness range indicated.

cially reckless when defending their territory, and they may crash into reflecting windows during their rambunctious chases around the garden. I've even had some enter the house in search of food. The best thing to do if that should happen is to let them alone to find their own way out, if you can stand it. If it looks as though they are battering themselves to death at the window, catch them gently and take them outdoors. Release them in a cool part of the garden, away from any predators, to give them a chance to recover.

Avoid using insecticides and other toxic chemicals if you are interested in watching the hummingbirds. They eat insects as well as nectar, and destroying this vital food source is unwise. Furthermore, the hummingbird's life may be endangered if chemicals coat the flowers it feeds on.

Wildlife Gardens

Some of the most successful wildlife gardens are unplanned and informal. If you have an area of the yard that you can leave relatively undisturbed, you have the makings of a thriving natural community. Plants native to your area that bear fruit and provide shelter are the best choices for a wildlife garden; these plants need little maintenance and are naturally preferred by local critters. The more variation in the plant life you can provide, the more varied will be your guests. Some open areas, bordered by thick shrubbery and occasional tall trees, attract a large number of different wild creatures.

You need to supply four things in order for your wildlife garden to prosper: food, water, cover, and reproductive areas.

Food. Plant bushes and vines that yield fruit or berries, and the animals will soon arrive. Leave the edges of the yard to nature. Rather than mowing grasses and wildflowers, allow them to mature and provide seeds. Scatter seeds, nuts, and crumbs during the winter, or when natural food is scarce.

Water. Even the shyest creatures will draw near your nature preserve if you provide water. A birdbath will suffice, but a pool or pond will get wildlife through drought times and encourage less common animals to visit. Along with the birds and butterflies, frogs, toads, and small mammals appreciate a constant water supply.

Cover. This is crucial. Give your wild friends something to hide in and shelter from the rain and cold. This is especially necessary near feeding areas and travel lanes. Most wild animals need to move from their habitat to their feeding area without being exposed to natural enemies.

Reproductive areas. Wildlife also need sheltered areas for raising their families. These reproductive areas must be safe, inaccessible places such as brush piles, thick shrubs, and tall grasses. Even your discarded Christmas tree can serve as a home for many birds and small animals, especially during long winters.

Not everyone loves wild animals. Your neighbors might complain when you attract raccoons, opossums, and squirrels to the neighborhood. If problems arise, perhaps they can be worked out. Keep your wildlife area away from your neighbors' fruit trees and vegetable gardens. Maybe the wild critters will prefer your natural food to your neighbor's corn. (I doubt it, but you can try!) There may be other problems, too. Your wildlife area may look a little *too* natural to the "weed police." Add attractive wildflowers and keep rampant plants under control to ward off complaints.

One man's pets are another man's pests! If your neighbor has a hunting cat or a chasing dog, it may spoil your wildlife sanctuary. Keep your own domestic pets penned or indoors during the prime early morning or evening feeding times. Letting your neighbor know about your special garden may solve the problem of wandering pets. Most people respect other's property and interests and are cooperative. If you still have problems, encourage a neighbor's pesty pet to leave your garden with a blast of water from the hose. A loud noise might work, too, but that will disturb the wildlife as well.

Be patient when you start your wildlife garden. The creatures may be slow about establishing their homes in your yard, but when they find things to their liking, they'll arrive and remain. You'll have hours of enjoyment watching your wildlife friends.

Many organizations encourage the establishment of wildlife habitats. One of the most well known is National Wildlife Federation's "Backyard Habitat Program," which promotes the creation of habitats in suburban yards. They will certify your yard as an official Backyard Habitat, if it meets certain criteria for providing food, water, and shelter. A packet of information may be obtained by writing the National Wildlife Foundation Backyard Habitat Program, Department ME1, 1412 16th Street N.W., Washington, DC 20036-2266.

WATER GARDENS

No garden is too small for a bit of water. The sight and sound of water have always been soothing to the weary gardener. A natural pool or a running stream may be beyond the realm of a suburban garden, but small manmade pools or even "puddle plantings" bring the serenity of water to any garden.

Pools can be made of brick, concrete, stones, or plastic. Also available are small, ready-made, completely self-contained pools with fountains. You simply plug them in and the water recirculates as long as the system is on. These fountains are ideal for a small deck and can even be used indoors.

WATER PLANTS

COMMON NAME	BOTANIC NAME	HARDINESS ZONES*
Horsetail	*Equisetum hyemale*	3
Lotus	*Nymphaea lotus*	10
Japanese iris	*Iris kaempferi*	4
Papyrus	*Cyperus papyrus*	9
Umbrella plant	*Cyperus alternifolius* cv. 'Gracilis'	10
Water-lily	*Nymphaea* spp.	3–10
Water snowflake	*Nymphoides indica*	9

* Chart shows coldest hardiness zone tolerated by a species. Where a specific species is not named on the chart, look for a species appropriate to the hardiness range indicated.

Preformed plastic or fiberglass pools are also relatively easy to install, either above or below the surface of the soil. Most come with pumping and recirculating systems. Concrete bowls, ceramic pots without drainage holes, and half barrels make good waterlily pools or reflecting ponds.

Even small water gardens take some maintenance. They need to be emptied and scrubbed at least once a year. If water in your area is high in mineral content, the recirculating system may need an occasional flushing to keep it running freely. If you have water plants, they may need to be thinned and perhaps pulled up and protected during the winter.

Puddle Plantings

Miniature water gardens bring the pleasures of outdoor gardening to the indoor gardener. Puddle plantings also do well on a patio, as long as they are protected from full sun and not allowed to dry out. Any waterproof container will support a small water garden. The best ones are stone containers that will look more natural when they eventually grow a bit of moss.

▲ *A small manmade pool creates an area of serenity in this suburban garden.*

Water should be at least 2 inches deep. A layer of charcoal topped with a 1-inch layer of gravel is a good base for a ½-inch layer of soil. Fill the pool carefully with water and let everything settle. Moss-covered rocks and pieces of driftwood add an artistic touch.

Use small plants in your miniature pool — this is no place for the lotus or horsetail. Small grasses or small floating ferns, like *Salvinia* or water lettuce *(Pistia stratiotes)*, work well in these little gardens. Plant Kenilworth ivy *(Cymbalaria muralis)*, violets, and ajuga around the edge to make a tiny, serene landscape. Experiment with water-tolerant plants for different effects.

THE AIR GARDEN

If you're tired of lifting pots and moving soil, try a garden that's as light as air. Hundreds of attractive, easy-to-care-for plants grow best when their toes are free, and, in fact, resent being confined to containers or restricted by soil. Among these *epiphytes* are certain orchids, bromeliads, Christmas cacti, and some ferns. In nature, these plants grow high in trees, where they get moisture and nutrients from rainfall, dew, and humid air. Since shady rain forests are the natural habitat of many epiphytes, they adapt well to low-light indoor situations. Air plants grow hanging on a wall, in a basket, on a windowsill, or simply resting on a shelf. Because they need little care, they are ideal for those who enjoy being surrounded by growing things, but have little time or energy to invest in a conventional garden.

Although air plants tolerate a wide range of climatic conditions, most, especially those with variegated leaves, prefer filtered sunlight. If potted, the roots should be kept slightly moist, but they don't like continuously wet feet. Bromeliads need fresh water standing in their vaselike centers. Other epiphytes like a daily misting. No need to cart heavy water cans around, however — just keep a spray bottle near your air garden for convenience. If your plants are in the kitchen, give them a spritz when you do the dishes. If possible, plunge the air plant in water once a month, to keep the osmunda and/or sphagnum moss moist. Mist it daily.

Air plants don't need much fertilizer; a light, monthly feeding with a fish-and-seaweed-based organic fertilizer or a synthetic, water-soluble, complete fertilizer is sufficient to keep your air garden happy. Because many air plants absorb nutrition through their leaves, foliar feeding is particularly successful. Use a fertilizer that contains specially formulated nutrients that are easily absorbed by plant foliage. Mix at one-quarter strength, and mist it on plants with a spray bottle.

Air plants don't require much pruning, either; occasion-

★ Air gardens can be planted

  In bird cages

  In picture frames

  On tree limbs

  In macramé slings

  On trellises

  In stones, shells, and dish gardens

★ Epiphytic plants combined with sphagnum moss make beautiful Easter baskets.

★ Green- and red-leaved bromeliads are ideal Christmas table decorations and gifts.

★ Moss and air plants attached to a tree-shaped Styrofoam base with fishing line or florist wire make a small, living Christmas tree.

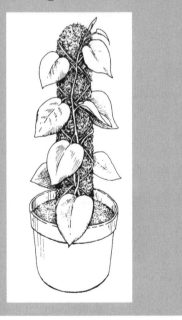

ally trim any dried tips or roots to keep them neat.

Many epiphytes have roots that grow from their base or stem. Because these *aerial roots* are above ground or outside the container, you can easily inspect them and judge whether the plants are healthy and growing well. The exposed roots should look plump, fresh, and white or light colored, with new, green tips. Dried brown roots indicate that a plant is suffering and needs more moisture or light. (Exception: Some ferns normally have dark-colored roots.) Don't be alarmed if the roots on a recently blooming air plant shrivel or brown a little. Several kinds of air plants need a break after blooming, and this may be a normal change. Cut back on moisture and fertilizer for most plants and let them rest for a few weeks at this time. (Check a garden encyclopedia for specific feeding requirements for different plants during dormancy.) When new growing tips appear, resume your usual watering procedures.

Supports for Air Plants

Unlike soil-grown plants that require frequent repotting, air plants can grow in the same place for years. With wire or fishing line, attach epiphytes to any of the materials described below, or place them in the shallow pockets of interesting rocks, hang them in baskets, wire them to tree branches, or suspend them in macramé slings.

Osmunda. Consisting of fibrous roots of osmunda ferns, this spongy material holds water, dries out slowly, and permits good air circulation. As it decomposes, it releases nutrients for plant growth. Osmunda can be pulled apart or cut with a knife. It is easier to handle if it has been soaked overnight in water. Obtain osmunda from indoor and orchid plant suppliers. Attached to bark, stone, or a tree branch with wire or fishing line, osmunda makes a good home for an air plant.

Sphagnum moss. Green or brown, lightweight, and easy to work with, sphagnum moss absorbs water readily. Live sphagnum retains water longer than dry sphagnum. Use sphagnum as a bed for your air plants or as filler in a fern column (see pages 219-221), dish, or wall garden. It can be found in almost any nursery.

Fir bark and **compressed wood.** Often cut into slabs and totem poles for vining philodendrons, these are great for growing air plants vertically. Attach the plant to the wood with wire or carve pockets in the wood and insert the plants.

Care of the New Air Garden

A newly created air garden needs a little extra care to get it established. After the plant is attached to the bark, slab, or other mount, soak it in a pan of water. You can't do this with tree branches or very large supports, of course, but it's a good way to increase the humidity around plants that are attached to smaller supports. Keep the plant in a bright place, out of direct sunlight, and mist it twice daily for the first two weeks. A high-humidity area, such as the bathroom or even a well-lit shower stall, is an ideal place to give newly planted epiphytes a good start. After about ten days, gradually expose the plants to brighter light. Mist the plants daily, and provide good air circulation. Within four to six weeks, new aerial roots will develop, and your air garden is on its way!

Air gardens are generally insect- and disease-free, and the few pests that do attack your plants are easily

---

Good Air Plants for Beginners

Bromeliads *(Tillandsia ionanthe, T. juncea, Vriesea malzinei)*

Christmas cactus *(Schlumbergera bridgesii)*

Easter cactus *(Rhipsalidopsis gaertneri)*

Orchids *(Brassavola glauca, Bulbophyllum lobbii)*

Philodendrons *(Philodendron bipinnatifidum, P. soderoi)*

banished. Overdry or overwet conditions are the most common causes of insect or disease attack.

Kinds of Air Plants

Bromeliads. Usually rosette-shaped, bromeliads are members of the Pineapple Family and a good choice for the beginning air-gardener. Some have plain green or gray leathery leaves, and others are dramatically variegated. Although some bromeliads have beautiful blooms, the flowers are often hidden and not nearly as showy as the leaves. Bromeliads are easy to maintain because they keep their own emergency supply of water in a vaselike cup in the center of the plant. Care of bromeliads involves keeping this vase filled with water and misting the plant two or three times weekly. Bromeliads make an elegant table decoration or, attached to an interesting branch, a lovely indoor "tree."

Orchids. In nature, the majority of orchids are epiphytic

SOME PROBLEMS WITH AIR PLANTS

PROBLEM	CAUSE	CONTROL
Fine webs on underside of leaves Leaves mottled or dry looking	Red spider mite	Spray vigorously with water. Plunge plant in very dilute soap solution (¼ teaspoon per gallon of water).
Swarming tiny moths	Whitefly	Same as above. Place a piece of bright yellow, petroleum-jelly-covered paper among the plants (flies will stick to it).
Cluster of little brown, gray, or white clumps with hard shells	Scale	Wash as above. Scrub scale off with alcohol-dipped cotton swab.
Gray or watery leaves Green or yellow crown rot	Bacterial blight	Remove affected leaves and hope for the best. Remove from the vicinity of other plants. Prevent by avoiding overwet conditions.
Flowers, stalks, and leaves with burn spots or circles	Virus disease	Destroy plant.

plants. Because they naturally grow in the branches of trees, epiphytic orchids do best as hanging plants — it must remind them of home. At the base of their stems, many orchids have thick, fleshy, swollen parts, called *pseudo-bulbs,* which store food and water for periods of drought. Orchids need heat, humidity, and light. Because orchids come from tropical areas where the days are ten to fourteen hours long, place them where they will receive plenty of light. If necessary during the winter, supply artificial light to lengthen their day. Some gardeners attach orchid plants to pole lamps, which can be turned on in the evening. Consider purchasing special grow lights, which supply a natural spectrum of light; these fit into standard fixtures. Watch out for hot sunlight. Orchids are used to the shady canopy of a rain forest, and if you place your orchids in a window, too much light can damage the plants.

> **Good Orchids for Air Gardening**
> *Aerides crassifolium*
> *A. odorata*
> *Bifrenaria harrisoniae*
> *Brassa maculata*
> *Brassavola digbyana*
> *Brassavola glauca*
> *Bulbophyllum lobbii*

Watering air-grown orchids is easy. Mist them once a day, keep them in a humid atmosphere, and stand back to watch them grow! Orchids suffer more from overwatering than from a lack of water, so don't worry if you miss a day or two.

A proper balance of warmth and humidity is essential for successful orchid cultivation. Follow this rule of thumb: The higher the temperature, the higher the humidity should be. If your house is extra warm, therefore, plan on misting more frequently than usual. Increase humidity by hanging your plants just above a tray of wet gravel or keep them in a naturally humid room, like the kitchen or bathroom. When you boil water for tea, your orchids benefit from the steam, or a hot shower in the bathroom will surround orchids with a warm mist.

Orchids need to be fed only when they are actively growing, usually during the summertime. Keep fertilizer solutions light, and give plants a rest right after they bloom.

Ferns. Ferns are decorative, undemanding air plants. *Davallias* like to have their "feet" hanging out. *Platyceriums*

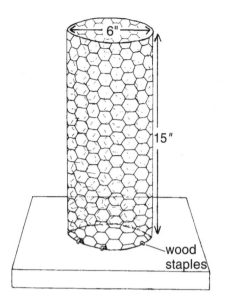

6"

15"

wood
staples

▲ *To make a column for air-grown fern, form a cylinder of chicken wire and staple it to a wooden base. Fill with planting material.*

Good Ferns for Air Gardens

Adder's or wall fern *(Polypodium vulgare)*

Ball fern *(Davallia trichomanoides)*

Bear's-foot fern *(Humata tyermannii)*

Carrot fern *(Davallia spp.)*

Elk's-horn fern *(Platycerium hillii)*

Maidenhair fern *(Adiantum pedatum)*

Rabbit's-foot fern *(Davallia fejeensis)*

Resurrection fern *(Polypodium polypodioides)*

Squirrel's-foot fern *(Davallia mariesii)*

Staghorn fern *(Platycerium bifurcatum)*

Walking fern *(Adiantum caudatum)*

grow best on a slab. Even the difficult maidenhair fern *(Adiantum pedatum)*, if grown in a humid environment, will happily live in the pocket of a rock; because they don't like to have water sprayed directly on their fronds, a terrarium or humid garden room is the best place to grow these. *Polypodiums* rarely succeed when planted in soil, but if grown in osmunda or on tree bark, they thrive.

A fern column, created by packing a wire-mesh tube with peat moss, shredded bark, or potting soil, is an interesting way to grow these plants with very little soil and water. It takes some patience to get started, but it's not hard. Form a piece of chicken wire into a 5- to 6-inch-diameter tube, and secure it to a platform to keep it upright. Make a solid, untippable base by sinking the tube in a containerful of plaster of paris, or by inserting the tube in Styrofoam or Sahara (a material used for dry floral arrangements), anchored to a heavy dish or container with florist tape. To contain the planting mix, wrap some damp sphagnum moss around the bottom part of the chicken wire. Using a funnel or an empty paper towel roll, pour a little crushed charcoal (available from indoor plant suppliers) into the bottom of the mesh tube; this helps drainage and keeps the soil mix sweet. Add moist peat moss or potting soil, to a depth of about 4 inches. Plant small ferns around the bottom of the fern column by inserting them through the sphagnum-covered wire and burying their roots in the soil mix. Continue to add sphagnum, potting soil, and ferns up the length of the column until it is filled. Mist the finished fern column thoroughly. To care for your ferns, water through the top of the column once in awhile, and mist daily. For a no-maintenance fern garden, place your column under a glass dome. Although not precisely an air garden, the fern column is a fun way to grow ferns.

Cactus. You might think that all cactus plants need to grow in sandy soil, but Christmas cactus and Easter cactus are epiphytes, and a number of cactuslike plants grow on supports rather than in pots. Don't pass up *Epiphyllum* — it has beautiful flowers. Cactus's needs are similar to orchid's: proper moisture, good humidity, and bright light.

Philodendrons. Even some philodendrons can be treated as air plants. Give their aerial roots good support on a bark slab or pole, and treat them like other epiphytic plants. Suitable plants include *Philodendron andreanum* (black-gold), *P. bipinnatifidum*, *P. cordatum* (heart-leaf), and *P. imperialis.*

Good Cacti for Air Gardens
Christmas cactus *(Schlumbergera bridgesii)*
Easter cactus *(Rhipsalidopsis gaertneri)*
Rattail cactus *(Aporocactus flagelliformis)*
Red orchid cactus *(Epiphyllum ackermannii)*
Spice cactus *(Hatiora salicornioides)*

THE SIT-DOWN GARDEN

Whether you use a wheelchair or are interested in finding ways to garden sitting down, there are any number of creative gardening projects you can enjoy.

Gardens Overhead

Hanging plants are perfect for sit-down gardening. Suspend the plants at eye level or hang them higher and use a pulley system to bring them within reach.

Supports for Hanging Plants Outdoors
★ A sturdy A-frame made of weather-resistant cedar or redwood
★ A child's swing set, with the swings removed
★ Commercially available hangers attached to a wall or a fence

▲ *Rig up a pulley system so that you can lower your hanging plants for easy maintenance.*

Plants for Hanging

Asparagus fern *(Asparagus setaceus 'Sprengeri')*

Baby's-tears *(Soleirolia soleirolii)*

Burro's tail *(Sedum morganianum)*

English ivy *(Hedera helix)*

Herbs (various)

Ivy geranium *(Pelargonium peltatum)*

Petunia *(Petunia spp.)*

Rosary vine *(Ceropegia woodii)*

Wandering Jew (bronze) *(Zebrina pendula purpusii)*

Plastic, clay, wood, and wire containers make fine hanging baskets. Plastic and moss-covered wire baskets are lighter than wood or clay. Some unusual containers for hanging plants include old birdcages, coconut shells, and pieces of driftwood. See pages 49-51 for more information on plant containers.

Hanging containers need more protection from the sun and wind than containers that are on the ground. Double-potting and other insulating techniques, such as lining a pot with moss, protect the suspended plants from heat and reduce evaporation. A moisture-retentive potting mix is suitable for most hanging plants, except cacti. Garden soil is too heavy and not porous enough for hanging containers, so stick with the commercial mixes for the best results. Fill the container to 1 inch from the top — no closer, to be assured of some watering room.

Hanging baskets require more watering than most container plants. An extension device attached to your hose will make overhead watering easier. An automatic drip irrigation system is a very attractive option (see pages 51-52). If possible, remove the plants from their hangers once a month, and plunge them in large containers of water to soak.

Because frequent watering washes nutrients out of the containers, keep plants growing vigorously by fertilizing them on a regular basis.

Wall Gardens: Espalier and Other Vertical Gardening Techniques

Even in the smallest spaces you can garden vertically. Not only do vertical gardens conserve space, but they bring your garden within reach. Staking, trellising, caging, and espalier are all good ways to create vertical gardens.

Espalier. Espalier not only saves space, it makes fruit growing easier. Fruit yields are high, trees begin bearing early, and fruits mature quickly (with less foliage, each fruit receives plenty of light). In addition, pruning, picking, and pest control are simplified, because everything is within easy reach.

Apples and pears are the easiest fruit trees for espalier. For best results, start with a young tree. Espaliers don't always have to be planted against a wall, but they do need a sturdy trellis or wire support. Build the trellis or wire support before you plant the tree. Espaliered trees can be grown even in containers, as long as a stout support is provided. Container-grown espaliers are easiest for sit-down gardening, because you can reach the plant from all sides.

There are several traditional training styles. A single straight branch, run vertically, horizontally, or at an angle, is called a *cordon*; for best fruiting and easy care, many growers choose the angled cordon. Another popular espalier shape has a main stem with four horizontal branches; this shape fits nicely against a wall or in a container (see drawings, at right).

To start the training process for the latter style, cut the main leader to the height of

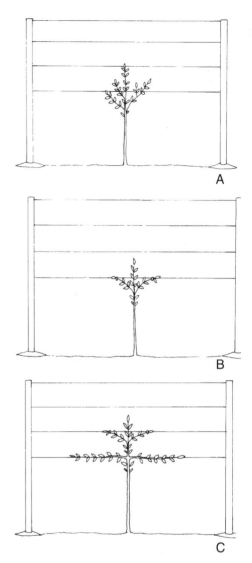

▲ *To train a single-stem cordon espalier, (A) plant tree midway between concrete-based posts in front of tautly stretched wires; (B) with strips of cloth, tie two side shoots to the lowest wire, leaving a third shoot to grow as the trunk; and (C) during the second spring of growth, train two more side shoots to the second wire, leaving a shoot to continue trunk growth.*

▲ *A single-stem cordon espalier grown against a wall.*

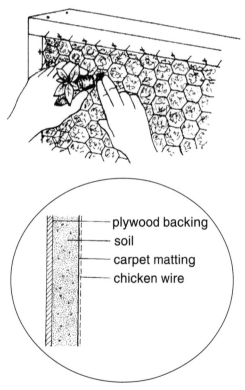

- plywood backing
- soil
- carpet matting
- chicken wire

▲ *To create a wall garden, plant seedlings into the soil contained between the backing and the chicken wire.*

the first cordon, or arm. This will stimulate side shoots that you can train horizontally along the trellis or wires. Allow a center shoot to grow to the height of the next horizontal support, and pinch it off. Again, allow side shoots to develop, and train one along each horizontal support. Your tree now has a center trunk and four arms. Continue to pinch off excess shoots. Allow the lateral arms to grow until they have reached the length desired, at which time pinch the growing tips. Fruiting spurs will eventually grow off these main stems.

Wall gardening. Another kind of wall garden is suitable for such plants as lettuce, herbs, strawberries, impatiens, and petunias. Fill a shallow box with soil. Cover the soil with a sheet of carpet matting, plastic, or sphagnum moss, and fasten chicken wire or lattice over the top to keep it all together. Cut plant-sized holes in the matting or plastic, and insert seedlings into the box. Stand the box on end, creating a wall of plants. For easiest watering, install drip irrigation before you plant, or situate it near a sprinkler.

Caging and trellising. Sweet peas and other climbing plants are perfect for your sit-down garden. Simply place a tomato cage in a container, secure it with stakes so it doesn't tip over, and sow your seeds. Other vertical supports for container-grown plants include stakes and twine, bamboo poles, or even old branches or dried brush. For more information, see pages 150-151.

Miniature Fruits and Vegetables

Pint-sized plants are perfect for an edible sit-down garden. There are two types of diminutive plants — dwarf plants and midgets. *Dwarf plants* are smaller than average, but they produce normal-sized fruits and vegetables. *Midgets* are not only very small plants but they also produce extra-small fruits and vegetables. Remember: The size of a plant determines the size of its yield; smaller plants, with fewer leaves and stems, will produce fewer fruits. In addition, fewer leaves producing sugars often result in poorer quality fruit. Dwarf and midget plants aren't for everyone.

Tiny vegetables will grow in containers on a table top, in raised beds, or in hanging baskets. These plants can be grown closer together than standard-sized plants. For instance, a bushel basket holds twelve wee lettuce plants or four midget tomatoes; dwarf corn, which grows only 3–4 feet high, will flourish in a 4-foot-square raised bed; one large strawberry jar can hold all your salad plants — midget tomatoes, spinach, lettuce, and some chives in the pockets, and miniature carrots and some radishes in the top.

How about sitting right next to your apple tree to harvest it? Dwarf trees are easy to prune, spray, thin, and harvest, and they often produce a crop much earlier than standard trees. Dwarf fruit trees can grow in pots no larger than a half-barrel. Containers that can be taken apart are the most practical, because container-grown trees must be removed from their pots every two to three years for root-pruning. If you're constructing your own containers, make them easy to break down by attaching the sides with screws instead of nails.

Container-grown fruit trees should be grown in a rich humus that drains well. Enrich commercial mixes with compost, if possible. Water and fertilize dwarf fruit trees on a regular schedule. Half-strength fertilizer, applied every two weeks, makes up for nutrients that are leached out of the soil by frequent watering. Once every three months, water the container heavily to wash out fertilizer salts and build-up. Add a top

Vegetables in a Pot

ALL-AMERICA SELECTIONS

You can also grow full-size vegetable plants, such as eggplant, bush beans, peas, and peppers, in containers. Bush cucumbers, squash, and tomatoes require containers that are at least 18 inches in diameter. Water well and fertilize regularly.

◀ *Cucumber F$_1$ 'Salad Bush'*

mulch of stones, compost, or bark to reduce evaporation and watering chores. Consult a garden encyclopedia for specific pruning recommendations for each type of fruit grown.

Not all dwarf fruit trees are self-fertile, so find out if the plant you choose needs a "buddy" to produce fruit.

Protect dwarf fruit trees from the birds by throwing netting or row cover over the tops of them after the blossoms have been pollinated.

The Bulb Garden

One gardener I know of plants only bulbs for year-round color. No stem cutting, root pruning, or seed-starting for this gardener — his plants increase without his help. Now and then he digs up a few in order to separate the bulbs and give them more room. He plants the extras in containers for gift-giving. A long-time gardener, my friend tells me he began growing bulbs when he started to have trouble seeing and handling tiny seeds. He grows bulbs indoors and out, in containers and in the ground. Bulb growing is so easy and satisfying that he won't waste his time with seed-grown plants anymore.

There are bulbs to suit every garden situation — some that grow in shade, others in the sun; some in dry conditions, others in wet. If the bulbs you like do not grow well in your climate, it's easy enough to give them what they need: If you live in a warm climate, send your winter-loving bulbs to the refrigerator for a chilly vacation; if you live where winters are cold, grow tender, heat-loving bulbs in the house.

Hardy Bulbs

Crocus, daffodils, hyacinths, tulips, muscari, Dutch iris, and true lilies are among the most familiar bulbs. These are known as hardy bulbs because they can stay safely in the ground all winter.

Bulbs are the storage units of the plants-to-be. Inside that compact unit are the embryonic leaves, stems, flowers, and ample nutrients to sustain a full-grown plant. Because of this self-sufficiency, most bulbs bloom the first season, even when planted in poor growing conditions; they have stored up the necessary elements during their last growing season. To eliminate the need for plant maintenance, some gardeners prefer to buy new bulbs each year, but if hardy bulbs are given proper care and sufficient food, they will grow and thrive in your garden year after year.

As soon as bulbs are planted, they form roots that will generate food to sustain the plant during the next season. When spring arrives, new shoots come up and flowers bloom, all fed by the energy stored in the bulb. After blooming, the leaves take in light from the sun and the roots absorb nutrients from the soil to replenish the bulb for next year's bloom. During this same period, bulblets are formed; if you wish, you

Tiered Container Gardeners
Make an impressive display of bulbs by piling bowl-shaped containers on top of each other, starting with the largest container at the bottom and working up to the smallest size.

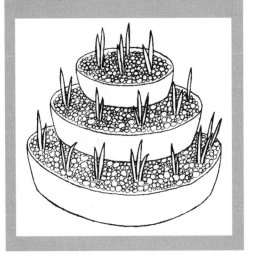

can separate these from the mother plant and use them to grow new plants. When the foliage dies back, the bulb has completed its cycle and will remain dormant until the next flowering season.

When, Where, and How to Plant Bulbs

Hardy bulbs should be planted in late summer or early fall, when they will have enough time before winter to establish a good root system. Although bulbs can also be planted in spring, as soon as the soil can be worked, spring-planted bulbs don't have as much time to establish a good root system, and they may not be able to store enough food for a good bloom in the following season. Most stores and mail-order sources offer bulbs in the fall. Plant them as soon as you get them. If you must store them for a short period of time, keep them in a cool, dry place.

Bulbs are not finicky about where they grow, but they do require well-drained soil. Use raised beds or containers if your soil remains too wet.

Most bulbs thrive in full sun, but they will tolerate partial shade as long as they get five to six hours of strong light every day. Grape hyacinths, Siberian squill, winter aconite, wood hyacinths, snowdrops, and crocuses will tolerate filtered sunlight. Shade-loving bulbs include true lilies, lilies-of-the-valley, and begonias.

Good soil preparation is important to keep a healthy bed of bulbs producing blooms every year. In addition to a well-drained location, bulbs grow best in a light soil that is rich in humus. Tulips do best in soil that is not overly rich. Add peat moss, compost, or commercial amendments to loosen and improve poor soil. Bonemeal is a good source of phosphorus for bulbs; it helps them produce good root systems. Bulbs prefer a soil with a neutral pH. If your soil is acid, add limestone or compost to modify it.

In most cases, cover bulbs with soil to a depth three times their diameter. There are exceptions to this rule, however, and it's a good idea to check a garden catalog or encyclopedia for specific recommended planting depths. In very cold climates, delay too-early blooming by planting bulbs deeper than suggested.

To create a clump of bulbs, dig a hole large enough to hold a handful or more of bulbs. Condition the soil that you remove from the hole. Place the bulbs in the bottom of the hole, spacing them according to recommendations for their size. Backfill the hole, and firm the soil to eliminate air pockets. This technique works best with bulbs that require identical planting depth and care. Another method is to make individual holes with a trowel or special bulb-planting tool and plant the bulbs one by one.

Naturalized bulbs are those grouped to look accidentally or informally arranged, as they would grow in nature. This technique is sometimes referred to as creating a *drift*. To naturalize, take a handful of bulbs and cast them across the planting area. Then, dig holes individually, and plant the bulbs where they fell. Daffodils, crocuses, wood hyacinths, and snowdrops are favorite bulbs to plant in this manner. These bulbs will thrive and increase in the same area for many years without special care. Overplant the area with grass, ground covers, trailing plants, or short annuals to hide the unattractive foliage after the blooms have passed.

After planting, water the bulbs to settle the soil. Continue to water occasionally to encourage root formation.

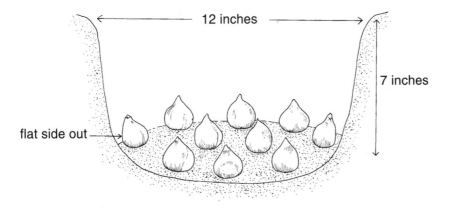

◀ *To plant a clump of bulbs, dig a hole wide enough to hold a handful of bulbs; place the bulbs, flat side out, at a depth about three times their diameter; and backfill with improved soil.*

Maintenance

Bulbs are some of the most carefree plants you can grow. All they need, once planted, is adequate moisture, fertilizer once a year, and an occasional dividing to keep them from becoming overcrowded.

Apply fertilizer in early spring, before the plants have bloomed. Scatter the fertilizer on top of the soil, or use a foliar feed, such as a seaweed solution, that is high in phosphorus.

After the bulbs have bloomed, remove the spent flower heads and allow the leaves to mature. When the leaves are yellowed and withered — but not before, because the bulb is storing energy for next year's bloom — you can cut them off at the base.

If the flowers look small and sparse, your bulbs have outgrown their bed. Divide hardy bulbs right after the foliage has matured. Dig up the clump, using a garden fork to avoid injuring the bulbs. Break the clump apart and replant the larger bulbs, giving them more room to grow. This is a good time to add soil amendments or slow-acting fertilizer, such as bonemeal. The smaller bulblets can be separated from the larger bulbs and planted in an inconspicuous place until they mature enough to bloom, usually in a year or two.

Growing Bulbs in Containers

Because the root systems of bulbs are not extensive, they make good subjects for container gardening. If you intend to discard the bulbs after blooming, fill the container with peat moss, sand, vermiculite, or gravel. Plant bulbs that you plan to carry over from season to season in rich, well-drained soil, and give them more room to grow. Water them regularly, and care for them as you would other container plants. After blooming, and while the leaves are maturing, move the container to an out-of-the-way place where the leaves will receive proper light and moisture, but where, in their unattractive state, they will be hidden from view.

Forcing Bulbs Indoors

Some bulbs can be forced to bloom ahead of their normal schedules. In the wintertime, treat yourself to the fresh fragrance, bright color, and beautiful blooms of spring and summer.

The secret to success in tricking bulbs to bloom out of season is a pot full of roots. The roots must be developed before any other growth takes place. Spring-flowering bulbs can be potted up from September to December. Forcing usually takes about twelve weeks. By planting different kinds of bulbs, with different natural bloom times, you can have indoor color from late December through April. Use only top-grade, fully mature bulbs for forcing.

Any container can be used to force blooms, but clay pots, which allow for good drainage, are preferred. They should be at least twice the depth of the bulb. A layer of gravel or perlite in the bottom of the container ensures good drainage. Use a loose soil mixture, and bury the bulbs topside up with the bulb tips just below the rim of the pot. Water the pot thoroughly, and let the excess water drain out. Label each pot and either wrap it in moist newspaper or put it in a plastic bag so it retains moisture.

▲ *To force container-grown bulbs, place a layer of gravel in the bottom of a clay pot. Bury bulbs with their tips just exposed in a loose soil mix.*

To start the forcing process, store the planted pots in a cool, dark place, such as an unheated garage, cold frame, root cellar, or refrigerator. A temperature of 40°–50°F is best. Check the plants occasionally, and water them only if the soil has dried out. After eight to twelve weeks of cold temperatures, the bulbs should have developed a good root mass which may be poking out of the bottom of the container. By now, the tops have probably sprouted, and it's time to move the bulbs into a warmer place, to encourage more active growth.

Gradually move the plants into a warmer area and

brighter light. If exposed to very bright light too soon, the flower stalks will be stunted. Water the pots as necessary to maintain moisture. Move them to a sunnier spot when the flower buds have developed. Once the flowers open, prolong their bloom by keeping them in a cool place out of direct sunlight. After blooming, cut off the flowers and move the pot outdoors to a sunny spot. If you like, plant the bulbs in the garden after the foliage withers. Do not try to force the same bulbs again next year; they will need a season or two to recover.

Hyacinth, crocus, and narcissus bulbs can be forced in water. Store the bulbs in the refrigerator until about six to eight weeks before you want them to bloom. Fill an attractive vase, jar, or bowl with gravel and water, and set the bulbs on top of it. If necessary, stabilize the bulbs with florist's tape, or pour just enough gravel around them to keep them from tipping out of the container. Place the container in a cool (50°–60°F), dark place until you see good root development. When the sprouts are about 2 or 3 inches high, move the bulbs into bright light and then eventually into direct sunlight. Maintain the water level. Discard these water-grown bulbs after blooming; they rarely recover.

Tender bulbs, such as amaryllis, freesia, ranunculus, and calla lilies can be grown indoors in colder climates. Tender bulbs need good soil and frequent watering during their period of active growth. To reduce watering chores, group individual pots in a larger container filled with moist peat moss.

A GARDEN THAT LASTS FOREVER

When you have dried flowers on hand, you can enjoy your garden year-round. Easy to grow and a snap to prepare, they can be made into decorative wreaths, garlands, and baskets that are welcome gifts. The cost is minimal and so is the effort. With a little planning, anyone can have a garden that lasts forever.

What to Grow

Some of the most colorful everlastings are annuals that need little more than average soil and minimal care. There are varieties to suit all sorts of garden conditions — some grow well in cool, shady conditions; others thrive in hot, sunny areas. Scatter the large-seeded ones over the garden bed for a colorful cottage-garden effect. If your garden is small, tuck everlastings in among the vegetables or in containers. If you use perennials, which return year after year, and plants that self-sow, you won't have to reseed each year.

When choosing everlastings for your garden, pick the brightest flowers you can find, because sometimes colors fade as the plants dry. If you plant a variety of flower forms, you will have tall, fluffy, short, and twisted blooms for interesting arrangements. My favorites are larkspur, all the *Limoniums* (especially pink pokers), nigella, bachelor's-buttons, and baby's-breath. These are no-fail everlastings that should do well in any garden. Try different kinds to see what grows best for you.

How to Grow Everlastings

Nurseries and garden centers offer a surprising variety of everlastings. Look for statice, lavender, strawflowers, larkspur, nigella, celosia, salvia, and dusty miller. To obtain the most unusual dried flowers, grow your own plants from seeds. Many mail-order houses offer packets of mixed everlastings that are a real bargain. This is a good way to find out which plants you like best, without having to buy more costly individual selections.

Because some everlastings need long growing periods to develop interesting seed heads and pods, start seeds indoors to get a jump on the season. (See pages 97-105 for information about starting seeds indoors.) When it is time to transplant seedlings to the garden, harden them off by exposing them to the outdoors slowly. Transplant on a cloudy day or use lath or shade cloth to protect the plants on their first

COMMON NAME	BOTANIC NAME	COLOR	ZONES*/PLANT TYPE
The Easiest			
Baby's-breath	*Gypsophila paniculata*	Pink, white	2
Bachelor's-button	*Centaurea cyanus*	Blue, pink	HA
Chives	*Allium schoenoprasum*	Pink, purple	2
Delphinium	*Delphinium* spp.	Blue, pink, white	4–7
Globe amaranth	*Gomphrena globosa*	Pink, purple, white	HHA
Larkspur	*Consolida regalis*	Blue, pink, white	HHA
Love-in-a-mist	*Nigella damascena*	Blue, pink	HA
Pink poker	*Limonium suworowii*	Pink	HHA
Starflower	*Scabiosa stellata*	Blue	HA
Statice	*Limonium sinuatum*	Blue, purple, white, yellow	HA
Strawflower	*Helichrysum bracteatum*	All except blue	HHA
Plants for Dry, Shady Places			
Bergenia	*Bergenia*	Pink, white	2
Honesty	*Lunaria annua*	Silvery seed head	HB
Pearly everlasting	*Anaphalis margaritacea*	White	3
St.-John's-wort	*Hypericum* spp.	Yellow	3–7
Yarrow	*Achillea filipendulina*	Pink, yellow, white	2
Plants for Moist, Shady Places			
Foxglove	*Digitalis purpurea*	Pink, white	4
Goldenrod	*Solidago* spp.	Yellow	4
Meadowrue	*Thalictrum* spp.	Gray-green leaves, pink flowers	2–5
Plants for Dry, Sunny Places			
Acroclinium, sunray	*Helipterum* spp.	Pink, yellow, white	HHA
Baby's-breath	*Gypsophila paniculata*	Pink, white	2
Clary sage	*Salvia sclarea*	Pink, red, white	HA
Cockscomb	*Celosia cristata*	Pink, purple, yellow	HHA
Dusty miller	*Artemisia stellerana*	Yellow flowers, white stems	2
Lavender	*Lavandula angustifolia*	Purple	5
Sea holly	*Eryngium maritima*	Blue	5
Yarrow	*Achillea filipendulina*	Pink, yellow, white	HP/2

COMMON NAME	BOTANIC NAME	COLOR	ZONES*/PLANT TYPE
Plants for Wet, Sunny Places			
Beebalm	*Monarda didyma*	Pink, red	4
False goat's-beard	*Astilbe biternata*	Pink, red	5
Forget-me-not	*Myosotis sylvatica*	Blue	HA
Foxglove	*Digitalis purpurea*	Pink, purple, white	4
Loosestrife	*Lythrum alatum*	Rose	3
Herbs That Dry Well			
Bay leaves	*Lauris nobilis*	Leaves	7
Chives	*Allium schoenoprasum*	Flowers, seed heads	2
Feverfew	*Chrysanthemum parthenium*	Flowers	5
Lamb's-ears	*Stachys byzantina*	Leaves	5
Lavender	*Lavandula angustifolia*	Flowers	5
Rosemary	*Rosmarinus officinalis*	Leaves, flowers	8
Rue	*Ruta graveolens*	Seed heads	4
Sage	*Salvia officinalis*	Leaves, flowers	4
Sweet marjoram	*Origanum majorana*	Flowers	9
Tansy	*Tanacetum vulgare*	Flower heads	4
Thyme	*Thymus vulgaris*	Leaves	4
Wormwood	*Artemisia absinthium*	Leaves	4
Yarrow	*Achillea* spp.	Flower heads	HP

PLANT TYPE: HA = Hardy Annual, HHA = Half-hardy Annual, HP = Hardy Perennial, HHP = Half-hardy Perennial, HB = Hardy Biennial

* Chart shows coldest hardiness zone tolerated by a species. Where a specific species is not named on the chart, look for a species appropriate to the hardiness range indicated.

couple days out in the garden. Water them carefully and don't let them dry out for the first ten days. After that, they should be established and give you no trouble.

Harvesting

Harvest plants before full bloom to preserve the best shape and color; blossoms begin to fade as soon as they are fully opened. I always seem to wait too long because I want to see the flower at its best. Blossoms may continue to open for a few hours or even a day after they are picked, and full bloom is often reached when the plant is hanging upside down in the garage. Harvest in the late morning when the plants are dry and the flowers are still fresh. After cutting, don't leave them out in the sun where they can quickly lose shape and color.

Air Drying Plants

Plants are easy to handle when they are fresh, but they become brittle when dry and should be separated and prepared while they are still flexible. Tie them in color-coordinated bunches for convenient grab-off-the-rafters bouquets.

The easiest way to dry everlastings is to hang them, upside down (so their stems will dry straight), in a well-ventilated, dark place. To prepare them for hanging, strip off the excess leaves. Gather the stems in bunches small enough to allow good air circulation. Tie the stems firmly because as the plants dry, they shrink and the bunches may fall apart if tied too loosely. Store the drying flowers out of traffic areas; fragile blossoms shatter if they're knocked around too much. Hang the bunches from beams or joists, or use clothespins to hang them on lines or folding clothes racks. You can also lay them on old window screens, or stand them upright in cans or baskets. If you dry them right side up, place the bunches in cardboard cylinders (such as paper towel tubes) to keep the stems straight. Weight the container, so it doesn't tip over.

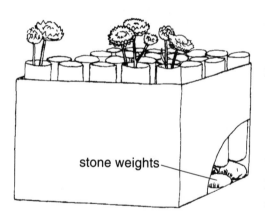

stone weights

▲ *You can dry flowers standing up if you place them in cardboard cylinders to keep their stems straight.*

To avoid mildew and decay, provide good air circulation. If you want them for kitchen decoration, be sure they are thoroughly dry before hanging them where steam and cooking oils will cling to the blossoms, delay drying, and dirty the plants. To preserve colors, dry plants in a dark place.

The stems of some flowers, such as hollyhocks and strawflowers, are short or don't dry well. For these plants, it's better to remove the stems and insert florist's wire into the back of the flower while it's still fresh; during drying the flower will shrink around the wire and hold it in place. When it's dry, add a touch of glue for more security.

Drying with Desiccants

Silica gel, cornmeal, perlite, sand, and borax can be used to dehydrate blossoms.

Silica gel. Although expensive, silica gel is the best material for preserving shape and color. It is recommended for roses, camellias, delphiniums, dahlias, hellebores, and daffodils, whose blossoms tend to lose their form and color when air-dried. Put a layer of silica gel in the bottom of a box, place blossoms face up, and gently sprinkle more silica over the blossoms to cover them. Seal the box tightly to keep out moisture. Dehydration takes anywhere from a few days to a few weeks. Test the blossoms occasionally; when they feel crisp, they're dry and ready to use.

Cornmeal and borax. Combine ten parts of white cornmeal to three parts borax and mix thoroughly. This mixture can be used much like silica gel.

Sand and borax. Mix one part sand to three parts borax. Although heavy, this mixture can be used instead of cornmeal and borax to dry sturdy flowers.

Perlite. Perlite is a fast-acting and inexpensive drying medium. Get very fine-textured perlite or crush it into small grains. Perlite is sometimes difficult to remove completely after the plants are dry. A soft brush or a hairdryer set at "low" may overcome this problem.

▲ *Lay flowers on silica gel, gently sift more silica over them until they are covered, and then cover the container tightly.*

Drying by Microwave

If you're in a hurry, use silica in a microwave oven to dry flowers. The heat of the microwave evaporates moisture in the plant material and then the moisture is absorbed by the silica.

Prepare the flowers in the same way as for silica drying. Put an inch or two of silica gel in the bottom of a microwave container, place the plant material on top, and sprinkle silica in between all the petals until the blossom is covered. Then add another 1½ inches of silica on top. Put the *uncovered* container in the microwave. Use a low setting of 200–300 watts for drying. Drying time takes from 2½ to 6 minutes, depending on how much silica is used and how many blossoms are in the container. As a rule of thumb, ½ pound of silica with flowers takes 2 to 2½ minutes, 2 pounds of silica takes 5–6 minutes and 3½ pounds takes about 6–7 minutes. After microwaving, let the plants cool for 10–30 minutes to evaporate the moisture fully. Cover the container when you take it out of the oven to keep atmospheric moisture out. Remove silica by shaking the flowers gently or touching them with a paintbrush. Store your dried flowers as described below. Microwave drying doesn't work for all flowers, so experiment.

Storing Dried Flowers

After your plants are dried, lay them carefully in labelled boxes or hang them upside down in a paper bag to keep them clean. If you'll be using them regularly, leave them hanging uncovered in a relatively dust-free place.

Arranging Everlastings

Containers. Use ornamental bowls, baskets, terra-cotta pots, or even paper bags for interesting dried arrangements. Earth-tone or neutral-colored containers look best with most dried plant material, but a bright-colored container filled with wheat grasses and seed pods is charming, too. Try different combinations, and since you don't have to worry about water or seepage, many unusual containers can be used.

Anchoring Materials. Because dried plant material is lightweight, it needs something to keep the stems upright and in position. Here are some suggestions:

Styrofoam is inexpensive and easy to find. Since it is also quite light, fix it to the bottom of the container with tape or florist's clay. To prevent the brittle stems from breaking, poke holes in the Styrofoam with a narrow stick or nail before inserting the dried material. Styrofoam comes in many shapes. Make attractive hanging arrangements with balls, circles, hearts, or cones.

Sahara is an earth-colored material available in hobby shops or florist-supply houses. Similar to Oasis, which can be moistened and used in fresh floral arrangements, Sahara is better suited to dried materials. As with Styrofoam, wedge or anchor it into the bottom of a container to keep it in place. Most stems can be poked directly into Sahara, since it is softer than Styrofoam, but you still may have to predrill holes for especially brittle stems.

A kenzan (Japanese) or pinholder is a flower-arranging device that keeps dried materials in place. Kenzans and pinholders come in many shapes and sizes; some are weighted to keep them stable. Heavy pinholders work well in shallow containers.

Marbles, sphagnum moss and even crumpled paper keep dried materials upright and in position. Camouflage unsightly base material with Spanish or sphagnum moss, straw, or wood excelsior. For low-cost fillers, save packing material and

Basic Tools for Arranging Dried Flowers

★ *Wire cutters* — for cutting artificial stems and wires that hold anchoring materials

★ *Bread knife* — for cutting Styrofoam and Sahara

★ *Spool wire or fishing line* — for anchoring background materials on wreaths and garlands

★ *Fast-drying glue* or *glue gun* — for quickly attaching plant material on wreaths, garlands, hanging balls, and swaths

★ *Floral tape* — for wrapping wire stems

★ *Scissors* — for clipping and shaping plant materials

★ *Florist pins or hair pins* — for anchoring materials to wreaths and other forms

★ *Florist's clay* — for fixing Styrofoam or Sahara to the bottom of a container

the "grass" from Easter baskets.

Putting it all together. Choose a color theme, and then add a spot of contrasting color to brighten the arrangement. Too many different colors, unless combined well, can look busy. Use pinks, blues, and purples for a cool theme or yellows, reds, and browns for a warm theme.

Because the blossoms are fragile and the stems break easily, dried plants are messy to work with. Work outside or spread a drop cloth under your work area for easy clean up.

What to Make

★ Weave dried flowers into the garlic braids or pepper strings for a special gift.

★ Create a hanging herb or flower ball on a Styrofoam base.

★ Glue bright-colored blossoms to basket handles and rims, and fill baskets with pretty dishtowels for a housewarming gift.

★ Make everlasting May baskets, and fill them with home-baked muffins.

★ Make a garland with a thick cotton rope as a base (rope is available at fabric or hobby stores). Cover the rope with raffia, or dye it a natural color. Use fishing line and hot glue to attach dried plant materials to the rope. For a Victorian look, drape the garland over a doorway or window.

★ Make a framed flower picture by gluing plant material to a dark-colored velvet or felt background. Place it in a frame deep enough to cover the arrangement with glass to protect it from dust.

★ Make a wreath on a Styrofoam, cardboard, or straw form, or tuck dried plants into a twisted vine wreath. Cover the form with moss or raffia, and glue, wire, or pin dried plants into place until the form is completely covered. Use large, colorful dried blossoms, such as statice or yarrow, as accents. White and pink- or yellow-flowered wreaths are sweet for a nursery. Bright-colored wreaths welcome guests in an entry hall, and dried herb wreaths with red berries are perfect for Christmas giving.

★ Use dried-flower trees as decorations during the winter season when fresh flowers are scarce. Tree forms made of twisted willow branches give an Oriental effect.

★ Arrange dried plant material on a plate or circle form to make a wreath around a candle.

★ For weddings, make dried-flower corsages, coronets, and bouquets. These last long after the wedding is over and make wonderful keepsakes.

★ In glass bowls or covered glass containers, make "terrariums" that never need water or replanting — these will bring grandmother's parlor to mind.

★ Create wall plaques on Styrofoam bases covered with mosses and stemless blossoms. Fill the gaps so that the background material doesn't show. Add some lavender or other scented material for a pleasant air-freshener in the bathroom.

▲ *Arrange a dried-flower wreath around the base of a candle.*

THE HERB GARDEN

If there is magic anywhere in the garden (and I believe there is), you'll surely find it in the herb patch. On a hot summer day, the very air around these aromatic plants shimmers with the scent of potent oils. It's no wonder that ancient healers looked to herbs for antidotes and elixirs. Grow these plants that were once used in ceremonies and religious rites in your own "magic garden."

Most herbs prefer a sunny location and well-drained, fertile soil. A raised bed or a rock garden is excellent for herbs. Don't despair if you can't find the perfect spot. Several herbs tolerate conditions that are not ideal, and some even grow where other plants "fear to tread." Many gardeners feel that less-than-perfect conditions actually improve herbal flavor and aroma. Perhaps it is as true in the herb garden as it is in life that a little adversity builds character.

Herbs grow best in soil that has a slightly acid or neutral pH. If your soil needs improvement, add compost or other organic material to modify the pH, increase the soil nutrients, and improve the texture. The best herb garden I ever had grew where I used to toss the kitchen scraps, in a lazyman's version of sheet composting.

Because herbs are often used to add zest to food, it's ideal to situate your herb garden near the kitchen. It's so much easier to lean out the back door for a snippet of parsley or sage than to go tromping out to the back forty for it. If you don't have a garden bed close by, plant herbs in containers, hanging baskets, strawberry jars, wall gardens (see page 224) — even a windowbox will do. Most herbs don't mind cramped quarters, and they can be trimmed radically to keep them within bounds. In fact, they are good subjects for standards or bonsai.

Some herbs, including basil, coriander, dill, feverfew, and parsley, are easily grown from seed. A few, such as French tarragon, do not come true from seed and must be started from stem cuttings or division in order to preserve their distinct flavor. Mint, pennyroyal, and horseradish can be grown from root cuttings. They will, in fact, grow anywhere a little bit of root is dropped and can quickly wander right out of their proper growing place.

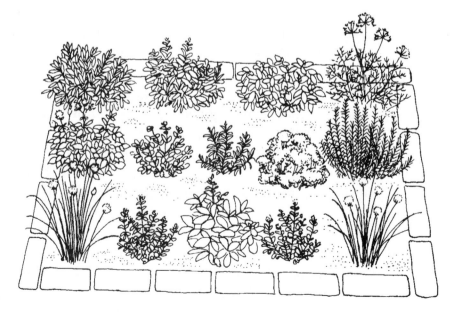

▶ *A small kitchen herb garden: (from left to right) (back) sage, peppermint, marjoram, dill; (middle) oregano, thyme, tarragon, parsley, rosemary; (front) chives, thyme, basil, thyme, chives*

If you buy nursery-grown plants, you can be sure of the variety and flavor. Plant them in the garden at the proper time, and treat them as you would any new transplants.

Once the herbs have become established, most are hearty plants, resistant to disease and insect pests. The few problems that do occur in the herb garden are usually the result of drought or overwatering. Mint plants are subject to rust diseases and are often attacked when they are weakened by lack of adequate moisture. When drainage is poor or humidity is quite high, tarragon, marjoram, and oregano may fall victim to molds and fungus.

Ten Best Herbs for the Kitchen

Basil (*Ocimum basilicum*). Traditionally called the herb of love, basil is said to cause a young man to fall in love with any maiden who gives him a sprig. Basil is wonderful sprinkled over pasta with butter, in pesto, in stew, and, especially, in any tomato sauce.

Basil grows anywhere that tomatoes or beans grow. The richer the soil, the lusher the basil. Its flavor is strongest in plants that grow in full sun. Basil can be started indoors in containers or sown in the garden after the last frost. It tolerates transplanting well when quite young, but older transplants tend to be stunted and go to seed prematurely. For a long harvest, plant basil every three weeks. To preserve the best flavor, freeze basil by placing the clean, dry leaves on a cookie sheet and putting the sheet in the freezer. When the leaves are frozen, store them in jars in the freezer. The leaves turn gray and lose their texture when thawed, but the flavor is unimpaired and fine for soups, stews, and sauces. Although you can also easily hang and air dry basil, it will not be as tasty as fresh or frozen basil.

Bay (*Laurus nobilis*). Bay was so esteemed by the ancient Romans that it was used to make crowns and wreaths for heroes and poets. Luckily for the kitchen gardener, bay tolerates container-growing, although in its natural state it is a large tree. On my patio in southern California sits a bay

GROW AN HERB AS A STANDARD

A *standard* is a shrub or tree that has been trained to a single stem with a bushy head. It looks very much like a lollipop or a miniature tree. Bay, rosemary, geranium, sweet myrtle, santolina, lavender, and lemon verbena all can be grown as standards. To create a standard, start with a young plant or a well-established cutting. Choose a main upright stem and remove all others. Clip the leaves from the bottom of the stem and leave the growing tip. As the plant grows, pinch back all new lower leaves, shoots, and lateral branches. Keep it growing straight by tying it to a vertical support. When the main stem reaches the desired height, pinch off the growing tip to stop the plant's upward growth. Allow leaves to develop to round out the top, but keep the lower stem clean of growth.

plant that has been growing in the same pot for five years. It requires little pruning, probably because of its cramped roots, but it keeps on giving me wonderful bay leaves. Use bay in soups, stews, and sauces. Remember to remove it before serving the food, because the leaves are sharp and can damage a sensitive mouth or esophagus.

Chives (*Allium schoenoprasum*). Clumps of chives seem to last forever. These small members of the onion family are pretty enough to decorate the edge of a garden or sit on a windowsill. Start them from seeds or plant bulbs obtained from the nursery; divide the clumps to increase them. Use chives to flavor potatoes, cottage cheese, fish, pasta, and salad dressings, or mix them with chervil, parsley, and tarragon to make the classic French *fines herbes*. Chives freeze well, but lose a good deal of their flavor when dried.

Garlic (*Allium sativum*). Garlic couldn't be easier to grow. Buy some garlic bulbs at the nursery or even at the grocery store, separate the cloves, and push each one about

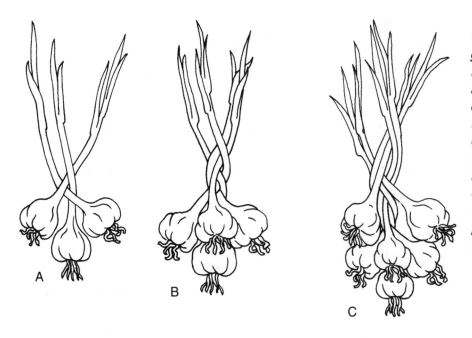

◄ *To make a garlic braid, begin to braid with three heads, as at A. Add a fourth head at the center and continue braiding (B). Add two more heads on the outside, as at C. Continue in this pattern until braid is desired length.*

1 inch into well-cultivated, humus-rich soil. Water occasionally, and about six months later, when the stalks start yellowing, harvest your home-grown garlic. Let the bulbs dry in the sun for about three days, then braid the tops together, and hang the braid in the kitchen for convenient garlic-grabbing. Or, store garlic in mesh bags or in baskets; just allow for good air circulation and keep the bulbs dry.

Oregano (*Origanum vulgare hirtum* or *O. vulgare* cv. Viride). Don't try to grow oregano from seed. Although many plants called oregano will grow nicely from seed, none of them is the culinary plant that gives us the right flavor for spaghetti sauces and meat dishes. Go to the nursery and pinch a leaf to see if it suits your taste. There are Greek, Mexican, Italian, and golden oreganos. Of Mediterranean origin, oregano is accustomed to mild winters. If your winter is harsh (zone 4 or colder), protect your oregano plants, or pot them and bring them inside for the winter. Give oregano a hot, dry place in the garden and it will flourish.

Parsley (*Petroselinum crispum*). Well-loved because of its flavor and its attractive, bright green leaves, parsley is another herb that was used by ancient officers to crown victo-

A Rosemary Ball

Rosemary makes a long-lasting herb ball for holiday gift-giving. Cut florist's foam (Oasis) into a ball shape, and wrap the ball with sphagnum moss. Wind fishing line around the moss to attach it firmly, and leave a long piece of line for hanging the finished decoration. Soak the ball in a pan of water for about one hour, then gently squeeze out the excess moisture. Poke rosemary cuttings into the ball, covering it all around. Decorate with a bright-colored ribbon, and hang the ball from the ceiling.

rious warriors. A tidy plant, parsley is especially suitable for a small herb garden. It is notoriously slow to germinate, and many a gardener gives up in disgust, only to find, a few weeks later, parsley volunteers popping up right next to the nursery-grown plant just planted. Parsley has a long season of harvest; start picking it as soon as it makes a few leaves. Leave the plants in place after they go to seed, and, with a little luck, the parsley will self-sow.

Rosemary (Rosmarinus officinalis). The scent of rosemary is cool and invigorating, almost a little piney. In the language of flowers, it is the herb of remembrance. In mild-winter areas, rosemary is nearly indestructible; I've never seen an insect or disease damage this plant. In cold-winter areas, keep rosemary in a pot and enjoy it indoors during the winter months. The blue blossoms and narrow, dark-green leaves make this a beautiful background plant for pink-flowered creeping thyme. Rosemary is found in large or dwarf plants, upright bushes or trailing plants. It can be started from stem cuttings. In the kitchen, sprinkle rosemary on potatoes, or use it to flavor poultry and meat, especially lamb.

Sage (Salvia spp.). The botanic name of this herb, *Salvia*, is derived from the Latin verb *salvere*, meaning *to heal*. Sage was supposed to give long life, help the nerves, and be good for the brain. The Chinese once valued this herb so highly that one pound of it was worth three pounds of tea in trade. Today, sage is associated with holiday feasts. A sage-scented turkey roasting in the oven brings thoughts of a warm, cozy house filled with family and friends. A little sage goes a long way, so be discreet when using it fresh.

Sage is a sun and heat lover; give it a bright, protected place in the garden. It is easily grown from seed and can also be started from stem cuttings and root division. In mild-winter areas, sage is a long-lived perennial. In cold-winter areas, older plants sometimes succumb to freezing temperatures. If your sage plant gets a little ragged and floppy looking, give it a good trim, and it will grow back upright and bushy.

Tarragon *(Artemisia dranunculus).* French chefs consider tarragon absolutely essential. Be sure to buy the true culinary tarragon, *Artemisia dranunculus,* and not Russian tarragon. The word *tarragon* comes from a French word meaning *little dragon.* Like many herbs, its lore is filled with myth and magic. Take a nibble of it, and you may experience a slight numbing of your tongue. Perhaps this is what gained it a reputation for relieving the pain of bites and stings of venomous beasts and mad dogs. It adds a clean, fresh, aniselike taste to sauces, mayonnaise, salad dressings, and vinegar, and tarragon butter makes a wonderful topping for any vegetable. Tarragon freezes well, but it loses most of its flavor when dried. Tarragon grows well in any sunny, well-drained location. Avoid overwet soils, which can cause crown and root rots. The plants can be increased by division in early spring.

Thyme *(Thymus* spp.) The word *thyme* comes from a Greek word meaning *fumigate;* its sweet smell made it useful for perfuming rooms and linens. "To smell of thyme" was an expression of praise. Its antiseptic properties were recognized even in ancient times.

There are so many kinds of thyme that whole gardens have been devoted to this plant alone — thymes with flowers that are pink, red, and white; leaves that are green, yellow, and variegated; and scents that are lemon, lavender, orange, and balsam, not to mention thyme-scented. The plants come in many forms — creeping, tall, short, and spreading. They require average garden soil and full sun. Most thymes are drought-tolerant, and with some protection, will survive all but the coldest winters.

Because each type of thyme has a particular scent and flavor, purchase plants at a nursery so that you can experi-

USING HERBS OUTSIDE THE KITCHEN

If you're not a cook and culinary herbs don't interest you, try some of these herbs for their special characteristics.

COMMON NAME	BOTANIC NAME	ZONES*/PLANT TYPE
Herbs for Fragrance		
Lavender	*Lavandula angustifolia*	5
Lemon balm	*Melissa officinalis*	4
Lemon verbena	*Aloysia triphylla*	9
Mints	*Mentha* spp.	5
Myrtle	*Myrtus communis*	9
Pennyroyal (American)	*Hedeoma pulegioides*	HA
Pennyroyal (European)	*Mentha pulegium*	5
Pineapple sage	*Salvia elegans*	TA
Scented geraniums	*Pelargonium* spp.	TA
Southernwood	*Artemisia abrotanum*	4
Sweet woodruff	*Galium odoratum*	3
Herbs for the Ornamental Garden		
Artemisia	*Artemisia* spp.	4–5
Calendula	*Calendula officinalis*	HA
Chamomile (German)	*Matricaria recutita*	HA
Chamomile (Roman)	*Chamaemelum nobile*	3
Feverfew	*Chrysanthemum parthenium*	5
Germander	*Teucrium chamaedrys*	5
Rosemary	*Rosmarinus officinalis*	8
Rue	*Ruta graveolens*	4
Sage	*Salvia officinalis*	4
Yarrow	*Achillea millefolium*	2
Herbs for Bees, Birds, and Butterflies		
Anise	*Pimpinella anisum*	HA
Beebalm	*Monarda didyma*	4
Borage	*Borago officinalis*	HA
Dill	*Anthemum graveolens*	HA
Sage	*Salvia officinalis*	4
Thyme	*Thymus vulgaris*	5

COMMON NAME	BOTANIC NAME	ZONES*/ PLANT TYPE
Everlasting Herbs to Dry		
Artemisia	*Artemisia* spp.	4–5
Feverfew	*Chrysanthemum parthenium*	5
Goldenrod	*Solidago* spp.	4
Lavender	*Lavandula angustifolia*	5
Rue	*Ruta graveolens*	4
Sweet marjoram	*Origanum majorana*	9
Tansy	*Tanacetum vulgare*	4
Yarrow	*Achillea millefolium*	2

PLANT TYPE: HA = Hardy Annual, TA = Tender Annual

* Chart shows coldest hardiness zone tolerated by a species. Where a specific species is not named on the chart, look for a species appropriate to the hardiness range indicated.

ence what you are buying. Thyme is increased by dividing or by taking stem-cuttings. Culinary thyme, *Thymus vulgaris*, grows easily from seed. Use it to flavor meats, vegetables, poultry, sauces, soups, and stews. This herb dries easily, but the flavor is best when fresh.

How to Dry Herbs

Harvesting herbs makes me feel in touch with the magic of the garden. Tying up armloads of fresh-scented foliage or pushing the bees aside to cut a few lavender stems, inspires thoughts of times when herbs were used for healing and sorcery, as well as for flavoring foods and scenting our homes. Drying herbs is not hard work, you don't need any special equipment, and in one day you can gather enough material for a year's worth of seasonings and gift-making.

Harvest herbs that are grown for their leaves at the first sign of flower buds. Aroma and flavor will be lost to flower formation if they are left to mature. Wait until late morning, after the dew has dried but before the heat of the afternoon

▲ *To dry herbs, tie them in small bundles and hang them in a dark, warm place with good air circulation.*

has set in. You can remove up to two-thirds of an herb plant's top growth.

Clean the herb leaves by rinsing them in a bucket of water. Shake off the excess water and tie the stems together. Short-stemmed plants or individual leaves can be dried on screens or on sweater-drying racks. Hang the tied bundles of herbs from joists or clotheslines, where air can reach them from all sides. If there is too much light in your drying area, put a brown paper bag over each bunch of herbs to preserve the color. The best drying spot is quite warm — at least 75°F or as high as 100°F. Temperatures over 100°F, however, sap the plant of its essential oils and destroy flavor and fragrance. A hot attic, porch, or garage may be just right. The high heat dehydrates the leaves before they rot; keeping the herbs away from sunlight protects their color.

After about a week, if the leaves crumble when you touch them, they are dry enough to strip from the plant. Store the dried herb leaves in a tightly sealed container placed in a dark place. Herbs for dried arrangements and gift projects can be left hanging in the garage or some other protected place for future use.

How to Freeze Herbs

If you don't have the room or the inclination to dry herbs, try freezing them. Studies show that frozen herbs retain more flavor than most dried ones. You can get away with simply tossing clean herbs right from the garden into the freezer, but blanching them first results in the best flavor. To blanch, dunk a bundle of herbs head-first into boiling water. When the herbs' color turns bright, remove the bundle and shake off the water; put it aside to cool. Wrap herbs in separate layers of paper towels, roll them up, put them in a freezer bag or other container, label each container, and freeze them. Use the herbs for cooking directly out of the freezer; there's no need to thaw them first.

If you prefer to skip the blanching process, put chopped, fresh herbs into ice cube trays, cover them with water and freeze. Drop these herb cubes into soups, stews, and sauces for fresh-herb flavor. Combine your favorite herbs for instant herbal seasoning mixes. Pack the herbs tightly into the trays, so as little extra water as possible is added to your stew.

Gifts You Can Make with Herbs

Herb vinegars. Bruise fresh herb leaves, and place them in clean, sterilized glass jars or bottles. Pour hot, but not boiling, vinegar over the herbs; cover the jars tightly; and allow the mixture to steep at room temperature for about ten days. Give the bottle a daily shake to stir the mixture. Strain the mixture, put the vinegar and a few fresh herb sprigs or leaves for decoration back into the bottle, reseal, and store the finished vinegar in a cool, dry place.

Herb sachets. Lovely scented herb sachets make delightful gifts. Fill small muslin or cotton bags with dried lavender or chamomile flowers, or scented geranium, lemon verbena, and rosemary leaves. Decorate the bags with ribbons and artificial flowers. Fill larger bags for herb pillows. Cover them with a soft, comfortable fabric for handy aromatherapy and sweet-scented naps.

Dried herb wreaths. Cover a moss-filled wire or Styrofoam foundation with herbs by poking their stems into the foundation or by fastening them in place with fishing line or florist's pins. Rue, sage, lavender, rosemary, thyme, santolina, chile peppers, and garlic bulbs are good herbal-wreath material. Allow the herb wreath to dry in a warm, dark place.

An Everlasting Project with Young Friends

Annual everlasting flowers are so easy to grow that they are especially suitable for children's gardens. Creating an everlasting garden and making gifts and decorations from the harvest is a great way to introduce and share with your young friends and family the joys of gardening.

▲ *Make an herb basket by weaving fresh herbs through a wire basket frame. Cover the mesh completely.*

Tie a ribbon on it to make a charming gift for the kitchen. As long as you have not used toxic insecticides in your garden, herbs may be removed from the wreath and used for cooking.

Herbal baths. Depending on the herb you use, a warm herbal bath can be soothing, healing, refreshing, or invigorating. Tie some herbs in cheesecloth, and drop the bag in a hot tub of water. Let the water steep for five minutes and then climb in. Adding a handful of oatmeal to the herbal mixture will soften your skin. A soak in a lemon verbena- or mint-scented bath after a hard day of gardening can renew your spirits and relieve your aching muscles.

Woven herb baskets. Start with plenty of *fresh* flexible herbs and a wire-frame basket. Weave the herbs tightly in and out of the frame ribs. Mix varying colors and leaf shapes. Press the stems together firmly and bind them with fishing line, if necessary, to keep them together. Make a handle out of woven stems or grape cuttings. Hang or prop the basket upside down to dry. Since the material shrinks as it dries, fill in gaps with Spanish or sphagnum moss. Add some decorated eggs for a lovely, gray and green, richly scented Easter basket.

Harness the magic of your garden — plant herbs for beauty, for flavor, for healing fragrance, and for gifts to share with friends and family.

MOBILE HOME GARDEN

The convenience and easy care of mobile homes and condominiums are well-suited to modern-day living, but mobile-home lots can be a real challenge to the gardener. The average lot is about 50 by 75 feet, and as much as two-thirds of that may be taken up by the home itself. Many mobile-home gardeners have only the minimum setback area — 10 feet all

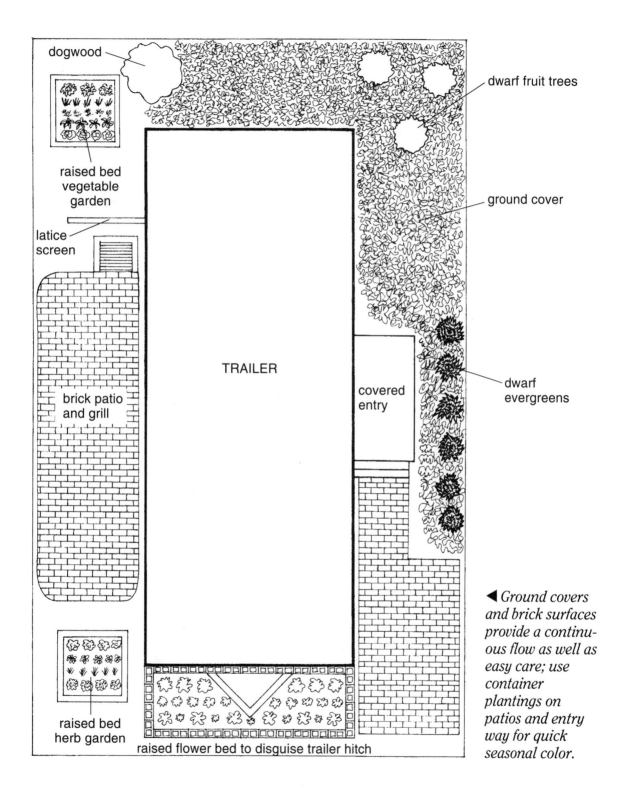

dogwood

raised bed
vegetable
garden

latice
screen

brick patio
and grill

raised bed
herb garden

TRAILER

covered
entry

dwarf fruit trees

ground cover

dwarf
evergreens

raised flower bed to disguise trailer hitch

◄ *Ground covers
and brick surfaces
provide a continu-
ous flow as well as
easy care; use
container
plantings on
patios and entry
way for quick
seasonal color.*

around — in which to garden. In addition to the space limitations, park administrators sometimes restrict landscape designs and types of plants; very large trees and flamboyant landscape features, for instance, may be prohibited. Usually small trees, shrubs, and flowers, however, are acceptable.

SHRUBS FOR SMALL GARDENS

COMMON NAME	BOTANIC NAME	LIGHT REQUIREMENTS	LEAF	HARDINESS ZONES*
Aucuba	*Aucuba japonica*	Shade	Evergreen	7
Azalea	*Rhododendron* spp.	Partial shade	Evergreen/ Deciduous	2–9
Barberry	*Berberis* spp.	Sun	Evergreen/ Deciduous	3–7
Boxwood	*Buxus* spp.	Sun/Shade	Evergreen	5–7
Camellia	*Camellia japonica*	Partial shade	Evergreen	7
Cotoneaster	*Cotoneaster* spp.	Sun	Evergreen/ Deciduous	4–7
Cypress	*Cupressus* spp.	Sun	Evergreen	5–8
Euonymus	*Euonymus* spp.	Sun	Evergreen/ Deciduous	3–6
Firethorn	*Pyracantha* spp.	Sun	Evergreen	6–8
Forsythia	*Forsythia* spp.	Sun	Deciduous	4–5
Heather	*Calluna, Erica* spp.	Sun	Evergreen	3–7
Heavenly bamboo	*Nandina domestica*	Sun/Partial shade	Evergreen	7
Hydrangea	*Hydrangea* spp.	Partial sun	Deciduous	4–7
Juniper	*Juniperus* spp.	Sun	Evergreen	2–7
Podocarpus	*Podocarpus* spp.	Sun/Shade	Evergreen	7–9
Privet	*Ligustrum* spp.	Sun/Shade	Evergreen/ Deciduous	3–7
Rosemary	*Rosmarinus officinalis*	Sun	Evergreen	8

* Chart shows coldest hardiness zone tolerated by a species. Where a specific species is not named on the chart, look for a species appropriate to the hardiness range indicated.

Although some folks resent not being able to express themselves freely in the garden, these rules protect neighborhood aesthetics in a space-limited community.

The Entry Garden

In many parks, streetside gardens are quite small and difficult to make attractive. First impressions are always important, and neatness counts. Low-maintenance ground covers are an excellent choice for ease of upkeep and year-round beauty. The right ground cover can pull a garden design together; instead of a bush here and a plant there, a ground cover establishes a flow from one part of the garden to another. Combine them with dwarf evergreens, which grow

══ GROUND COVERS FOR SMALL GARDENS ══

COMMON NAME	BOTANIC NAME	LIGHT REQUIREMENTS	HARDINESS ZONES*
Baby's-tears	*Soleirolia soleirolii*	Shade	9
Bearberry	*Arctostaphylos* spp.	Sun	7–10
Bugleweed	*Ajuga* spp.	Partial or full shade	2
Campanula	*Campanula* spp.	Partial or full shade	3–6
Corsican mint	*Mentha requienni*		7
Creeping thyme	*Thymus* spp.	Sun	4–5
Honeysuckle	*Lonicera* spp.	Sun	3–7
Ice plant	*Mesembryanthemum* spp.	Sun	10
Spike moss	*Selaginella* spp.	Sun/Partial shade	10
Pachysandra	*Pachysandra* spp.	Partial to full shade	4–5
Periwinkle	*Vinca* spp.	Partial to full shade	4–7
St.-John's-wort	*Hypericum* spp.	Sun/Partial shade	3–7
Sedum	*Sedum* spp.	Sun	2–10
Star jasmine	*Trachelospermum jasminoides*	Sun	8

* Chart shows coldest hardiness zone tolerated by a species. Where a specific species is not named on the chart, look for a species appropriate to the hardiness range indicated.

slowly, require little or no pruning, and are available in many forms and colors. Some gardeners like to add a few containers of flowering annuals or bulbs for color and seasonal interest.

Proportion is important in designing a mobile-home garden. Choose plants that will not outgrow the garden. In a small-space garden, you don't need full-sized trees. Shrubs provide privacy, define boundaries, soften the edges of a building, and beautify a garden with attractive flowers and berries.

Instead of greenery, many mobile-home gardeners opt for paving materials and mulches to keep the streetside garden neat. Paving materials, such as *brick, tile, concrete, and stone,* work well in small entry areas. Loose-fill materials, such as *gravel, cinder, crushed brick,* and *wood chips,* are also popular landscape coverings for people who want a low-maintenance entry yard. Ornamental statues and decorated mailboxes can also individualize this public area.

The Private Garden

The typical lot has two side sections and a back section, as well as a front entry area. Each of these areas might have a separate garden theme. For instance, I know one mobile-home gardener who created a tea garden in her quiet back area. She placed an interesting rock next to a carefully pruned dwarf Japanese maple, added some mossy ground cover, and then filled in the bare spots with wood chips. She erected a small pergola and set up a little wooden table with chairs. The garden, which measures only 10 by 12 feet, has the serene effect of a Japanese tea garden and requires little maintenance. On the other side of the yard, this same gardener made a sunny herb garden. Most of that area is paved with flagstone. The herbs grow in between the pavers and in containers along the edges of the garden. On warm days she sits here, sips her fresh mint-flavored lemonade, and watches the birds and butterflies visit the herb blossoms. The third side of her lot is the outdoor cooking area. A barbecue grill is set on some flagstone paving. Creeping thyme grows in the center of the area, and around the edges she has planted bright flowers. A few lawn chairs and a table make this a comfortable garden for entertaining.

Small Garden Tricks

Use color to give a small garden the feeling of depth and distance. Artists have learned that pale, cool colors seem to recede, and rich, hot colors advance. One gardener I know planted shrubs with colored foliage to achieve the effect of distance. With purple and dark green shrubs in the foreground, blue-green and gray-green shrubs behind, and light green and silvery-leafed shrubs in the background, his garden seems to go on forever. The same effect can be accomplished with flowers, using dark colors in front, graduating to pastels in the rear. Stay in the same color family to avoid confusion and a messy-looking garden. For instance, use bright yellow blossoms in the foreground, fading to medium yellow, then creamy yellow in the middle, and finally white in the background. If you're addicted to a multicolored garden, plant different colors at different seasons: blues in the spring, yellows in the summer, then bronze, red, and orange in the fall.

Another way to create an illusion of space is to use lattice, a shrub, or even a large perennial to screen part of your yard. When you can see the whole garden at once, you observe how small it is, but it will seem larger if you give the beholder the feeling that there may be a hidden garden behind the screen.

Vines will work for you in several ways. They can hide such undesirable views as chain-link fences, tree stumps, drain pipes, or blank house walls, or they can be used on a trellis to partition a small garden or give a feeling of depth. When planting close to your mobile home, don't use vines that attach themselves under the siding or roof coverings and cause damage.

You need not do without home-grown fruits and vegetables just because your garden is tiny. In two 4-foot-square beds you can grow two tomato plants, two pepper plants, and a row each of lettuce, carrots, onions, and beans. You can also grow some of your vegetables in containers. A trellised climbing bean grown in a container on wheels makes a portable — and edible — privacy screen.

Where space is at a premium, don't forget that the ground is not your only option for planting. Cherry tomatoes and cucumbers will grow happily in a well-watered hanging pot. Combine them with petunias or nasturtiums, and your sky garden will be the envy of your neighbors. Mints, tarragon, rosemary, and scented geraniums also do well in hanging baskets.

Dwarf fruit trees grow nicely in containers, and, when trained against a wall or fence, take up little space. (See pages 223-224 for information on how to espalier.)

Some mobile-home parks have community gardens where residents grow vegetables in a shared space. This is a good place to grow those space-hogs — corn, squash, and melons. Neighbors can trade produce and share expenses. Harvest festivals and giant pumpkin-growing contests add a bit of spice to the group-gardening activities. You may also wish to share a community compost heap.

You can have as much fun with your mini-garden as other folks have with their acre lots. Plan carefully, keep proportion in mind when you're choosing plants, and don't crowd and clutter your yard. A few well-chosen, well-placed plants can make an elegant small garden.

My Mother's Garden

For as long as I can remember, my mother had wanted a garden. Recently, after many years of living in the city and gardening in containers on small apartment balconies, she retired from her city job and traded her balcony plants for a suburban yard. Forty years is a long time to wait for a bit of soil to dig and my mother is not as robust as she once was, but her enthusiasm is undiminished.

Her good-sized lot had almost no landscaping. The front yard had a small lawn with a beautiful dogwood tree; the large backyard was bare except for tall pines at the far end of the property and unkempt shrubbery screening a fence along the sides. A virgin garden!

Right after moving into her new home, my mother ordered a truckload of finely shredded wood chips, which my sister and her husband helped her spread over the bare backyard. This made an attractive, natural-looking ground cover that helped to keep the weeds under control until she was ready to create flower beds. The first spring, at planting time, she simply raked some of the bark aside and spaded a small area. Because the bark cover had kept the soil moist and soft, it was easy to dig. She broadcast an annual seed mixture, set a birdbath, and placed a few interesting rocks in the bed. She started a vegetable garden for sun-ripened tomatoes and fresh-picked beans. Hoping to keep insects under control, she hung an inviting feeder for the birds. She put an herb garden next to the back door. A couple of leftover tree stumps provided seating, and she watched her garden grow.

Her back occasionally gives her trouble, so she was careful to dig only a portion of the garden every day. Seed tapes and transplants from the local nursery helped to get her new garden off to an easy start. Since her area gets a lot of rain, her watering chores were few, and the bark helped keep weeds down. She sat on a stool and weeded, while she watched birds visit her feeder. A plastic bucket at her side was a convenient receptacle for the weeds. She found it easy to move her tools and equipment around the garden in a wheelbarrow.

Gardening is full of surprises, however, and they aren't always pleasant. As that first summer wore on, something seemed to be wrong in the vegetable garden. The tomato plants looked small and weak and set only a few fruits. The cucumbers and squash were puny, and other plants looked a little "peaked," even though my mother fertilized faithfully. What a disappointment! Her long-awaited garden appeared to be dying. The results from a home soil-test kit showed that the soil was far too acid for vegetables. She blamed the pine trees that grew nearby. Their needles had covered the ground for many years, acidifying the soil as they decomposed and perhaps adding a chemical that inhibits the growth of some plants.

Instead of trying to remake all that garden soil, my mother chose to plant her next crop of vegetables in raised beds. The following year, my brother and his wife built raised beds, which she filled with a combination of good topsoil (obtained from the front yard where no pines grew) and soil amendments. Her new raised beds are about 12 inches high — a more convenient height when she sits on her garden stool to work. The first vegetables planted in these raised beds gave

━━━ THE ABSOLUTELY EASIEST GARDEN ━━━

1. Find a sunny spot, near the house.

2. Prepare the soil by rototilling or digging in some premixed soil amendment and a time-release fertilizer.

3. Install a soaker hose to reach all areas of the garden bed. Attach a watering timer.

4. Plant perennials that are suited to your soil and climate from the list of long-lasting, easy-care plants, (see list, facing page).

5. For bright, all-season color, broadcast seeds of easy, re-seeding annuals (see list, facing page). Rake soil over the seeds and lightly water.

6. Apply bark or some other light mulch over the garden bed, covering the soaker hoses and seeds and filling in between the perennials.

7. Set up your chair and relax. You have just created a self-sowing, self-watering, weed-resistant garden that will bloom all season long.

her a bumper crop, and she did less weeding and had a neater-looking yard.

Her next project was to create "just a little piece of grass" in the backyard for her picnic table and garden chairs. She had found the bark dust to be a nuisance in rainy weather, because it clung to her shoes and got tracked into the house.

▰▰▰▰▰ Easy-Care Perennials ▰▰▰▰▰

COMMON NAME	BOTANIC NAME	ZONES*/PLANT TYPE
Baby's-breath	*Gypsophila paniculata*	2
Clary sage	*Salvia sclarea*	B
Columbine	*Aquilegia* spp.	3
Foxglove	*Digitalis purpurea*	4
Hollyhock	*Alcea rosea*	4
Lavender	*Lavandula angustifolia*	5
Michaelmas daisy	*Aster* spp.	2-7
Penstemon	*Penstemon* spp.	3–7
Rosemary	*Rosmarinus officinalis*	8
Viola	*Viola* spp.	

Easy-Care Annuals

COMMON NAME	BOTANIC NAME	ZONES*/PLANT TYPE
Calendula	*Calendula officinalis*	HA
Cosmos	*Cosmos* spp.	HHA
Gaillardia	*Gaillardia* spp.	HHA
Impatiens	*Impatiens* spp.	TA
Johnny-jump-up	*Viola tricolor*	HA
Marigold	*Tagetes* spp.	HHA
Salvia	*Salvia* spp.	HHA
Stock	*Matthiola* spp.	HA
Zinnia	*Zinnia* spp.	TA

PLANT TYPE: B = Biennial, HA = Hardy Annual, HHA = Half-hardy Annual, TA = Tender Annual

* Chart shows coldest hardiness zone tolerated by a species. Where a specific species is not named on the chart, look for a species appropriate to the hardiness range indicated.

This time her gardening buddies helped her plant a small lawn just in front of the back door, leaving bark as ground cover in the rest of the yard and in the pathways between the raised beds. She enjoys the exercise of mowing her small, easily maintained lawn with her lightweight mower.

She turned a little room off of her garage into her seed room, where she dries, sorts, and labels the seeds she saves. Her collection of nursery catalogs is kept there, too, right next to her rocking chair. She tells me that on rainy days she likes to sit there and plan her gardens-to-be. This is also where she grows her own transplants. A fluorescent light fixture, found at a garage sale, plus a small window, supplies enough light for germination. She moves the plants to a cold frame after they sprout, and then on to the main garden when the weather permits. She now grows both flowers and vegetables from her own saved seed and purchases only a few hybrid seeds and nursery-grown transplants.

As summers pass, my mother's garden continues to change and grow. She has plans for the front yard and also for a woodland garden under the pine trees in the back, where she'll grow plants that appreciate pine-mulched earth.

My mother has carefully designed a garden that she can take care of with little assistance, and she has eliminated chores that are too difficult or time-consuming. As her garden matures, so does she, and her garden is one she can enjoy throughout her life.

GARDEN POWER:
EXERCISES TO GET GOING
AND KEEP GOING

We've all seen joggers reaching for their ankles, football players touching their toes, and baseball players swinging bats. These athletes aren't just showing off — they're preparing their bodies for activity. Studies show that bending and stretching exercises increase blood flow to muscles, improve performance, and help prevent injuries. Good preliminary exercises also reduce next-day soreness and muscle stiffness. Bending and reaching in the garden put a lot of stress on back, shoulder, and leg muscles. It is just as helpful to warm up before gardening as it is to warm up before the Big Game.

Rules for Safe Exercise

★ Check with your doctor before starting any new exercise program or strenuous activity.

★ Start your exercise program gradually, beginning with one or two routines and building up your tolerance slowly.

★ *Do not* overdo it. You shouldn't feel too sore to go about your daily life after exercising. Take a hint from your body — if you feel worse instead of better after exercising, you have done too much.

★ If, while exercising or gardening, you feel short of breath or dizzy, stop and rest. Consult your physician if this happens regularly.

★ Always exercise both sides of your body, in order to keep muscle strength as equal as possible.

★ Be aware of proper posture and body position while exercising. Keep your joints in proper alignment to maintain balance and prevent injury.

★ *Do not* do deep-knee bends to strengthen your knees. Knee bends put undue stress on knee joints.

★ If you have arthritis, osteoporosis, or any mobility restriction, *do not* use weights while exercising, unless your doctor considers it safe.

★ Use hot packs or warm water to decrease morning stiffness. Washing dishes in hot water warms up hand and finger joints. Quick hot packs for the neck, knees, or hands can be made by tossing a towel in an automatic dryer for about five minutes or heating it in a microwave on "high" for one minute. Test the towel carefully before using it, so you don't burn yourself.

STRETCHING EXERCISES

Neck

Try touching your ear to your shoulder – without lifting your shoulder.

From a standing or sitting position, touch your chin to your chest and hold it there for five seconds, while you look at the ground. Very slowly, tilt your head backwards until you are looking up at the sky — hold that position for five seconds. Next, look as far to the right as you can, and then look to the left, holding each position for five seconds. To finish, try touching one ear to your shoulder. Don't cheat by lifting your shoulder to meet your ear. Repeat on the opposite side. Impossible? Yes! But it's a good stretch, so try it.

Shoulders

From a standing or sitting position, shrug your shoulders, lifting them as high as you can, and then lowering them as far as you can. Shrug five times.

Hold both arms out to the side and make circles — first clockwise, then counterclockwise. Make bigger and bigger circles as you repeat the movement, then work your way back down to small circles.

Hands

Sit next to a garden bed and press your hands flat against the soil. Spread your fingers and hold them there for five seconds. Grab a fistful of soil in each hand, and gently squeeze it. Repeat five times.

To warm up the wrists, make circles with each fist, first one way, then the other. Bend each wrist up, and then bend it down.

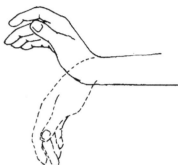

Warm up wrists by bending wrist up and then down.

Back

Toe-touches stretch your back and also the muscles, called hamstrings, that run up the back of your legs. If toe-touches are out of the question, sit on the floor with your legs together, and reach for your toes. When you feel the pull in the back of your legs, stop, and hold that position for five seconds. Repeat the exercise five times.

If getting up and down off the floor is hard for you, do this exercise from a chair. Place one foot on a stool in front of you and then reach for your toes. Hold the stretch and repeat as above.

Hoe Tricks

Use a lightweight garden hoe to help with the following warm-ups.

★ Grasp the hoe handle with both hands, and hold it out in front of you. Lift the hoe as high over your head as you can, hold it there for five seconds, and then let it down slowly.

While still grasping the hoe in both hands, move it to one side of your body, then to the other (in the old "and awaaaay we go" motion). Lift as high to each side as you can, hold that position for five seconds, and then relax. Next, hold the hoe behind your back, if possible, and lift backwards as high as you can. Hold this position for five seconds, and then relax. These exercises

▶ *"Awaaay we go."*

warm up shoulders muscles and maintain shoulder-joint mobility.

★ Hold the hoe handle across your shoulders, as if you were a scarecrow. Bend to each side as far as possible, and hold that position for five seconds. Return to the starting position, and repeat on the other side. Be careful to keep your body in good alignment and do not bend so far that you lose your balance. Bend to each side five times. From the starting scarecrow position, rotate from the waist, first to one side then the other, holding the ultimate position, as before, and repeating each direction five times. This exercise increases the flexibility of back and trunk muscles.

▶ *In the "scare-crow" position, carefully bend to the left and then to the right.*

★ For a safe back stretch, hold the hoe in one hand with the blade on the ground for balance. Slowly reach down and touch one knee, rounding your back as you do so. Switch hands, and do the same on the other side.

Knees

Knees get a lot of abuse in the garden, so take a minute to warm them up. Before you get started with garden chores, march around the garden, lifting your knees as high as you can. You can do this exercise from a chair, too, by lifting each knee as high as you can. You may need to grasp the seat of the chair for balance and leverage. A bicycle-pedaling motion from a seated position or from the floor is another good knee warm-up.

Remember to give your knees some relief while you're working. Straighten your legs every thirty minutes or so, or get up and walk around.

▲ *Stretch back muscles by leaning forward to touch knee while using hoe for balance.*

STRENGTHENING EXERCISES

Garden work challenges even the strongest backs and knees. Two simple exercises done once-a-day will increase your flexibility and gardening power.

Stomach

Because abdominal muscles support the trunk of your body, making these muscles stronger will take some of the stress off your back. In addition to strengthening your trunk, this simple exercise increases back flexibility.

Lie on your back with your feet flat on the floor and your knees elevated. A carpeted or padded floor is best for this exercise, but a firm bed will do. Very slowly raise one knee to your chest. Concentrate on keeping your back flat against the floor. Don't strain if you're not very flexible. You don't need to get your knee up under your chin to benefit from this ex-

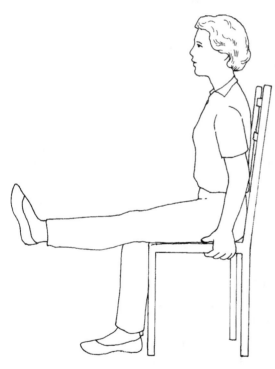

▶ *Strengthen abdominal muscles by raising knees, one at a time, toward chest.*

ercise; the effort of bringing your knee up slowly will work the abdominal muscles. When you've gone as far as you can, hold your knee in that position for five seconds, and then slowly let it back down. Repeat with the other knee. Alternate raising and lowering knees five times each.

Knees

Strong knees help you safely lift heavy loads and reduce the effort it takes to get up from a seat or the ground.

Do this easy exercise while you're watching TV or reading a book. From a seated position, raise one leg straight out to the front, hold it there for five seconds, and then lower it. Do the same with the opposite leg. Repeat this exercise five times to strengthen the muscles called *quadriceps* that are above your knees. These are the stair-climbing and lifting muscles.

Sitting with back straight, straighten each knee and hold for five seconds.

MEASUREMENTS FOR BARRIER-FREE DESIGN

Wheelchair dimensions

Length 42"
Open width 25"
Collapsed width 11"
Seat to floor 19½"
Armrest to floor 29"
Wheel Chair Access
Minimum turning space, 360° 60"
Minimum turning space, 180° 36"
Side reach limit, high 54"
Side reach limit, low 9"
Safest ramp slope 1:12
Table height 30"–33"

Entry Doors

Minimum clear opening 36"

Stairs

Maximum riser height 7"
Handrail height 32"

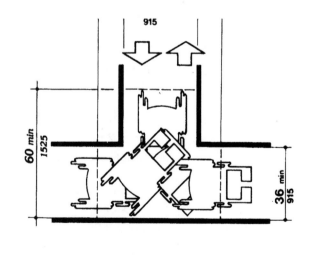

▲ *Tool shed designed for easy access from a wheelchair.*

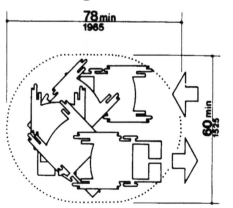

◀ ▲ *Requirements for turning spaces for wheelchairs.*

(American National Standards, U.S. Government publication)

METRIC CONVERSION CHART

Weight

1 pound = 454 grams, therefore:
_____ pounds x 454 = _____ grams
_____ grams x .002 = _____ pounds

1 pound = .454 kilograms, therefore:
_____ pounds x .454 = _____ kilograms
_____ kilograms x 2.2 = _____ pounds

1 pint (dry) = .55 liters, therefore:
_____ pints (dry) x .55 = _____ liters
_____ liters x 1.82 = _____ pints (dry)

1 pint (liquid) = .47 liters, therefore:
_____ pints (liquid) x .47 = _____ liters
_____ liters 2.11 = _____ pints (liquid)

Volume

1 quart (dry) = 1.1 liters, therefore:
_____ quarts (dry) x 1.1 = _____ liters
_____ liters x .91 = _____ quarts (dry)

1 quart (liquid) = .95 liters, therefore:
_____ quarts (liquid) x .95 = _____ liters
_____ liters x 1.06 = _____ quarts (liquid)

1 peck = 8.81 liters, therefore:
_____ pecks x 8.81 = _____ liters
_____ liters x 1.14 = _____ pecks

l bushel = 35.24 liters, therefore:
_____ bushels x 35.24 = _____ liters
_____ liters x .028 = _____ bushels

Dimension

1 inch = 25.4 millimeters, therefore:
_____ inches x 25.4 millimeters = _____ millimeters
_____ millimeters x .04 = _____ inches

1 inch = 2.54 centimeters, therefore:
_____ inches x 2.54 = _____ centimeters
_____ centimeters x .394 = _____ inches

1 foot = .305 meters, therefore:
_____ feet x .305 = _____ meters
_____ meters x 3.28 = _____ feet

1 ounce = 28.4 grams, therefore:
_____ ounces x 28.4 = _____ grams
_____ grams x .04 = _____ ounces

USDA ZONE MAP

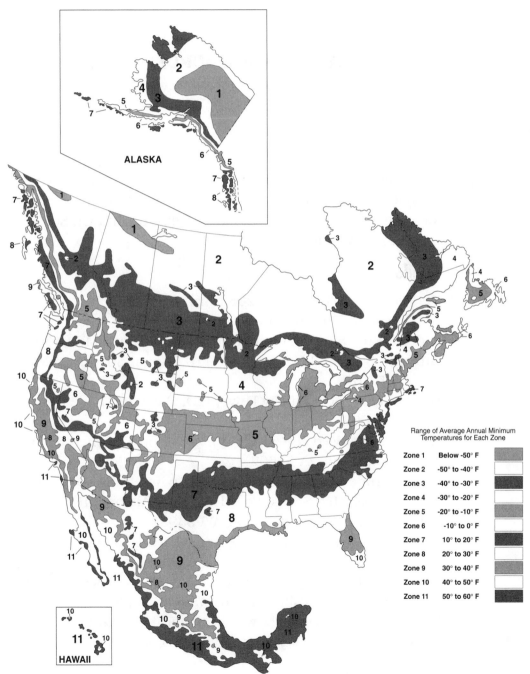

ALASKA

HAWAII

Range of Average Annual Minimum
Temperatures for Each Zone

Zone 1	Below -50° F
Zone 2	-50° to -40° F
Zone 3	-40° to -30° F
Zone 4	-30° to -20° F
Zone 5	-20° to -10° F
Zone 6	-10° to 0° F
Zone 7	10° to 20° F
Zone 8	20° to 30° F
Zone 9	30° to 40° F
Zone 10	40° to 50° F
Zone 11	50° to 60° F

MAIL-ORDER SOURCES

MAIL-ORDER SOURCES - U.S.

A complete list of the Mailorder Association of Nurseries members is available for $1.00 postage and handling from Mailorder Association of Nurseries, Department SCI, 8683 Doves Fly Way, Laurel, MD 20723.

Seeds

Earl May Seed & Nursery, 208 North Elm Street, Shenandoah, IA 51603

Fedco Seeds, 52 Mayflower Hill Drive, Waterville ME 04301

Gurney's Seed and Nursery Co., 110 Capital Street, Yankton, SD 57079

Harris Seeds, 60 Saginaw Drive, P.O. Box 22960, Rochester, NY 14692

Henry Field's Seed & Nursery Co., 415 North Burnett Street, Shenandoah, IA 51602

High Altitude Gardens, P.O. Box 4619, Ketchum, ID 83340

Johnny's Selected Seeds, Foss Hill Road, Albion, ME 04910

J.W. Jung Seed Co., Randolph, WI 53957

Nichols Garden Nursery, 1190 North Pacific Highway, Albany, OR 97321

Otis S. Twilley Seed Co., Inc., P.O. Box 65, Trevose, PA 19047

Park Seed Co., Cokesbury Road, Greenwood, SC 29647

Pinetree Garden Seeds, New Gloucester, ME 04260

Seeds Blüm, Idaho City Stage, Boise, ID 83706

Shepherd's Garden Seeds, 30 Irene Street, Torrington, CT
06790

Stark Brothers Nurseries and Orchards Co., Louisiana, MO
63353

Territorial Seed Co., P.O. Box 27, Lorane, OR 97451

The Tomato Seed Company, Inc., P.O. Box 323, Metuchen, NJ
08840

Thompson & Morgan Inc., P.O. Box 1308, Jackson, NJ 08527

W. Atlee Burpee & Co., 300 Park Avenue, Warminster, PA
18974

Heirloom Seeds

Johnny's Selected Seeds, Foss Hill Road, Albion, ME 04910

J.W. Jung Seed Co., Randolph, WI 53957

Seeds Blüm, Idaho City Stage, Boise, ID 83706

Shepherd's Garden Seeds, 30 Irene Street, Torrington, CT
06790

The Tomato Seed Company, Inc., P.O. Box 323, Metuchen, NJ
08840

Seed Starting Kits

Gardener's Supply Co., 128 Intervale Road, Burlington, VT
05401

Harris Seeds, 60 Saginaw Drive, P.O. Box 22960, Rochester,
NY 14692

Johnny's Selected Seeds, Foss Hill Road, Albion, ME 04910

Park Seed Co., Cokesbury Road, Greenwood, SC 29647

W. Atlee Burpee & Co., 300 Park Avenue, Warminster, PA
18974

Grow Bags (Pillow Packs)

Discount Garden Supply, Inc., E. 14109 Sprague, Suite 5,
Spokane, WA 99216

East Coast Hydroponics, 432 Castleton Avenue, Staten Island, NY 10301

Greenfield's Hydroponics and Indoor Garden Equipment,
8139 Milwaukee Avenue, Niles, IL 60648

Plants

Earl May Seed & Nursery, 208 North Elm Street,
    Shenandoah, IA 51603
Fedco Seeds, 52 Mayflower Hill Drive, Waterville, ME 04301
Gurney's Seed and Nursery Co., 110 Capital Street, Yankton,
    SD 57079
Henry Field's Seed & Nursery Co., 415 North Burnett Street,
    Shenandoah, IA 51602
High Altitude Gardens, P.O. Box 4619, Ketchum, ID 83340
Jackson & Perkins, 1 Rose Lane, Medford, OR 97501
J.W. Jung Seed Co., Randolph, WI 53957
Nichols Garden Nursery, 1190 North Pacific Highway, Albany,
    OR 97321
Park Seed Co., Cokesbury Road, Greenwood, SC 29647
Raintree Nursery, 391 Butts Road, Morton, WA 98356
Stark Brothers Nurseries and Orchards Co., Louisiana, MO
    63353
Thompson & Morgan Inc., P.O. Box 1308, Jackson, NJ 08527
W. Atlee Burpee & Co., 300 Park Avenue, Warminster, PA
    18974
Wayside Gardens, 1 Garden Lane, Hodges, SC 29695
White Flower Farm, Litchfield, CT 06759

Earthworms

Gardener's Supply Co., 128 Intervale Road, Burlington, VT
    05401
Growing Naturally, P.O. Box 54, 149 Pine Lane, Pineville, PA
    18946
Necessary Trading Co., 1 Nature's Way, New Castle, VA 24127
The Earthworm Co., 3675 Calistoga Road., Santa Rosa, CA
    95404

Beneficial Insects

Gardener's Supply Co., 128 Intervale Road, Burlington, VT
    05401
Gardens Alive!, Highway 48, Box 149, Sunman, IN 47041

Growing Naturally, P.O. Box 54, 149 Pine Lane, Pineville, PA 18946

Necessary Trading Co., 1 Nature's Way, New Castle, VA 24127

Territorial Seed Co., P.O. Box 27, Lorane, OR 97451

Garden Supplies

Alsto's Handy Helpers, P.O. Box 1267, Galesburg, IL 61401

Cumberland General Store, Route 3, Crossville, TN 38555

Earl May Seed & Nursery, 208 North Elm Street, Shenandoah, IA 51603

Gardener's Eden, P.O. Box 7307, San Francisco, CA 94120

Gardener's Supply Co., 128 Intervale Road, Burlington, VT 05401

Harris Seeds, 60 Saginaw Drive, P.O. Box 22960, Rochester, NY 14692

Henry Field's Seed & Nursery Co., 415 North Burnett Street, Shenandoah, IA 51602

High Altitude Gardens, P.O. Box 4619, Ketchum, ID 83340

J.W. Jung Seed Co., Randolph, WI 53957

Langenbach, P.O. Box 453, Blairstown, NJ 07825

Lehman Hardware and Appliances, 4779 Kidron Road., P.O. Box 41, Kidron, OH 44636

Nichols Garden Nursery, 1190 North Pacific Highway, Albany, OR 97321

Park Seed Co., Cokesbury Road, Greenwood, SC 29647

Plow & Hearth, 301 Madison Road, P.O. Box 830, Orange, VA 22960

Raintree Nursery, 391 Butts Road, Morton, WA 98356

Smith & Hawken, 25 Corte Madera, Mill Valley, CA 94961

Walt Nicke Co., 36 McLeod Lane, P.O. Box 433, Topfield, MA 01983

W. Atlee Burpee & Co., 300 Park Avenue, Warminster, PA 18974

Drip Systems

Gardener's Supply Co., 128 Intervale Road, Burlington, VT 05401

Ringer, 9959 Valley View Road, Eden Prairie, MN 55344
Smith & Hawken, 25 Corte Madera, Mill Valley, CA 94961
W. Atlee Burpee & Co., 300 Park Avenue, Warminster, PA
    18974

Fertilizers

Gardens Alive!, Highway 48, Box 149, Sunman, IN 47041
Growing Naturally, P.O. Box 54, 149 Pine Lane, Pineville, PA
    18946
J.W. Jung Seed Co., Randolph, WI 53957
Necessary Trading Co., P.O. Box 305, New Castle, VA 24127
Ringer, 9959 Valley View Road, Eden Prairie, MN 55344
Territorial Seed Co., P.O. Box 27, Lorane, OR 97451

Row Covers

Gardener's Supply Co., 128 Intervale Road, Burlington, VT
    05401
Gardens Alive!, Hwy 48, Box 149, Sunman, IN 47041
Growing Naturally, P.O. Box 54, 149 Pine Lane, Pineville, PA
    18946
Harris Seeds, 60 Saginaw Drive, P.O. Box 22960, Rochester,
    NY 14692
W. Atlee Burpee & Co., 300 Park Avenue, Warminster, PA
    18974

Composters

Alsto's Handy Helpers, P.O. Box 1267, Galesburg, IL 61401
Gardener's Eden, P.O. Box 7307, San Francisco, CA 94120
Gardener's Supply Co., 128 Intervale Road, Burlington, VT
    05401
Growing Naturally, P.O. Box 54, 149 Pine Lane, Pineville, PA
    18946
Johnny's Selected Seeds, Foss Hill Road, Albion, ME 04910
Langenbach, P.O. Box 453, Blairstown, NJ 07825
Plow & Hearth, 301 Madison Road, P.O. Box 830, Orange, VA
    22960
Ringer, 9959 Valley View Road, Eden Prairie, MN 55344

Smith & Hawken, 25 Corte Madera, Mill Valley, CA 94961

W. Atlee Burpee & Co., 300 Park Avenue, Warminster, PA
  18974

Special Tools

Alsto's Handy Helpers, P.O. Box 1267, Galesburg, IL 61401

adaptAbility, P.O. Box 515, Colchester, CT 06415

Comfortably Yours, 61 West Hunter Avenue, Maywood, NJ
  07607

Creative Enterprises, Inc., P.O. Box 3452, Idaho Falls, ID
  83403-3452

Cumberland General Store, Route 3, Crossville, TN 38555

Gardener's Eden, P.O. Box 7307, San Francisco, CA 94120

Gardener's Supply Co., 128 Intervale Road, Burlington, VT
  05401

J.W. Jung Seed Co., Randolph, WI 53957

Langenbach, P.O. Box 453, Blairstown, NJ 07825

Lehman Hardware and Appliances, 4779 Kidron Road, P.O.
  Box 41, Kidron, OH 44636

Pinetree Garden Seeds, New Gloucester, ME 04260

Plow and Hearth, 301 Madison Road, P.O. Box 830, Orange,
  VA 22960

Raintree Nursery, 391 Butts Road, Morton, WA 98356

Smith & Hawken, 25 Corte Madera, Mill Valley, CA 94961

Walt Nicke Co., 36 McLeod Lane, P.O. Box 433, Topfield, MA
  01983

W. Atlee Burpee & Co., 300 Park Avenue, Warminster, PA
  18974

Garden Software

Garden Journal Plant Library, Heizer Software, 1941 Oak Park
  Boulevard, Suite 30, P.O. Box 232019, Pleasant Hill, CA
  94523 (Macintosh)

Gardenview, Mindsun, R.D.2, Box 710, Andover, NJ 07821
  (IBM and IBM compatibles)

Gardenwise, 4021 McIntyre Road, Trumansburg, NY 14886
  (Macintosh)

Hortis Opus, J. Mendoza Gardens, Inc., 18 East 16th Street, New York, NY 10003 (IBM, IBM compatibles, and Macintosh)

Infopoint Software Finder, Infopoint Software, P.O. Box 83, Arcola, MO 65603 (IBM and IBM compatibles)

Just the Right Rose, Rosebud, 3707 SW Coronado Street, Portland, OR 97219 (IBM and IBM compatibles)

Mum's the Word, Terrace Software, P.O. Box 1236, Cambridge, MA 02238 (Macintosh)

The Plant Database Library, Taxonomic Computer Research, P.O. Box 12011, Raleigh, NC 27605 (IBM and IBM compatibles)

Adaptive Devices

adaptAbility, P.O. Box 515, Colchester, CT 06415

Comfortably Yours, 61 West Hunter Avenue, Maywood, NJ 07607

Foster House, 141 Foster Building, Peoria, IL 61632

Hanover House, Hanover, PA 17331

Harriet Carter, Dept. 32, Plymouth Meeting, PA 19462

Keepsakes, 329 Main Street, Ames, IA 50010

Maxi-Aids, 86-30 102nd Street, Richmond, NY 11418

Miles Kimball, 41 W. Eighth Avenue, Oshkosh, WI 54901

Park Seed Co., Cokesbury Road, Greenwood, SC 29647

Spencer Gifts, Spencer Building, Atlantic City, NJ 08411

Sunset House, Sunset Building, Beverly Hills, CA 90215

Walter Drake and Sons, Drake Building, Colorado Springs, CO 80901

W. Atlee Burpee & Co., 300 Park Avenue, Warminster, PA 18974

Mail-Order Sources - Canada

Seeds, Plants, and Garden Supplies

Aimers Seeds, 81 Temperance Street, Aurora, ON 14G 2R1

Aubin Nurseries, Ltd., Box 1089, Carman, MB R0G 0J0

The Alpine Garden Club of British Columbia, P.O. Box 5161, Main Post Office, 349 West Georgia Street, Vancouver, BC V6B 4B2

Butchart Gardens, Box 4010, Station A, Victoria, BC V8X 3X4

The Canadian Wildflower Society, c/o James French, 35 Crescent, Unionville, ON L3R 4H3

Corn Hill Nursery Ltd., R.R. 5, Peticodiac, NB E0A 2H0

Cruickshank's Inc., 1015 Mount Pleasant Road, Toronto, ON M4P 2M1

Dacha Barinka Seeds Ltd., 46232 Strathcona Road, Chilliwack, BC V2P 3T2

Wm. Dam Seeds, Box 8400, Dundas, ON L9H 6MI

Dig This: Gifts and Gear for Gardeners, 45 Bastion Square, Victoria, BC V8W 1J1

Dominion Seed House, Box 2500, Georgetown, ON L7G 5L6

Elk Lake Garden Centre, 5450 Patricia Bay Highway, Victoria, BC V8Y 1T1

Gardenimport Inc., P.O. Box 760, Thornhill, ON L3T 4A5

Heritage Seed Program, R.R. 3, Uxbridge, ON L8C 1K8

Island Seed Mail Order, P.O. Box 4278, Station A, Victoria, BC V8X 3X8

Natural Legacy Seeds, R.R. 2, C-1 Laird, Armstrong, BC V0E 1B0

Pacific Northwest Seed Company, P.O. Box 460, Vernon, BC V1T 6M4

Pickering Nurseries Inc., 670 Kingston Road, Pickering, ON L1V 1A6

Richters, Box 26, Highway 47, Goodwood, ON L0C 1A0

Riverside Gardens, R.R. 5, Saskatoon, SK S7K 3J8

Rocky Mountain Seed Service, P.O. Box 215, Golden, BC V0A 1H0

Saltspring Seeds, Box 33, Ganges, BC V0S 1E0

Sanctuary Seeds/Folklore Herbs, 2388 West 4th Avenue, Vancouver, BC V6K 1P1

Seed Service, P.O. Box 215, Golden, BC V0A 1H0

Territorial Seeds Ltd., Box 46225, Station G, 3760 West 10th Avenue, Vancouver, BC V6R 4G5

Stokes Seed Company, 39 James Street, Street Catharines, ON 12R 6R6

Heirloom Seeds

Aimers Seeds, 81 Temperance Street, Aurora, ON L4G 2R1

Aubin Nurseries Ltd., Box 1089, Carman, MB R0G 0J0

Butchart Gardens, Box 4010, Station A, Victoria, BC V8X 3X4

Corn Hill Nursery Ltd., R.R. 5, Peticodiac, NB E0A 2H0

Cruickshank's Inc., 1015 Mount Pleasant Road, Toronto, ON M4P 2MI

Wm. Dam Seeds, Box 8400, Dundas, ON L9H 6MI

Dominion Seed House, Box 2500, Georgetown, ON L7G 5L6

Hortico Inc., R.R. 1, Robson Road, Waterdown, ON L0R 2H0

McConnell Nurseries, Port Burwell, ON N0J 1T0

Pickering Nurseries Inc., 670 Kingston Road, Pickering, ON L1V 1A6

Richters, Goodwood, ON L0C 1A0

Riverside Gardens, R.R. 5, Saskatoon, SK S7K 3J8

Stokes Seed Company, Box 10, Street Catharines, ON L2R 6R6

Composters

Bonar Inc., 311 Alexander Avenue, Winnipeg, MB R3A 0M9

Century Plastics, 12291 Horseshoe Way, Richmond, BC V7A 4V5

Dominion Seed House, Box 2500, Georgetown, ON L7G 5L6

Stokes Seed Company, 39 James Street, Street Catharines, ON 12R 6R6

Wireman Products Inc., 5780 Production Way, Langley, BC V3A 4N4

OTHER SOURCES OF INFORMATION

U.S. SOURCES

Gardening Agencies

American Horticultural Therapy Association, Wightman Road, Suite 300, Gaithersburg, MD 20879

Chicago Horticultural Society, "Books" Horticultural Therapy Dept., P.O. Box 400, Glencoe, IL 60022

Gardens for All, 180 Flynn Avenue, Burlington, VT 05401

Hydroponic Society of America, P.O. Box 6067, Concord, CA 95524

National Council for Therapy and Rehabilitation through Horticulture, 9041 Comprint Court Suite 103, Gaithersburg, MD 20877

National Gardening Association, 180 Flynn Avenue, Burlington, VT 05401

Other Agencies and Organizations

American Association of Retired Persons, National Headquarters, 1909 K Street, NW, Washington, DC 20049

American Occupational Therapy Association, 1383 Piccard Drive, Rockville, MD 20850

American Physical Therapy Association, 1111 North Fairfax Street, Alexandria, VA 22314

Association for the Advancement of Rehabilitation Technology, 1101 Connecticut Avenue, NW, #700, Washington, DC 20036

Association for Persons with Severe Handicaps, 7010 Roosevelt Way NE, Seattle, WA 98115

Council on Aging, 600 Maryland Avenue SW, Washington, DC 20024

Michigan Center for a Barrier-Free Environment, 6879 Heather Heath, West Bloomfield, MI 48033

Rehabilitation Services Administration, Department of Education, Switzer Building, #3024, 330 C Street, SW, Washington, DC 20202

Publications

Ability Magazine, Majestic Press, P.O. Box 5311, Mission Hills, CA 91345

Accent on Living, Accent Publications, P.O. Box 700, Bloomington, IL 61702

A quarterly publication started in 1956 to provide information to people with physical disabilities about new devices and easier ways to do things

A Positive Approach, 1600 Malone Street, Municipal Airport, Millville, NJ 08332

A bi-monthly magazine for the physically challenged; positive profiles on living and creating a barrier-free environment

Arthritis Today, Arthritis Foundation , 1314 Spring Street, NW, Atlanta, GA 30309

Monthly magazine with upbeat personality profiles, tips on easy living, nutrition, and life-style articles

Breaking New Ground, Dept. of Agricultural Engineering, Purdue University, West Lafayette, IN 47907

Quarterly newsletter written specifically for agricultural workers with physical handicaps and for rehabilitation professionals; lots of good tips for adapting farm machinery and tools

Independent Living, 44 Broadway, Greenlawn, NY 11740

Quarterly magazine for persons with disabilities and home health-care dealers, manufacturers, and health-care professionals; up-to-date news and ideas

National Gardening, 180 Flynn Avenue, Burlington, VT 05401

Monthly magazine covering all aspects of gardening; personal experience articles, novel ideas, science news, and techniques for making gardening easier; of interest to gardeners of all ages and abilities

Organic Gardening, 33 East Minor Street, Emmaus, PA 18098

The "grandaddy" of popular organic gardening publications; published nine times a year; includes home gardening tips, garden research, new and old garden wisdom, and ideas from readers; "down-home" editorials fun to read

CANADIAN SOURCES

Gardening Agencies

Canadian Horicultural Council, 1101 Prince of Wales Drive, Suite 310, Ottawa, ON K2C 3W7

Other Agencies and Organizations

Canadian Association of Retired Persons, 27 Queen Street East, Suite 1304, Toronto, ON M5C 2M6

Canadian Occupational Therapy Foundation, 110 Eglinton Avenue West, 3rd Floor, Toronto, ON M4R 1A3

Canadian Association of Occupational Therapists (CAOT), 110 Eglinton Avenue West, 3rd Floor, Toronto, ON M4R 1A3

Canadian Association of Physical Medicine and Rehabilitation, 505 Smyth Road, Ottawa, ON K1H 8M2

Canadian Rehabilitation Council, 45 Sheppard Avenue East, Suite 801, Toronto, ON M2N 5W9

Canadian Paraplegic Association, 520 Sutherland Drive, Toronto, ON M4G 3V9

National Advisory Council on Aging, Ottawa, ON K1A 0K9

Disability Information Services of Canada, 501 18th Avenue SW, Suite 304, Calgary, AB T2S 0C7

Publications

Caliper, Canadian Paraplegic Association, 1500 Don Mills Road, Don Mills, ON M3B 3K4

The Canadian Plant Sourcebook, 93 Fentiman Avenue, Ottawa, ON K15 0T7

Harrowsmith, 7 Queen Victoria Road, Camden East, ON K0K 1J0

Heritage Seed Program, R.R. 3, Uxbridge, ON L8C 1K8

Seniors Today, 395 Berry Street, Suite 11, Winnipeg, MB R3J 1N6

Today's Seniors, 1091 Brevik Place, Mississauga, ON 14W 3R7

Canadian Gardening, 130 Spy Court, Markham, ON L3R 5H6

TLC...for Plants, 1 rue Pacifique, Ste-Anne-de-Bellevue, PQ H9X 1C5

FURTHER READING

Arthritis Foundation. *Arthritis and Farmers: A Guide to Daily Living.* Atlanta, GA: Arthritis Foundation.

_____. *Guide to Independent Living for People with Arthritis.* Atlanta, GA: Arthritis Foundation, 1988.

Arthritis Health Professionals. *Self-Help Manual for Patients with Arthritis.* Atlanta, GA: Arthritis Foundation, 1988.

Ball, Jeff. *Jeff Ball's Sixty-Minute Garden.* Emmaus, PA: Rodale Press, 1985.

Bartholomew, Mel. *Square Foot Gardening: A New Way to Garden in Less Space with Less Work.* Emmaus, PA: Rodale Press, 1983.

Breaking New Ground. Agricultural Tools, Equipment, Machinery and Buildings for Farmers and Ranchers with Physical Handicaps. West Lafayette, IN: Department of Agricultural Engineering, Purdue University, 1986.

Harkness, Sarah, and James N. Groom. *Building without Barriers for the Disabled.* New York: Watson-Guptill Publications, 1976.

Lorig, Kate, R.N., and James F. Fries, M.D. *Arthritis Helpbook.* New York: Addison-Wesley Publishing Co., 1986.

Moore, Bibby. *Growing with Gardening.* Chapel Hill and London: The University of North Carolina Press, 1989.

Raymond, Dick. *Joy of Gardening.* Pownal, VT: Garden Way Publishing, 1982.

Riotte, Louise. *Successful Small Food Gardens.* Pownal, VT: Garden Way Publishing, 1993.

Stout, Ruth. *How to Have a Green Thumb without an Aching Back.* Exposition-Phoenix Press, Inc., 1955. New York: Cornerstone Library, Simon and Schuster, 1971 (reprint).

Yepsen, Roger B., Jr. *The Encyclopedia of Natural Insect & Disease Control.* Emmaus, PA: Rodale Press, 1984.

INDEX

Numbers in *italics* indicate photographs and drawings; numbers in **boldface** indicate tables.

Gloves, 37, 135, 184
Gloxinia (*Gloxinia* spp.), **61,
70**
Goldenrod, **206, 234**
Goldfinches, 207–8
Gomphrena globosa. See
Globe amaranth
Gooseberries, **206**
Gophers, 176
Grape, 198, **206, 207**
Grape hyacinths, 228
Grasses, 80, **206**
Grass shears, 31, *31*
Gravel paths, 23
Greenhouse (window), 65–71,
99, *99*
Green lacewing, 159, *159,*
162, 163, 164
Green manure, 79–80
Grip
doors to compensate for, 22
tools to enhance, 29–30, *30,*
31–32
Ground beetle, **162,** 164
Ground covers, 174, **193,**
204, **255**
Ground-feeding birds, 204
Groundhogs, 177
Grow lights, 60
Guzmania, 218
Gypsophila paniculata. See
Baby's-breath
Gypsum, 75, **77,** 105–6

Hand exercise, 265, *265*
Hanging plants, 221–22, 225,
258
Hardening off, 114–16, 120
Hardy bulbs, 227–28
Hare's-tail grass, 196, *196,*
197
Harlequin bug, **173**
Harvesting, 235–36, 249–50
Hatiora salicornioides. See
Spice cactus
Hawaiian ti plant, **61**
Haworthia (Haworthia spp.),
59
Hearing garden, 196–98

Heart-leaf philodendron, 221
Heather, **254**
Heavenly bamboo, **254**
Hedeoma pulegioides. See
Pennyroyal (American)
Hedera canariensis. See
Algerian ivy
Hedera helix. See English ivy
Hedera spp. *See* Ivy
Heeling in plants, 25, *25*
Heirloom seeds, 95, 273, 280
Helianthus spp. *See* Sun-
flower
Helichrysum bracteatum. See
Strawflower
Heliotrope, **192,** 194–95, **201**
Heliotropium arborescens. See
Heliotrope
Heliotropium spp. *See* Helio-
trope
Helipterum spp. *See*
Acroclinium
Hemerocallis spp. *See* Daylily
Herb(s), **70,** 71, 163, 209,
222, 224, 241–52, *244,*
248, *250, 252*
in outdoor containers, 55,
56
as plant-disease inhibitors,
185–87
teas for repelling insects,
165
Herbal bath, 252
Hibiscus (*Hibiscus* spp.), 147,
196, **210**
Hillside lot, 17
Hippeastrum hortorum. See
Amaryllis
Hoe, 35
exercises with, 265–66, *266*
Holly, 174, **207**
Hollyhock, **210,** 236–37, **261**
Honesty, 196, **197, 234**
Honeybee, **162**
Honeysuckle, 191–93, **192,
206, 207, 255**
Hordeum jubatum. See
Squirreltail grass
Hornets, 161

Horseradish, **164, 166,** 242
spray, 186
Horsetail, **213**
Hosta (*Hosta* spp.), **197**
Hoverfly, 160, *160,* **162**
Howea forsterana. See Kentia
palms
Howea belmoreana. See
Sentry palm
*How to Have a Green Thumb
Without an Aching Back*
(Stout), 135–36, 143–45
Hoya carnosa. See Wax plant
Hoya spp. *See* Wax plant
Humata tyermannii. See
Bear's-foot fern
Hummingbird gardens, 208–
11
Hyacinth, **58, 192,** 193, 232,
227
Hyacinthus spp. *See* Hyacinth
Hybrids, 95
Hydrangea (*Hydrangea* spp.),
147, **254**
Hypericum. See St.-John's-
wort

Iberis spp. *See* Candytuft
Ice plant, **255**
Icheumonia wasps, **162**
Ilex spp. *See* Holly
Impatiens (*Impatiens* spp.),
61, 206, 224, **261**
Indoor container garden, 57–
65, 194–96
Information sources, 281–82
Insect gardens, 202–3
Insecticides, 36, 157–59, 166–
68, 198, 202, 203, 211
Insects
beneficial, 159–64, 274–275
companion planting and,
164–66, **164**
control of, 157–59
disease prevention and, 180
pests, 168–71, **173**
Insect traps, 158
Interplanting crops, 157
Ipomoea purpurea. See

California bay
Umbrella plant, **213**
Umbrellas for sun protection, *19*, 20
Umbrella tree, **61**
USDA zone map, *271*

Vaccinium spp. *See* Blueberry
Vanilla-scented sprays, 167
Vegetables, 55, *56*, **70**, 71, 94, 224, 225–26, 257
  fertilizing, 132
  transplanting to garden, 117
Verbascum spp. *See* Mullein
Verbena *(Verbena* spp.), **202**
Vertically grown plants, 150–51, 223–24, *224*
Verticillium wilt, **181**
Vetch, 80
Viburnum *(Viburnum* spp.), **207**
Vinca spp. *See* Periwinkle
Vines, 174, **192**, 257, 258
Viola, **58**, **261**
Viola spp. *See* Viola; Violet
Viola tricolor. See Johnny-jump-up
Violet, 191, **192**, 200, **201**, 214
Virginia creeper, **207**
Viruses, **67**, **181**, 182, **218**
Visually impaired
  container gardening for, 55
  garden design for, 12, 22
  tools for, 35, 37
Vitamin-B solution for seedlings, 104
Vitis spp. *See* Grape
Vriesea, 218
Vriesea malzinei. See Bromeliads

Walkers, 7, 37–38
Walking fern, 220
Wall fern, 220
Wall gardens, 223–24, *224*
Wandering Jew, 222
Water
  to attract wildlife, 211–12

for bird gardens, 205
for butterfly gardens, 201
for dwarf fruit trees, 225–26
garden, 213–14
garden design and, 9, 20
plants, **213**
Watering, 51–52, *52*, 124–31
air plants, 215, 217
bulbs, 229, 232
container gardens, 51–53, 225–26
disease prevention and, 184
equipment for, 33–34, *33*, 131
hanging plants, 222
indoor gardens, 62–63
orchids, 219
seedlings, 101–2, *102*, 104–5, 111–12
seeds, *102*
transplants, 118, 120
wall gardens, 224
window greenhouse, 69
Watering cans, 33, *34*
Water lettuce, 214
Water-lily, **213**
Water meter, 62
Water nozzles, 33
Water snowflake, **213**
Water sprays, 167
Water stress, 126, 180
Wax begonia, **61**
Wax plant, **61**, **70**, **192**
Weak fingers, tools to compensate for, 30, 31–32
Weak grip
  doors and, 22
  moistening soil technique, 99–100
  tools to compensate for, 29–30, *30*
Weather, 9, 126
Weed control, 134–42
  tools for, 34–36, *35*
Weeds, disease and, 183
Weeping fig, **61**
Weeping willow, **197**
Wheelchair(s)
  customizing, *19*, 20–21, 38

dimensions, **269**
garden design and, 7, 18–24, *20*, 43–44, *44*
turning space requirements, *269*
White clover, 80
Whiteflies, 65, **66**, 69, 180, 194–95, **218**
White plastic mulch, 137, **140–41**
Wide-row planting, 106–8, *107*
Wild ginger, 187
Wildlife garden, 211–13
Willow, 198, **201**. *See also* Pussy willow; Weeping willow
Window gardening, 64–71
Window greenhouse, 65–71, **70**
Windowsill gardening, 57–60
Windowsill greenhouses, 99, *99*
Wind protection, 119–20, 222
Winter aconite, 228
Winter barley, 80
Winter rye, 80
Wisteria *(Wisteria* spp.), **192**, 193
Woodchucks, 177
Wood hyacinths, 228, 229
Wood preservative, 45
Woodwardia spp. *See* Chain fern
Woolly thyme, **193**, 196, **197**. *See also* Thyme
Worms. *See* Earthworm(s)
Wormwood, **164**, **166**, **235**
Wrist-saving tools, 31–32

Yarrow, **234**, **235**, **248**
Yellow jacket, 161, *161*
Yew pine, **59**

Zebrina pedula purpusii. *See* Wandering Jew
Zinnia *(Zinnia* spp.), 200, 207, **206**, **210**, **261**